The Secret Lore of London

The Secret Lore of London

EDITED BY JOHN MATTHEWS

With Caroline Wise

CORONET

This edition first published in Great Britain in 2016 by Coronet.
An imprint of Hodder & Stoughton
An Hachette UK company

3

Copyright © Nigel Pennick
John Matthews
Caroline Wise
Caitlín Matthews
Carol Clancy
R.J. Stewart
Bernard Nesfield-Cookson
Gareth Knight
Robert Stephenson
Geraldine Beskin
Chesca Potter
William Stukeley
Lewis Spence
Harold Bayley
Alan V. Insole
Ross Nichols
2016

A CIP catalogue record for this title is available from the British Library

ISBN: 978 1 473 62024 7
Ebook ISBN: 978 1 473 62028 5

Typeset in Bembo MT by Hewer Text UK Ltd, Edinburgh
Printed and bound by CPI Group (UK) Ltd, Croydon, CR0 4YY

Hodder & Stoughton policy is to use papers that are natural, renewable
and recyclable products and made from wood grown in sustainable forests.
The logging and manufacturing processes are expected to conform
to the environmental regulations of the country of origin.

Hodder & Stoughton Ltd
Carmelite House
50 Victoria Embankment
London EC4Y 0DZ

www.hodder.co.uk

Contents

PART III: STORIES FROM LONDON'S PAST

List of Illustrations

Acknowledgements

The editors and authors wish to thank the following people who have helped in various ways and at various times in the completion of this book:

Mark Booth for taking it on; Caitlín Matthews, Andrew Collins and Steve Wilson for help with various researches; to all the contributors (old and new) for taking the time to update their original work and for generally supporting our efforts to bring this book back into print in its shining new form.

'London in the Time of Arthur' by Lewis Spence originally appeared in *Legendary London*, Robert Hale, 1937.
'Great St Helen' by Harold Bayley originally appeared in *The Lost Language of London*, Jonathan Cape, 1935.
'Britannia and St Paul's' by Alan V. Insole originally appeared in *Immortal Britain*, The Aquarian Press, 1952.
'Parliament Hill and the Druids' by Ross Nichols is published with the permission of the Order of Bards, Ovates and Druids.

The ideas expressed in the various essays are not necessarily those of the editors.

All illustrations are by Chesca Potter unless otherwise stated.
All photographs are by Caroline Wise unless otherwise stated.

[Frontispiece: St Helen, Magna Mater.]

FOREWORD

London: First, Last and Always City

Iain Sinclair

B URIED IN EVERY cell of our being, the folk memory of London as a unitary organism is under constant threat from history-denying improvers. And yet we cling to the notion of this special city as a field of force interrelated in all its particulars. Previous invaders, exploiting the broad river-road of the Thames, acknowledged the potency of the founding settlement as sovereign territory, the head and crown of the land. Danish and Saxon warriors and Dutch fire-fleets on the Medway seemed to anticipate the sinister flock of Second World War bombers who shadowed the snaking river to Silvertown, Millwall and Wapping. All those raiders, in their primitive savagery, were honouring the place.

With the passage of centuries, London leaked, spreading promis-cuously beyond the original walled camp into a confusion of overlap-ping localities. The imperatives of our digital age, the bias towards information over knowledge, gossip over experience, favour the establishment of a corporate theme park in place of half-forgotten legends based on seasonal rituals and earth magic. Generic structures without adequately embedded roots are commissioned: hospitals that look like universities, that look like leisure centres. And all of them aspiring to the post-architectural paradigm of the airport. London, divided between the entitled few and the invisible host, tears down structures with complicated pedigrees in favour of non-stick storage units purchased as investment.

The point of a vanity project like the Shard is simply to be a *point*: a slender silhouette like the outline of Hawksmoor's Christ Church looming over the Georgian roofs of Spitalfields. A point that is higher than any other point, with no purpose beyond the boast of domi-nance. The Shard is not attached to the body of a church. It is

non-denominational. It promotes a form of architecture as a genera-
tor of similes. Nothing in itself, the mirrored pyramid is *like* a sail, *like*
a steeple in the medieval city of churches. And that is the problem to
be confronted in any serious account of London, the Mithraic nest of
doubled and conflicted identities: how to understand occulted
impulses in the politics of the real. And how to find an urgent poetic
in a terrain dedicated to its exclusion.

The task, at this critical moment, is to turn our attention back to
the founding myths of city as polis, to the sacred. *The Secret Lore of
London*, a wide-ranging collection assembled by John Matthews and
Caroline Wise, is not so much about originality of tone as origin
itself. Without an adequate chart of first things, we have nothing.
Our secrets are hidden in full sight. But it takes witnesses of this cali-
bre to reveal them. We have to know that we can trust the teller as
well as the tale. This book is a valuable map of monuments, hollows,
burial stones; nominated sites that act like hot needles puncturing the
membrane of indifference and lighting up fresh neural pathways.

I am brought back to 1974, when a copy of Elizabeth Gordon's
Prehistoric London, Its Mounds and Circles was pressed into my hands.
The plan of the triangulation of sacred mounds didn't distract from
what was now visible, but it demonstrated a method for coping with
it. *The Secret Lore of London* is an equally provocative text to carry into
the multiverse of Michael Moorcock, where time eddies and flows in
impossible vortices. To the city of words forged by Peter Ackroyd,
Aidan Dun, China Miéville, Will Self, Nick Papadimitriou. Here is
the plural river of David Jones: sign and symbol. And the eternal
Golgonooza of William Blake. Contemporary scholars, geomancers,
ley-line dowsers and antiquarians report on their expeditions, while
rescuing texts that have vanished from view. They re-introduce us to
the living substance of the temenos that grew from the sediment of
the Thames: living London. We are reminded, finally, that there are
no secrets, just re-discoveries. Places and patterns waiting to be admitted to the light.

Iain Sinclair

Introduction

John Matthews and Caroline Wise

L ONDON IS AN ancient city, whose foundations date back to the legendary prehistory of these islands. Not surprisingly it has accumulated a large number of stories, both historic and mythical, during this period, many of which, though faithfully recorded at the time, have lain almost forgotten in dusty libraries throughout the city. The original editors, whose own interest in legendary London sprang from personal exploration of many of the ancient sites, found that there was an increasing amount of interest in these stories and tales, and that others were researching them just as keenly. They conceived the idea of asking some of these people to get together and produce a guide to the lore and legends, which would include a discussion of their importance as part of the oral tradition of Britain, combining prehistoric, Celto-Arthurian, Roman, Saxon and Norman levels – each of which has contributed to the many-layered life of the city.

The present book is the result. The first part, **The Legendary City**, contains a selection of essays by experts in their fields, each of whom possesses an abiding interest in the legends of these islands, and who have written widely on associated themes.

Thus in 'Legends of London', Nigel Pennick investigates the basic foundations of myth and folklore which surround and interpenetrate the ancient city of London on every side; and John Matthews in 'New Troy: London Before History' examines the substratum of ancient legends which look to another city, ruled by giants, to which Aeneas, the Prince of Troy, found his way, and where his son Brutus ruled, sacrificing to an altar of Diana which may still lie beneath present-day St Paul's Cathedral.

In 'The Goddesses of London', Caroline Wise looks back to the earliest strata of mythology connected with London and finds a multitude of sacred figures whose titles are recalled by the names of churches and streets, gardens and crossroads through the heart of the city. She urges us to return to these often-neglected sites and to reawaken their slumbering *genia locii*, bringing new life to the tired heart of the metropolis and perhaps inspiring ourselves in the process.

This is followed by 'The Guardian Head', in which Caitlín Matthews, looking at the mysterious Celtic legend describing the burial of the head of Bran beneath the White Hill – now the site of the Tower of London – finds an underlying archetype that is still active in our own time.

Nigel Pennick then offers a second contribution, on 'Templar London', tracing the connections between this tragically reviled group of warrior priests and the city in which they were once acknowledged great.

Carol Clancy next looks at another neglected aspect of London's forgotten history: that of the witches who once lived within its streets and plied their trade – for a time – unmolested. A strange and fascinating catalogue of the practitioners of magic takes us back to another age – which is not so far removed from our own.

In 'Merlin's in London', R.J. Stewart writes of an all-but-forgotten site known as 'Merlin's Cave', where in the gracious age of Queen Caroline and the Prince Regent members of high society met to have their fortunes told by someone purporting to represent the mighty prophet and wizard himself. Beneath this lies a deeper mystery, which is explored in this fascinating chapter.

We hear much, today, about 'urban blight' and 'architectural desecration' in the city. But, as Bernard Nesfield-Cookson shows, such ideas are not new. The poet and prophet William Blake (1757–1827) understood London in terms that would be recognized by conservationists as much as those concerned with the 'inner' history of the city. For Blake, London was the outward representation of the dark, oppressive world humanity had constructed for itself, where love, kindness and honesty were overwhelmed by hatred, greed and analytical reasoning.

As he walked the filthy, disease-ridden streets, Blake saw only 'marks of weakness, marks of woe' on the faces of people he met. Another visionary poet, William Wordsworth, writing in 1802, noted:

The wealthiest man among us is the best:
No grandeur now in nature or in book
Delights us. Rapine, avarice, expense,
This is idolatry; and these we adore:
Plain living and high thinking are no more . . .
Lines written in London, September 1802

While again, in 1922, T.S. Eliot could still see where:

A crowd flowed over London Bridge, so many,
I had not thought death had undone so many.
The Waste Land, 1922

For Blake, the answer was to build the New Jerusalem 'in England's green and pleasant land', to make a 'spiritual four-fold London' – Golgonooza, the city of Art – where the monstrous metropolis stood. Imagination, the power of artistic endeavour, would be shield and spear in this endeavour.

Just how much of Blake's vision has been implemented we may judge for ourselves. The city within the city still remains, though few are aware of it. Those best able to see it are individuals, who see reality best from a personal perspective.

Next comes Gareth Knight's consideration, in 'Towers of Sound and Light' of the esoteric significance of the many towers and spires of London's churches and cathedrals, which still dominate the skyline despite the intrusion of modern tower blocks.

Geraldine Beskin gives a lively account of one of the oldest surviving traditions of London, the Beating of the Bounds and finally Robert Stephenson chronicles 'A Long Tradition' of extraordinary and sometimes bizarre folklore observances, which form an immensely important part of the living kaleidoscope of the city's legendary life – a life which has never really ceased its endless movement and mutability.

That these ancient customs should be remembered and celebrated today is evidence of the deep-seated sense of ritual that is present in all men; particularly, it seems, in Londoners. As Robert Stephenson notes, it would be a pity if these observances were to cease. Happily, they show no sign of doing so, but are apparently as keenly celebrated now as at their original moment of inception. We may not always understand them – perhaps wisely so, since to uncover too much meaning can destroy something as tenuous as these folk-customs – but we are as willing as ever to acknowledge their power to intrigue and inspire.

The second part of the book, **A Guide to the Sites**, consists of a 'gazetteer' of the sites discussed which are still in existence, together with various other sites of associated interest. Here the reader will find brief references to many of the legends mentioned in Part I, with details of how to find the way there and how to explore them at first hand.

Finally, in Part Three, **Stories from London's Past**, we have assembled a selection of excerpts from older writings about London, discovered by earlier students of the city's mythological heritage. These complement the work of the more recent authorities in a fascinating way. Although new evidence has come forward in great quantity during the last decade alone, much of the speculative thinking of these earlier investigators remains valid, and continues to make intriguing reading. There is much cross-tracking of sources and information between both the older writers themselves and that of the recent commentators. This in itself shows the continuing vitality of the legendary background, and forms a fascinating web of mystery and insight regarding the ancient capital city.

Thus the great antiquarian William Stukeley's extraordinary document 'The Brill' relates to the ancient prehistoric sites around the area of present-day St Pancras, and excerpts from the two best-known earlier works on legendary London, by Lewis Spence and Harold Bayley, deal with the subjects of Arthurian London and the figure of the Goddess Elen; while Alan Insole spins an extraordinary pattern of ideas around the figure of Britannia and St Paul's, and Ross Nichols, the late Chief of the Order of Bards, Ovates and Druids, writes illuminatingly concerning the Druidic uses of Parliament Hill.

It was a revelation to us to discover that a Paleolithic axe and woolly mammoth's remains had been found at the bottom of King's Cross Road. Or that beneath the traffic of the City the River Fleet still ran, on whose banks healing wells once stood. The more we immersed ourselves in the hidden sacred areas, the more we felt that something of that sacredness still remained. London has suffered badly from the neglect and destruction of such sites, but if enough time is spent at those remaining, its ancient mystery can still shine through.

Though the well-known poem 'London Bridge is Falling Down' refers to a specific moment in history – when the bridge was destroyed by the Danes – there is something of a prophecy behind its familiar words. This version comes from an ancient collection of rhymes made by Joseph Ritson at the beginning of the nineteenth century:

> London bridge is broken down,
> Dance o'er my lady Lee;
> London bridge is broken down,
> With a gay lady.
>
> How shall we build it up again,
> Dance o'er my lady Lee;
> How shall we build it up again?
> With a gay lady.
>
> Silver and gold will be stolen away,
> Dance o'er my lady Lee;
> Silver and gold will be stolen away,
> With a gay lady.
>
> Build it up with iron and steel,
> Dance o'er my lady Lee;
> Build it up with iron and steel,
> With a gay lady.
>
> Iron and steel will bend and bow,
> Dance o'er my lady Lee;
> Iron and steel will bend and bow,
> With a gay lady.
>
> Build it up with wood and clay,
> Dance o'er my lady Lee;
> Build it up with wood and clay,

With a gay lady.

Wood and clay will wash away,
Dance o'er my lady Lee;
Wood and clay will wash away,
With a gay lady.

Build it up with maidens fair,
Dance o'er my lady Lee;
Build it up with maidens fair,
With a gay lady.

Build it up with stone so strong,
Dance o'er my lady Lee;
Huzza! 'twill last for ages long,
With a gay lady.

Altogether it is hoped that this book will provide a companion to many fascinating and rewarding journeys, not only through the physical streets of London, but also through the deeper, inner harmonics of the city which exist just below the surface, ready to be explored at any moment.

John Matthews and Caroline Wise
Oxford and Lud's Town, 2015

Goodly London

Michael Drayton (1563–1631)

T HIS EXTRACT COMES from a monumental poem by Michael
Drayton, a poet and playwright contemporary to Shakespeare,
who explored the mythology and legendary history of much of
Britain in his monumental *Poly-Olbion*. A new edition of this work
will be published in 2017; for now here is an extract that deals with
London, conjuring up some of her great mythic themes.

Poly-Olbion Song XVI

Besides; my sure abode next goodly *London* is,
To vent my fruitfull store, that me doth never misse.
And those poore baser things, they cannot put away,
How ere I set my price, nere on my chap-men stay.
When presently the Hill, that maketh her a Vale,
With things he had in hand, did interrupt her tale,
With *Hampsted* being falne and *Hie-gate* at debate;
As one before them both, that would advance his State,
From either for his height to beare away the praise,
Besides that he alone rich *Peryvale* survaies.
But *Hampsted* pleads, himselfe in Simples to have skill,
And therefore by desert to be the noblest Hill;
As one, that on his worth, and knowledge doth rely
In learned Physicks use, and skilfull Surgerie;
And challengeth, from them, the worthiest place her owne,
Since that old *Watling* once, o're him, to passe was knowne.
Then *Hie-gate* boasts his Way; which men do most frequent;
His long-continued fame; his hie and great descent;
Appointed for a gate of *London* to have been,
When first the mighty *Brute*, that City did begin.

7

And that he is the Hill, next *Enfield* which hath place,
A Forrest for her pride, though titled but a Chase.
Her Purlewes, and her Parks, her circuit full as large,
As some (perhaps) whose state requires a greater charge.
Whose Holts that view the East, do wistly stand to look
Upon the winding course of *Lee's* delightfull Brook.
Where *Mimer* comming in, invites her Sister *Beane*,
Amongst the chalky Banks t'increase their Mistresse traine;
Whom by the dainty hand, obsequiously they lead
(By *Hartford* gliding on, through many a pleasant Mead.
And comming in hir course, to crosse the common Fare,
For kindnes she doth kisse that hospitable *Ware*.)
Yet scarsely comfort *Lee* (alasse!) so woe begonne,
Complaining in her course, thus to her selfe alone;
How should my beauty now give *Waltham* such delight,
Or I poore silly Brook take pleasure in her sight?
Antiquity (for that it stands so far from view,
And would her doating dreames should be believ'd for true)
Dare lowdly lie for *Colne*, that sometimes Ships did passe,
To *Verlam* by her Streame, when *Verlam* famous was;
But, by these later times, suspected but to faine,
She Planks and Anchors shews, her errour to maintaine;
Which were, indeede, of Boats, for pleasure there to rowe
Upon her (then a Lake) the *Roman* Pompe to showe,
When *Rome*, her forces here did every yeere supply,
And at old *Verlam* kept a warlike Colony.
But I distressed *Lee*, whose course doth plainely tell,
That what of *Colne* is said, of me none could refell,
Whom *Alfred* but too wise (poore River) I may say
(When he the cruell *Danes*, did cunningly betray,
Which *Hartford* then besieg'd, whose Navy there abode,
And on my spacious brest, before the Castle road)
By vantage of my soyle, he did divide my Streame;
That they might ne're returne to *Neptunes* watry Realme.
And, since, distressed *Lee* I have been left forlorne,
A by-word to each Brook, and to the World a scorne.
When *Sturt*, a Nymph of hers (whose faith she oft had prov'd,

And whom, of all her traine, *Lee* most intirely lov'd)
Least so excessive greefe, her Mistresse might invade,
Thus (by faire gentle speech) to patience doth perswade:
Though you be not so great to others as before,
Yet not a jot for that dislike your selfe the more.
Your case is not alone, nor is (at all) so strange;
Sith every thing on earth subjects it selfe to change.
Where rivers sometime ran, is firme and certaine ground:
And where before were Hills, now standing Lakes are found.
And that which most you urge, your beauty to dispoile,
Doth recompence your Bank, with quantitie of soyle,
Beset with ranks of Swans; that, in their wonted pride,
Do prune their snowy plumes upon your pleasant side.
And *Waltham* wooes you still, and smiles with wonted cheere:
And *Tames* as at the first, so still doth hold you deer.
To much beloved *Lee*, this scarcely *Sturt* had spoke,
But goodly *Londons* sight their further purpose broke:
When *Tames* his either Banks, adorn'd with buildings faire,
The City to salute doth bid the Muse prepare.
Whose Turrets, Fanes, and Spyres, when wistly she beholds,
Her wonder at the site, thus strangely she unfolds:
At thy great Builders wit, who's he but wonder may?
Nay: of his wisedom, thus, ensuing times shall say;
O more then mortall man, that did this Towne begin!
Whose knowledge found the plot, so fit to set it in.
What God, or heavenly power was harbourd in thy breast,
From whom with such successe thy labours should be blest?
Built on a rising Bank, within a Vale to stand,
And for thy healthfull soyle, chose gravell mixt with sand.
And where faire *Tames* his course into a Crescent casts
(That, forced by his Tydes, as still by her he hasts,
He might his surging waves into her bosome send)
Because too farre in length, his Towne should not extend.
And to the North and South, upon an equall reach,
Two Hils their even Banks do somewhat seeme to stretch,
Those two extreamer Winds from hurting it to let;
And only levell lies, upon the Rise and Set,

Of all this goodly *Ile*, where breathes most cheerfull aire
And every way there-to the wayes most smooth and faire;
As in the fittest place, by man that could be thought,
To which by Land, or Sea, provision might be brought.
And such a Road for Ships scarce all the world commands,
As is the goodly *Tames*, neer where *Brute's* City stands.
Nor any Haven lies to which is more resort,
Commodities to bring, as also to transport:
Our Kingdome that enricht (through which we flourisht long)
E're idle Gentry up in such aboundance sprong.
Now pestring all this Ile: whose disproportion drawes
The publique wealth so drie, and only is the cause
Our gold goes out so fast, for foolish foraine things,
Which upstart Gentry still into our Country brings;
Who their insatiate pride seek chiefly to maintaine
By that, which only serves to uses vile and vaine:
Which our plaine Fathers earst would have accounted sinne,
Before the costly Coach, and silken stock came in;
Before that *Indian* weed so strong was imbrac't;
Wherin, such mighty summes we prodigally waste;
That Merchants long train'd up in Gayn's deceitfull schoole,
And subtly having learn'd to sooth the humorous foole,
Present their painted toyes unto this frantique gull,
Disparaging our Tinne, our Leather, Corne, and Wooll;
When Forrainers, with ours them warmly cloath and feed,
Transporting trash to us, of which we nere had need.
But whilst the angry Muse, thus on the Time exclames,
Sith every thing therin consisteth in extreames;
Lest she inforc't with wrongs her limits should transcend,
Here of this present Song she briefly makes an end.

PART I
The Legendary City

I

Legends of London

Nigel Pennick

T HE GREATER LONDON that exists today is a megalopolis that encompasses literally hundreds of once-separate villages and towns. Each of these centres has its own separate history, and once had its own customs and traditions. Every sacred site, extant and destroyed, possessed its associated lore and legends. To research these would take a lifetime, and to document them, a long series of volumes would be required. However, the definition of 'London' I use here is that of the medieval city and its immediate surroundings. Today, this area is represented by the historic City of London and the area to its west around the Strand, Westminster, Trafalgar Square and Marble Arch. Within this area, we can find important legends connected with major places and buildings. In London, there are legends of notable individuals, legends of places, legendary history, and modern, 'urban' legends. They are all the living media of our human experience of history and place.

Legendary History

Various London legends exist concerning the prehistoric kings of Britain, who, although recorded in medieval chronicles, are considered by the historians of today to be nothing more than fables. For example, Bladud, father of Leir, prototype of Shakespeare's King Lear, was reputed to be the first British monarch to die in an aviation accident. According to *The British History, Translated into English from the Latin of Jeffrey of Monmouth* by Aaron Thompson, London, 1743, 'This prince was a very ingenious Man, and taught Necromancy in his Kingdom, nor left off pursuing his Magical Operations, till he attempted to fly to the upper Region of the Air with Wings he had prepared, and fell down upon the Temple of Apollo in the City of *Trinovantium* [London], where he was dashed to pieces.'

His burial-place is not recorded, but that of King Lud is. In the nineteenth century, 'King Lud' was the pseudonym used by machine-breakers in their vain attempts to stem the tide of the Industrial Revolution. But, unlike an alternative name for machine-breakers, 'Captain Swing', this name was taken from one of the prehistoric kings of Britain, after whom London was supposed to be named. According to Geoffrey of Monmouth, 'When Lud died, his body was buried in the above-mentioned city [London], near the gateway which in the British language is still called after him "Porthlud", though in Saxon it bears the name Ludgate.' Although the legend is discounted now, in 1260 the gate was repaired and statues of Lud and his two sons, Androgeus and Tenuantius, were erected there. Not far away, Billingsgate, for many centuries London's fish market, is said to be named after King Belinus, for, when he died, his ashes were placed in a bronze (or golden) urn on top of the gate.

It is probable that the site of Lud's burial was the sepulchre of the old kings of Britain, now occupied by the church of St Martin-within-Ludgate. This is indicated by a strange legend that tells of the body of the Welsh King, Cadwal II (Cadwallon II of Gwynedd), penultimate King of Britain, being taken there for burial after his death in battle. He fell with his Welsh warriors fighting on the side of the pagan Mercians against the Christian Northumbrians at the Battle of Hefenfelth in the year 634. At the time, London was officially pagan, having expelled Mellitus, the Archbishop, on the death of King Sebert, first Christian King of the East Saxons, when London was re-paganized. Because of this, the archbishopric of the south of England, which followed the old Roman imperial organization in having London as its centre, was set up at Canterbury, where it remains to this day.

If the Cadwal story is true, then it was the last recognition that a British king should be buried at the traditional site, despite the change in rulership of London from Britain to Saxon. An earlier royal burial, of the Icenian Queen, Boudicca, is reputed to be located under platform 10 at King's Cross main-line station. The place where the station was built by the Great Northern Railway in 1852 was called Battle Bridge, the alleged site of her last, fatal, battle with the Roman army. Another of her reputed sepulchres, however, was a tumulus on Primrose Hill, which in 1811 was used by the Masonic architect John Nash as a survey-point for laying out Regent's Park.

A Legendary Foundation: The London Stone

The London Stone is an enigmatic, geomantic mark-stone that stood originally on the south side of Candlewick Street (Cannon Street), one of the two main parallel streets of the old city. It is ancient, having had its present name since the twelfth century, at the latest. In his *Britannia*, Camden claimed that this stone was the *Millarium*, the central mark-point from which the Roman roads radiated from the capital, and from which distances were measured. The first Lord Mayor of London, Henry Fitz-Aylwin (1189) had the surname or epithet de Londenestane because his house stood close to the stone.

In Elizabethan times, the stone was buried deeply in the ground with only the upper portion visible. But in 1742 the worn stump, which by then had a protective stone cover over it, was removed to the north side of Cannon Street. In 1798, being still in the way of traffic, 'a nuisance and obstruction', it was set in a stone housing on the southern external wall of St Swithin's Church, which had been built in 1405 by the Mayor of London, John Hinde, draper, as the 'Church of St Swithen by London Stone'.

There it remained until the Second World War, when St Swithin's was destroyed by bombs in the Blitz. The shell of the church was left derelict until 1961, when the wall with the stone was demolished. When examined, the stone was found to have a rounded top, with two deeply incised grooves. Its material was identified as Clipsham limestone. Redevelopment of Cannon Street saw its insertion in a new niche in the wall of the Bank of China. According to tradition, the London Stone was originally a temple altar-stone, laid by none other than Brutus the Trojan, mythical founder of Britain. Because of this, it was considered to be a sacred object, upon which oaths were sworn. The stone was also the point from which authoritative proclamations were made.

[Figure 1: The London Stone, from *Old and New London*,
Walter Thornbury, first published 1872–8.]

The tradition of striking one's sword against the stone as a symbol
of sovereignty was observed in 1450 by the Kentish insurgent, Jack
Cade. On striking his sword on the stone, he declared himself Lord
of the City. The London Stone is a typical survivor of the thousands
of mark-stones that used to exist at important geomantic points in
medieval cities. In mainland Europe, they are often 'blue stones'.
One exists at St Andrew's in Scotland, upon which the Jacobite

soldiers struck their swords on their way to fight at Culloden in 1746. It is said that so long as Brutus's stone is safe, so long shall London flourish.

St Peter's-upon-Cornhill

The medieval street plan of London was laid out according to a grid, based upon two main parallels of Cannon Street and Cheapside, a furlong apart, across which, at right angles, other straight alignments were surveyed. The two main parallels appear to be orientated with regard to the Roman basilica and forum, although on a slightly different axis. The church of St Peter's-upon-Cornhill stands on one of these parallels. This ancient church is said to have been founded in the second century of the present era by King Lucius. In his *Survey of London* (1598), John Stow wrote that it was reputed to have been the chief church of Britain until the coming of St Augustine.

According to the tradition, Thean, the first Archbishop of London, built the church with the aid of Ciran, Lucius's butler. The second Archbishop, Eluanus, built a library next to the church and converted many of the Druids, 'learned men in the Pagan law', to the Christian religion. The folk tradition that St Peter's was founded during the Roman occupation has some archaeological reality, for it was built over Roman foundations. It is on the most important geomantic point in Roman London, on the basilica in the location customary for the municipal shrine. This is a typical example of the continuity of sacred sites from pagan to Christian times. Perhaps the Roman Christians' legend has more truth in it than some have claimed.

Westminster Abbey

The original church at Westminster, later Westminster Abbey, was reputed to have been consecrated supernaturally. Its location, the Isle of Thorney, was formed by a bifurcation in the stream known as the Tyburn at its confluence with the Thames. Its name is often said to mean 'the isle of thorns', but it is possible that it was so-called because the Saxons recognized that it was shaped like the protective rune *thorn*. The island was reputed to have held a Roman temple of Apollo, demolished by an earthquake in the fifth century. This was the site of the fall of King Bladud in his ill-fated attempt to fly. Subsequently, Thorney may have been a pagan sanctuary of the Anglo-Saxon god Thunor (Thor). In the year 610, King Sebert founded a church there, which he dedicated to St Peter.

According to legend, on the night before the church was due to be consecrated, St Peter came down from heaven to do the job himself. Unfortunately, St Peter's navigation was rather inaccurate, and, unlike his heavenly choir, which arrived at Thorney, St Peter ended up at Lambeth, on the south side of the river. Fortunately, there he met a fisherman named Edric, who agreed to ferry him across the river. Peter went to the church, and Edric witnessed the building effulgent with light and heard the sound of angelic voices singing heavenly chants. The phenomenon lasted for about half an hour, after which all was dark and silent. St Peter asked to be rowed back to Lambeth, and Edric obeyed. On the journey back, the saint asked the fisherman to go and see Mellitus, Archbishop of London, and inform him that the church was consecrated now by miraculous agency. When the ecclesiastics visited the church, they found evidence that the fisherman was telling the truth.

This legend was accepted as a true account as late as the time of King Edward III (1359), when Westminster was described as 'the place which in ancient days received its consecration from Blessed Peter the Apostle with the ministry of angels'. At the Reformation, this story was discredited as an example of 'popish superstition', but more modern thought on 'earth energies' interprets the illuminated building in terms of 'earth lights'. These terrestrial light phenomena have been seen in more recent times in connection with sacred buildings constructed on sites of intense geological activity. The reputed earthquake of the fifth century may indicate this. Other London earthquakes, in 1580, 1692, 1750 and 1884, have been felt at Westminster. Perhaps the Isle of Thorney was one such 'place of power'. No investigations of this possibility have been conducted yet.

[Figure 2: St Peter consecrating Westminster
Abbey, from a medieval manuscript.]

St Paul's Cathedral

The metropolitan cathedral of London is St Paul's, named after the
patron saint of the city. It is the East Minster by reference to which
Westminster is named. Like the latter abbey, St Paul's is reputed to
stand on the site of an earlier pagan temple, dedicated to the Goddess
Diana. 'Some have imagined a temple of Diana stood here,' wrote
Camden in the *Itinerarium Curiosum*, 'and their conjectures are not
unsupported. The neighbouring old buildings are called in the church
records, *Camera Dianae*, and in the reign of Edward I were dug up in
the churchyard . . . an incredible number of ox heads, which were

held by the multitude with astonishment as remains of heathen sacrifices . . .'

In medieval times, there was a ceremony which appears to have been the continuation of pagan hunting rites associated with Diana, or her Northern Tradition counterpart, Frigga or Freyja. It involved a ceremony that entailed laying a slaughtered deer on the cathedral altar, and carrying the head of a buck on a spear or pole, accompanied by the blowing of hunting horns inside the church. This association is reinforced by the names of two streets close to the cathedral in medieval times: Friday Street and Distaff Lane. Friday is the sacred day of Frigga, and one of her sacred attributes is the distaff. If we accept the legend, then Westminster Abbey (Apollo) is a solar site, and St Paul's (Diana) is a lunar one.

The Tower

In Celtic times, more than a millennium before the Tower of London was built, the site was a holy hill, Bryn Gwyn. Such white hills were formerly sacred to the Great Mother Goddess. On this hill, the great Norman main keep of the castle, the 'White Tower' stands. This was the place where, according to legend, the severed head of the hero-god Bran was buried along with Brutus, founder of Britain. It was believed that while Bran's head remained buried there, Britain was inviolate from conquest. But King Arthur, scorning 'pagan superstition', dug up the magically protective head, and Britain fell to the Saxon conqueror. However, to this day, a number of ravens, the sacred bird of Bran, are kept at the Tower of London. Their wings are clipped and they strut about on the lawns, for so long as there are ravens there, it is said, the Tower will never fall.

Perhaps because of the Bran legend, the Tower was the place where execution by beheading took place. The name of a street close to the Tower is associated with a beheading that took place at the Tower in the early eleventh century. The future King, Canute, promised Earl Edric that he would give him the highest place in London if he would assassinate King Edmund Ironside (981–1016). After the bloody deed had been done, as a reward, Canute had Edric beheaded. His head was stuck on a spear on the Tower, the highest point in London, and his body was thrown into a nearby ditch, to be eaten by the dogs. This ditch is now replaced by the street called Houndsditch. Elsewhere in the Tower of London, ghost legends abound, as befits a place of imprisonment, torture and execution. The Traitors' Gate, the water gate of the Tower of London, was built against the wishes of London's people. The spirit of St Thomas à Becket took sides with the London citizens to prevent it, even causing the works to collapse several times during its construction. But, finally, even the wraith of the people's saint could not prevail, and it was completed.

St Bartholomew's

For seven centuries, the greatest fair in London, Bartholomew Fair, was held in Smithfield, in the precinct of the Priory of St Bartholomew, at Bartholomewtide (24th August). According to legend, the priory originated when Rahere, jester to King Henry I, became disgusted at his profession, and undertook a pilgrimage to Rome. When he arrived at Rome, he was stricken with a life-threatening illness. Believing that he was a terminal case, he made a vow to God that, if he were spared, he would found a hospital for poor men. Regaining his health, he returned to England, where he had a vision of St Bartholomew, who commanded him to found a church dedicated to him in Smithfield. Rahere went to the King, who gave permission for a church to be constructed in what was the royal market of Smithfield. The place where the church was founded was swampy ground that had been pointed out a century and a half earlier to King Edward the Confessor as a good location for a religious house. The marsh was drained, and in 1123, the Priory of St Bartholomew was founded there. Rahere became prior, and collected around him a number of religious men.

During the life of Rahere, many miracles are reputed to have occurred. The monastery gained a reputation for healing, and it is said that many lame, sick and blind people visited St Bartholomew's, and were cured. Their thanks in kind and money soon made the monastery wealthy. At sea, the customary saint whom London-based mariners would call upon to quell storms was Bartholomew, and many gifts of silver ships were presented at Smithfield in gratitude to the saint. Perhaps remembering his jesterly origins, Rahere also instituted the famous Bartholomew Fair. This was held over a three-day period: the eve of the saint's day, the day itself, and the day after. It soon became the major cloth-sellers' fair in London. When the religious house was suppressed, the fair continued under the tutelage of the Mayor and Corporation.

After the Tudor period, however, its importance as a cloth fair declined, and the entertainment side, always present, became its main reason for existing. 'Monsters, motions, drolls and rarities' became the new attractions. Many famous plays, and even more infamous ones, were put on at 'Bartlemy Fair', as it was known popularly. Ben Jonson's play *Bartholomew Fair* depicts the humours and abuses of the carnival. The fair was so popular that even Cromwell did not suppress it, at a period when the Puritans even made the celebration of Christmas illegal. In the late seventeenth century, the fair was extended in length to a fortnight. The fair became increasingly disorderly over the years, often beginning in a riot on the night before it was due to open. The last major riot was in 1822. In 1840 the booths were demolished by order of the City Solicitor, and finally, by the ruse of buying up the land where the fair was held, the Court of Common Council was able to suppress it. Like the sanctuary of the Temple (see Chapter 5), this is another example of popular continuity of use of a sacred site long after the original function of the place was suppressed. Bartholomew Fair was declared officially extinct in 1855.

Dick Whittington's Stone and Cat

A London legend that has reached the status of fairytale and pantomime is that of Dick Whittington and his cat. As if to verify this legend, on top of Highgate there is a milestone topped by a bronze cat. This is the reputed site where Dick Whittington, hearing the bells of London ringing, turned again towards the city where he was to make his fortune. As explanation of the legend, it has been suggested that the 'cat' was actually a type of ship used in the coal trade, on which a large part of Whittington's fortune was founded. A mummified cat, ascribed to Whittington, was formerly displayed in the church of St Michael Royal, on College Hill. Although the church was originally founded by Sir Richard Whittington, 'four times Mayor of London Town', it had been rebuilt in 1687–91, before being bombed in the Second World War. After the war, during repairs, the mummified cat was found in a sealed passage under the roof. Immediately it was discovered, it was declared to be none other than Dick Whittington's famous cat. In 1949 it was placed in a glass case near the church door above a chest used for collecting money to repair the war damage. Subsequently, it was stolen, and its whereabouts are unknown now.

Legends of Execution-Places

As befitting a large city, old London had several execution-places. In the medieval period, the central site of Cornhill was an important place. Judicial killings also took place at the Elms (whose location is now unknown), Tower Hill (for traitors and nobility) and Smithfield, on the site of Bartholomew Fair, where executions took place as late as 1656. Occasionally, hangings also took place closer to the site of the crime. The aftermath of the 'Mug House Riots' from November 1715 to July 1716 saw the hanging of five 'Jacks' (Jacobites) at the end of Salisbury Court, Fleet Street for an attack on Read's Mug House. Hogarth's engraving of a bonfire near Temple Bar, perhaps the anti-Catholic celebrations held for many years on Queen Elizabeth I's birthday on 17 November, has a hanging figure, perhaps just an effigy, but, in a more barbarous age, perhaps not. All of these places were deemed special in some way, being affected by the violent act and preserving there some place-memory of the event. Perhaps even today they are locations where psychical phenomena occur.

The most important place of execution in later times was at Tyburn, a place of legend and romance, especially in connection with the flamboyant highwaymen who died there by the rope. The place name comes from the stream, now a sewer, which flowed from there to Westminster, where it formed Thorney Island. Perhaps Tyburn is named after the Saxon divinity Tiw, god of justice. The gallows there was located at the intersection between the Oxford Road (now Oxford Street) and the Edgware Road. The first recorded execution at Tyburn took place in 1196, when the popular agitator, William Fitzosbert, better known as Longbeard, was killed. When he was hanged, there was a scuffle to obtain shreds of his clothing, and hair from his head. Earth at the foot of the gallows on which he was hanged was collected by women from surrounding counties, to be used magically. A hair from his beard was believed to have power against evil spirits, and a fragment of his clothing was a charm against aches and pains.

The original Tyburn scaffold was made from two poles with a crossbeam, erected when needed, the traditional form of the gallows still seen in the Tarot as Trump XIII, The Hanged Man. In 1571, the rising number of the condemned made a larger gallows necessary, and the notorious 'triple tree' was constructed. This triangular gallows enabled the authorities to perform mass executions, for up to twenty-four people could be hanged at once.

The site either already had a reputation as a sacred place or gained it through the presence of the scaffold. An old print exists showing Queen Henrietta Maria (wife of King Charles I) praying beneath the triple tree, and probably collecting a sample of magic soil, too. One night in 1678, the triple tree fell down. It was said to have been 'uprooted by its ghosts', of which doubtless there were many. The ceremonial 'Road to Tyburn', along which the condemned were taken to their death, began at Newgate, from whence the carts carrying them left between ten and eleven o'clock in the morning.

The procession halted outside St Sepulchre's for the prisoners to hear the Bellman's final proclamation. Each prisoner was given a floral wreath here. Then the procession proceeded down Snow Hill, across the Fleet River (like the Tyburn, now a sewer), and up to High Holborn, where a stop was made for the condemned to have a last drink at the George Inn. The procession then proceeded by way of the church of St Giles-in-the-Fields and along the Oxford Road to Tyburn, arriving around midday. Such ceremonial routes were a common part of medieval European geomancy, either for condemned criminals, or for taking the dead along a prescribed route – as in the *Hellweg* at Soest in Germany – to a sacred place of disposal.

In London, executions took place eight times a year (the old pagan eightfold division), and were accompanied by festivities known as the Tyburn Fair. People came from miles around, treating the grisly proceedings as an outing for the family, and possibly an opportunity to get a relic or two. A permanent grandstand existed at Tyburn for the accommodation of spectators. In the eighteenth century, grandstand tickets sold for two shillings and sixpence officially and a lot more from the ticket touts, who attended the Tyburn Fair as their spiritual descendants do today at Wembley and Wimbledon. The record 'gate' for Tyburn was double that of a modern Wembley Cup final – 200,000.

The gallows at Tyburn was demolished in 1759, and the beams were used as beer barrel supports in a nearby inn. After that, a portable gallows was brought from Newgate and assembled at Tyburn. The final execution there occurred on 7 November 1783, and after that the execution place became the Old Bailey, which became as popular an entertainment as Tyburn had been. Public executions were discontinued in London in 1868, not for humanitarian reasons, but because of the riotous nature of the assembled multitudes. Subsequently, a turnpike tollhouse was erected on the site of the triple tree. This site is marked now by a stone plaque on a traffic island near Marble Arch. It is said that Speakers' Corner is a remnant of the right of the condemned to make a final speech to the assembled crowds at Tyburn.

Underground Legends

Since the middle of the last century London has undergone a massive expansion. As part of this expansion, new underground transport links have been dug. Sometimes these diggings have occasioned new urban legends. For example, when St Pancras station was being built in the late 1860s, an entire cemetery was burrowed through. It is said that the relatives of a Frenchman buried there demanded that his bones be returned to his native land. When the appropriate grave was dug up, the remains of several people were found. The foreman of the gang pointed out that the Frenchman's bones, belonging to a foreigner, would be darker than English bones, so the darker bones were sent to France for re-burial. In 1900 the crypt of Nicholas Hawksmoor's church of St Mary Woolnoth was dug out to accommodate the new Bank tube station. The skeletons and bones were all removed to consecrated ground elsewhere.

The underground railways in London have several legends. One is that a sudden, sharp curve in a line was laid out to avoid a 'plague pit', mass graves in which victims of the 1665 plague were buried unceremoniously. This story is told of the curve in the Piccadilly Line west of Knightsbridge station, just before the train arrives at South Kensington. It is also said of a sharp curve in the Central Line between Bank and Liverpool Street. Another Tube legend is told of the workmen, who, when driving a tunnel, suddenly saw a ghost, and fled. The workmen in this tale are usually said to have been 'superstitious' Irishmen, who then refused ever again to work underground.

One place where this was said to have happened was to the south of Moorgate station, where the extension to Lothbury being dug in 1904 was summarily abandoned after, it is said, an apparition was seen in the tunnel. This is the site of the disastrous 1975 Moorgate Tube disaster, where the train's driver, seemingly transfixed, accelerated his train into the end wall of the blank tunnel at the end of the station, killing forty-five passengers. Another site of subterranean apparition was in one of the running tunnels of the Victoria Line, south of Victoria, where a ghost was reported during construction in 1970. In 2014 the excavators of Crossrail discovered the cemetery of the Bethlehem Hospital (Bedlam) during the construction of the new station at Liverpool Street. It contained thousands of skeletons, but there have been no reports of ghostly appearances to date.

Old London Bridge

London Bridge is a legendary structure in more than one way. It is the subject of the famous rhyme 'London Bridge is falling down', and is said to be the reason why traffic drives on the left in Britain to this day. It is believed that the first London Bridge was built by the Romans at a place where the river could be forded at low tide. As the only reliable entrance to the city from the south, the bridge was defended by earthen banks and ditches known as 'the South Work', which has given its name to that part of London called Southwark. As inferred by the rhyme, the story of London Bridge is a catalogue of disasters. During the siege of London in the year 1009, the Battle of London Bridge was fought, where the Norwegians, under King Olaf, attacked the bridge, which was held by the Danes. Using the wattle-and-daub walls of houses as shields over their ships, the Norwegians were able to row up to the bridge, and to tear down its wooden piers, drowning some of its defenders and routing others. Hooks, axes and other weapons of this era, found in the Thames near London Bridge, are on display in the Museum of London.

In the year 1091, London Bridge was destroyed by a tidal surge during a storm which an old chronicle describes thus: 'On the sixteenth of November, the feast of St Edmund the Archbishop, in the year 1091, at the hour of six, a dreadful whirlwind from the south-east, coming from Africa [the wind-direction of Eurus in the *Rose of the Winds*], blew upon the City, and overthrew upwards of six hundred houses, several churches, greatly damaged the Tower, and tore away the roof and part of the wall of the church of St Mary-le-Bow, in Cheapside.'

Major disasters have always occurred throughout history, as today. In the following year, 700 houses were destroyed in London by a great fire. William II attempted to raise the money for reconstruction from the Church, but the Church refused, and so the hapless citizens were taxed, and a new, stronger bridge was erected. This was burnt in 1136 and was repaired, but in 1163 this bridge was no longer safe and another replaced it. This bridge was designed by Peter of Colechurch and had stone foundations. Founded in about 1176, it was to the west of the earliest bridge. Peter of Colechurch constructed a chapel as the first building on the bridge, and was buried in it in 1205 as a sort of foundation sacrifice. It has been thought that the 'my fair lady' reference in the rhyme may refer to an earlier foundation sacrifice of a woman. Foundation sacrifices of animals, and even humans, were common in the medieval period, especially with regard to bridges. The mummified cats found in a number of old London buildings, including the so-called Dick Whittington's cat, are later examples of this practice.

The bridge was completed in 1209, and another fire damaged it on 10 July 1212, when around 3,000 sightseers, who had gathered on the bridge to view a major fire raging in Southwark, were engulfed by flames or drowned in the river when they overwhelmed boats sent to rescue them. Only two years later, during a great drought, 'men walked dryshod' across most of the Thames at the ford close to London Bridge. The bridge next collapsed through neglect during a severe winter, probably that of 1282, when five arches were swept away by ice floes, and repairs were so shoddy that by 1289 many refused to cross the bridge, using boats instead. After some years of argument, the bridge was repaired again.

On 14 January 1437, the great stone gate at Southwark, the southern entrance to the bridge, fell into the river, tearing down two arches. In 1471, the 17,000-strong army of Thomas Nevil (Falconbridge) besieged the bridge and burnt the gate and all the houses as far as the draw-bridge, thirteen in all. In 1481, one of the new houses on the bridge, called 'Common Siege' fell into the river, killing five. In the late medieval period, traffic on the bridge grew to such a volume that it took well over an hour to cross it. To alleviate the problem, a rule-of-the-road was instituted, where it was made compulsory for carts and coaches to pass one another on the right. This is the origin of the British 'keep left' rule of the roads, still in force today.

Finally, in the nineteenth century, a new bridge, designed by John Rennie, was built and the old bridge was demolished in 1831. When the new bridge was founded, on 15 June 1825, the foundation sacrifice tradition was continued, though in the modern way by substituting money for an animal or human victim. As the sacrifice for the new bridge, the City Chamberlain deposited a set of new coins of the realm inside a cut-glass bottle in a hollow under the foundation stone. This was followed by a brass *depositum plate*, engraved with a pompous Latin inscription composed by the Master of Oriel College, Oxford. After the usual speeches, the four-ton Aberdeen granite foundation stone was lowered and the Lord Mayor tapped it into place with a ceremonial trowel.

Owing to subsidence of the foundations, by the 1960s Rennie's bridge was unsound and was demolished. It was taken down stone by stone, transported to the United States and re-erected at Lake Havasu

City in Arizona as a tourist attraction, where it now serves to carry people to an artificial island. Modern folklore tells of how the American purchasers were mortified when they found that they had purchased not, as they thought, the Victorian iron splendour of Tower Bridge, but a relatively undistinguished stone bridge!

London Maypoles

Standing in the middle of the Strand in its own churchyard is the beautiful eighteenth-century church of St Mary le Strand. A stone cross formerly existed in the Strand, and justices itinerant sat at the stone in 1294. But the most notable geomantic structure there was the 'Strand Maypole'. During the Commonwealth period, this maypole was demolished by order of Parliament 'as a last remnant of vile heathenism'. But the pole had been so popular that a new one was erected in the reign of King Charles II. The new maypole was no less than 134 feet high, so bulky and heavy that twelve seamen under the command of the High Admiral, James, Duke of York (later King James II), used cables, pulleys and anchors to erect the pole. It may have been the reinstitution of a (now forgotten) tradition of maypole rearing. A carved and gilded representation of the Royal Arms surmounted the pole. Immediately to the north was the street called Maypole Alley. The maypole was a notable feature of the liberties just west of the City of London, being mentioned in Gay's *Trivia* and Pope's *Dunciad*. This location was the first coach-stand in London, for in 1634 Captain Bailey started a hackney-coach service at the maypole in the Strand.

The maypole erected in Charles II's reign was decayed by 1713, when it was replaced by a new 125-feet pole, topped by two gilt balls and a weathervane. There is an artistically licentious version of the appearance of the maypole in the wall tiles of the Gents' lavatories subterraneanly situated close to the east of St Clement Danes. Presumably the phallic imagery is unintentional!

The original church of St Mary le Strand stood to the south of the Strand. First mentioned in 1147, it was demolished in 1549 on the orders of the Protector Somerset, who commandeered the land for his palace, Somerset House, and tore down many buildings to provide building materials for it. But when new churches were begun after 1711, the site of the Strand maypole was chosen for the replacement of St Mary's. This is, perhaps, the last example of the Christianization of a pagan site in Britain. When the church was under construction, the maypole was taken down and Sir Isaac Newton obtained it and had it transported to Wanstead Park to hold up a telescope that had been donated to the Royal Society.

Another notable London maypole was kept in the church of St Andrew Undershaft by Leadenhall Street. Each May Day it was erected with much revelry outside the south door of the church. But after a xenophobic riot by apprentices on May Day 1517 in which many lost their lives, it was hung along the wall in Shaft Alley. It remained there until 1550, when a rabble-rousing sermon preached at Paul's Cross, against pagan practices, led the drunken mob to attack the pole, saw it into sections and burn it.

2

New Troy:
London Before History

John Matthews

The Trojan Kings

Until the end of the Elizabethan era it was still a commonly held belief that Britain had been colonized by Brute or Brutus the Trojan, a grandson of the famous hero Aeneas. Even the sober, cautious John Milton, writing his *History of Britain* in 1670 reported that: 'Brutus in a chosen place builds *Troia Nova*, changed in time to Trinovantum, now London.'[1]

To trace this tradition back to its beginnings we have first to turn to the medieval writer Geoffrey of Monmouth, famed for what is perhaps the earliest novelization of the Arthurian legends in his *History of the Kings of Britain*, which begins, not with Arthur, but with Brute. The story he tells may be summarized as follows.

Aeneas, fleeing from Troy, took ship for Italy with his son Ascanius. There he was honourably received by King Latinus, whose daughter Lavinia he shortly married. Brutus was the grandson of Ascanius who, after he slew his father Sylvius accidentally in the hunting field, was exiled to Greece where he gathered about him the remnants of the Trojans who had escaped from the doomed city and who now flocked to him when they learned he was the grandson of the great Aeneas.

With the help of the army he had thus raised, Brutus defeated the Greek forces and having taken their King prisoner, demanded the hand of his daughter Ingoge in marriage and a fleet of well-equipped ships with which to seek a new homeland. Only two days out at sea, the fleet sighted a deserted island called Leogicia, where stood a ruined city with a temple to Diana at its heart.

Brutus made sacrifice there and that night dreamed of the goddess, who told him to seek a land beyond Gaul in the country of the setting sun.

Voyaging on, the fleet sailed first to Africa, then on to Mauritania, through the Pillars of Hercules and into the Tyrrhenian Sea, where they encountered a second Trojan colony ruled by Duke Corineus. Making common cause with them, the Trojans passed onward to Aquitaine and the mouth of the Loire River, where they were attacked by the Gaulish people. Several mighty battles ensued, in which the Trojans inflicted terrible losses on their enemy. But Brutus saw that he could not win in the end, and decided to follow the path of the sunset as the goddess had advised. A fair wind drove the fleet ashore at a place called Totness on an island named Albion after its gigantic ruler.

Falling in love with the rich land, Brutus and his followers established a colony there and began to build a city. They were harried by the race of giants who dwelled in the island and fought and killed several of them. Finally they captured one, whose name was Goemagot, and the Trojan Duke Corineus, who was a famous wrestler, challenged him to a bout. The giant was a mighty fighter and broke five of Corineus's ribs before the latter heaved him off the top of the cliffs into the sea, the place being thereafter known as Lamgoemagot or 'Goemagot's Leap'. After this the Trojans were left in peace and founded cities across the country. Brutus himself had three sons: Locrin, Albanacht and Camber, who became the governors of Cambria (Wales), Alban (Scotland) and Llogria (England), after the death of Brutus.[2]

Geoffrey goes on to extend the line of 'Trojan' Kings into a complex dynastic chain extending to Arthur himself. The following genealogical tree, which first appeared in a more detailed form in Acton Griscom's edition of *The History of the Kings of Britain*,[3] gives some idea of the extent of Geoffrey's schema – which in fact far outreaches any simple 'invention' such as his work, until recent times, has been consistently described. However much elaboration or decoration of his sources Geoffrey may be guilty of, he clearly had recourse to original material to produce a family of such magisterial proportions:

From this, the character known to all from Shakespeare's play *King Lear*, the line extends down to Arthur, 90th in succession from Aeneas of Troy. (An idea still being expressed in such great medieval Arthurian works as *Sir Gawain and the Green Knight*,[4] the opening of which describes Arthur's Trojan ancestors in detail.)

When Caesar arrived in Britain he found a tribe called the Trinovantes living in the south of the country – were they the descendants of Brutus and his men? Or did the whole idea of the Trojan

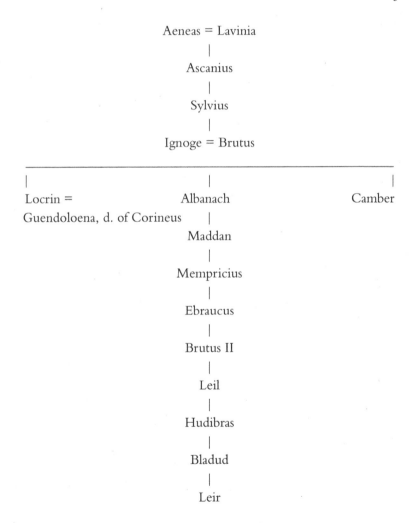

[Figure 3: The lineage of London's kings.]

colonization of the island spring from a medieval misunderstanding of the name Trinovante? It would seem, on the face of it, that we cannot know. Yet the tradition that Britain had been colonized by the Trojans is supported by a surprising detail. In Wales, as late as the eighteenth century, shepherd boys used to play a game called Caer Droea or 'Troy Town', which consisted of laying out a maze-like pattern on the ground and holding contests to see who could reach the city at the centre first. This is a very ancient game indeed, possibly stretching back to prehistoric times, when the maze or labyrinth was used for ritual purposes. Famous mazes in Crete and Egypt were described by classical writers, and were old even then. How there came to be such designs in Britain may be accounted for in a number of ways, including the assumption that a kind of universal religion was practised in the early world, or indeed that incoming conquerors (such as the so-called Trojans) brought the concept with them.[5]

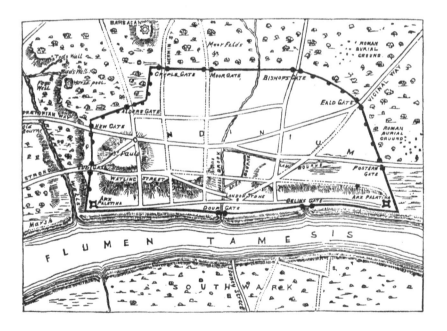

[Figure 4: Roman London, from *Old and New London*, Walter Thornbury, 1872–8.]

The final word on the question of a possible Trojan settlement in Britain must await further investigation. We can, however, note that the idea of tracing one's descent to Troy was by no means unusual. The Roman poet Virgil himself did so, for his own people, in the *Aeneid*,[6] and the classical writer Ammenius Marcianus wrote of the Gaulish belief that they were of Trojan descent; while as late as 1514 an oration over the coffin of Anne of Brittany traced her lineage back to Brutus.

Certainly archaeological evidence suggests that trade routes between the Mediterranean world and Britain were established from a significantly early date. So that there seems no difficulty in believing that a group of people escaping from the fall of Troy (wherever and whenever we take that event to have occurred) might indeed have sailed to these shores and established a colony here. Whether Brutus really extended his sway over the entire country, so that it became known as Britain after him, is less likely to be true – though even here we may still be seeing a distant memory of an event that actually occurred.

Lud's Town

With the connection of London with Lud, Brutus's descendant, we enter the realms of both myth and religion. Geoffrey of Monmouth describes the foundation of Trinovantum in Book I, Chapter 17. The Welsh *Brut* offers its own idiosyncratic version, and is worth quoting in full from Lewis Spence's translation:

> And when he found a place lovely and fulfilling his desires, he built a city there [beside the Thames] and called it Troyaf newydd, and thus it was called for a long time; and then, by corruption of that name it was called Trynofant. Afterwards it was possessed by Llydd, the son of Beli the Great, the brother of Caswallawn, the man who fought with Ilkassar [Caesar]. And when this Llydd got the kingship he strengthened the city with grants of lands and with walls of wondrous art and craftsmanship; and he ordered it to be called Caer-lydd, after his own name; and the Ssaissons [Saxons] called it Lwndwn . . . At this time Beli the Priest ruled in Judea and the ark of the covenant was in captivity to the Pilistewission [i.e. the Philistines].[7]

[Figure 5: Old Lud Gate, from a print of *c.*1750.]

The dating from the time when the Ark of the Covenant was in the possession of the Philistines is certainly startling – and just as certainly spurious – but it indicates the antiquity of the tradition, which was clearly seen as dating back to a very ancient past. Layamon, the Saxon poet who retold Geoffrey's book in English, offers the king's name as Lud, the tower as Caerlud, and adds:

[Figure 6: The Troy Town Maze – *Caer Droea*].

Afterwards came other dominion, and new customs, that men called it Lundin, over all this country. Subsequently came English men, and called it Lundene. Afterwards came the French, . . . with their country-manners, and Lundres it named. Thus has this burgh fared, since it first was reared.[8]

Once the city was founded Lud embarked on an intensive building plan, extending the existing town and instituting palaces and temples. Holinshed's *Chronicles* tells us more:

[Lud] himself caused buildings to be made between London Stone and Ludgate, and builded for himself not far from the said gate a fair palace, which is the Bishop of London's palace beside St. Paul's at this day, as some think . . . He also built a fairer temple near to his said palace, which temple (as some take it) was after turned into a church, and at this day called Paul's.[9]

The mention of the London Stone is interesting, as it reinforces other claims that this ancient monument was erected by Brutus himself (for which reason it was also called Brutus's Stone in other texts). It was believed to have been erected on the site of a temple to Diana, whom Brutus worshipped after she prophesied that he should find his way to Britain. The London Stone is discussed elsewhere in this collection (see pages 15–16 and 214–16), but we should note that a unique illustration exists in the thirteenth-century manuscripts of a work by

[Figure 7: *Brutus Sacrificing to Diana*, from Matthew Paris, thirteenth century, Corpus Christi, Cambridge, MS 26.]

Matthew Paris (see Figure 7) that shows Brutus sacrificing before the altar of a horned goddess – indication of the validity still attached to the idea even as late as the Middle Ages.

Ludgate, also mentioned in the quotation from Holinshed, is the most tangible evidence we possess for the connection of London with the Trojan dynasty. Accounts exist of its restoration in 1215, at which time bricks from the houses of purged Jewish citizens were used to affect the repairs. These were discovered in 1586 when the gate was pulled apart in order to rebuild it yet again.

In 1260 we hear of it being completely restored, with statues of Lud and other kings, though whether there were images present before we are not told. Later, during the troubled reign of Edward VI, these statues had their heads knocked off, and were not repaired until Mary Tudor ascended the throne in 1553. Finally, in 1586, when the 'Jewish' stones were recovered, the statues were again replaced with King Lud and others on the eastern side of the gate and a new statue of Elizabeth I on the western side. This cost the city the sum of more than £1,500, the equivalent of four times that amount in today's currency.

When the gates of the city were taken down in the eighteenth century the statues were bought by Sir Francis Gosling, who intended to install them in St Dunstan's Church, Fleet Street. But it was found that they would not fit, and in the end only the statue of Queen Elizabeth was erected in its new home, while Lud and his sons languished 'in the bone yard'. What happened to them after that is unclear. No one now seems certain of the precise origins of the statues that now stand in the porch of St Dunstan's Church. They are much damaged and rather sad in aspect, though Lud himself still has a certain dignity, despite a chipped face and vestiges of paint that indicate the images must once have been decked out in splendid colour.

As to Lud himself, there is every reason for believing that he may have been a god. The great Celticist Sir John Rhys stated in his *Hibbert Lectures*:[10]

The association of Llud, or 'King Lud', as he has come to be called in English, with London, is apparently founded on a certain amount of fact: one of the Welsh names for London is *Caer Lud* or Lud's Fort, and if this is open to suspicion as having been suggested first by Geoffrey, that can hardly be supposed possible in the case of the English name of Ludgate Hill. The probability is that as a temple on a hill near Severn associated him with that river in the west, so a still more ambitious temple on a hill connected him with the Thames in the east; and as an aggressive creed can hardly signalize its conquests more effectually than by appropriating the fanes of the retreating faith, no site could be guessed with more probability to have been sacred to the Celtic Zeus than the eminence from which the dome of St Paul's now rears its magnificent form.

Lud as a Celtic Zeus may cause a smile now, but there seems little doubt that Lud was indeed a god of some importance and power, and that his temple could well have been established in 'Lud's Town', even at the present site of St Paul's, which Holinshed thought to be the original site of Brutus's temple to Diana, and where archaeologists did indeed discover traces of such a place after the last war.[11]

Perhaps, if there was a real 'King Lud', descended from Trojan Brutus, he assumed something of the form and nature of an older god, much as the historical Arthur seems to have absorbed aspects of a primitive bear god named Artos. Spence thinks he may have been a corruption of the Welsh Gwyn ap Nudd, the god of the Underworld, but this seems to be stretching a point, since the pronunciation of Nudd is 'Nith' – although it must be allowed that the written form of the two names looks remarkably similar. However, there seems to be no precise overlay between the attributes of the Celtic god of the underworld and the guardian of Caer Lud, and in all probability we are looking at a figure of similar type to Gog and Magog, whose extraordinary history we must examine next.

Effigies of the Gods

One of the most intriguing references in Geoffrey's narrative, and one which touches most nearly on the legendary history of London, is the

[Figure 8: Gog and Magog.]

story of Corineus's battle with the giant Goemagog. The latter has an extraordinary and complex history, which is deeply connected with the mythic history of Britain, and with London in particular.

Although Geoffrey gives the giant's name as 'Goemagog', or even 'Goemagot', other sources, in particular the Welsh *Brut Tysilio*,[12] which derives in part from the *History of the Kings of Britain* but also contains independent material, give the more familiar 'Gogmagog', which the text's earliest editor, Peter Roberts, suggests was a corruption of Cawr-Madog – the Great Warrior of Madog. However, we may look further afield than this for the origins of the giant, digging back into the very foundation myths of this island.

Gogmagog (as we shall continue to call him) is the champion of the giant Albion, whose own legend stretches back to the mists of proto-history, where he is known as the son of Poseidon, the Greek god of the sea. Raphael Holinshed in his great *Chronicles of England, Scotland, and Ireland* declared that after the Flood, Albion the Giant led a company of giants descended from a son of Noah's named either Ham or Shem to Britain – though it was not called that at the time – and how he overcame the original inhabitants through skill and cunning in warfare. After this the island was named Albion, a title that has remained embedded in the consciousness of its people to the extent that it can still be evoked today.[13] The poet and prophet William Blake devised a whole mythology based on the Giant Albion, writing, in his *Jerusalem*:[14]

> *There is a Void outside of Existence, which if entered into*
> *Englobes itself & becomes a womb; such was Albion's couch,*
> *A pleasant Shadow and Repose call'd Albion's lovely Land.*
> *His Sublime & Pathos become Two Rocks fix"d in the Earth;*
> *His reason, his Spectrous Power, covers them above.*
> *Jerusalem his Emanation is a Stone laying beneath.*
>   *O behold the Vision of Albion.*

Elsewhere he writes: 'The stories of Arthur are the Acts of Albion applied to a Prince in the Fifth Century.'[15]

Here Albion has become the tutelary spirit of Britain, an inner guardian not unlike the later Bran (see pages 64–5). Or indeed like another titanic figure also associated with Britain – the Greek God Cronos, father of Zeus, who is supposed to have been imprisoned in a cave beneath the island in an enchanted sleep until, like Arthur, he is recalled in some future time.

The myth of the sleeping titan seems inextricably linked with Britain. In c.400 BC a Carthaginian explorer circumnavigated the island and, in his subsequent report, included that its sophisticated populace refer to their homeland as the 'island of Albiones'. While later, the Greek Pythias recorded (c.300 BC) a Western island known to be 'the abode of Albion'. Another Greek, Plutarch, described the sleep of Cronos, which had been 'devised as a bondage for him, and round about him are many demigods as attendants and servants.'[16]

In *The Mabinogion*[17] the demi-God Bran commands that his head be cut off and buried beneath the White Mount in London, from which point it will guard the land. Arthur later has the head disinterred, so that he alone should be the guardian, and after his passing he is indeed believed to be sleeping beneath the hills of Britain, awaiting his country's call to arms. To this may be added the figure of the Celtic King Cadwallo, who was embalmed and placed on the brazen statue of a horse above the Western gate into London – a position later to be assumed by Gogmagog – or rather, Gog and Magog after the giant became curiously divided into two characters, perhaps under the influence of biblical traditions which referred to two giants by this name mentioned in Chronicles, Ezekiel and Revelations.

Descriptions of the 1554 pageant welcoming Philip of Spain to England for his impending marriage to Mary Tudor describe two effigies as being carried through the streets. Normally they resided in London's Guildhall. A reference in a work entitled the *Orthoepia Gallica of 1593*[18] seems to indicate that one of the two was of Corineus, Brutus's heroic captain, while the other was still of Gogmagog. While in Plymouth at this time and originating at least as early as 1494 there were two gigantic figures cut in the turf of the Hoe. Carew, writing in the Elizabethan era, describes them as the portraiture of two men with clubs in their hands cut in the turf, 'the one bigger, the other lesser, whom they term Gogmagog and Corineus, intimating the wrestling to have been between these two champions and the steep rocky cliff affording aptitude for such a cast.'[19]

Sir E.B. Tylor, in his book *Anthropology* (1848), suggested that the idea of Gogmagog being thrown over the cliffs at Plymouth may have originated quite late on, as a result of fossilized dinosaur bones discovered there at various times. Lewis Spence, who has written most persuasively on the subject, quotes this information in his *Legendary London*. He also believes Corineus to have been an invention of Geoffrey of Monmouth, to form a link in the chain of semi-mythical kings he represented as ruling Britain before Arthur.

Spence, in another book, *The Mysteries of Britain*,[20] maintains the belief that Gog and Magog may have been the original (Celtic) deities connected with London, having their temples, or seats of power, on the twin hills either side of Walbrook: 'They might actually have been those "Fierce ones" alluded to by Dr Henry Bradley in his derivation of the [old Celtic] name "Londinos", from which the spot took its name.'

If this can be regarded as in any way true, we must immediately note that Magog may possibly be equated with 'Mother Gog', an interesting speculation that supplies us with a much more likely male and female set of deities indigenous to the City.

During the Fire of London in 1666 the effigies at Guildhall seem to have been destroyed, and we hear in 1669 that the hall was to be restored and that 'two new figures of gigantic magnitude will be as before'.[21] The statues then erected were apparently carved by Captain Richard Saunders of King Street, Cheapside, sometime after this date. J.T. Smith in his *Ancient Topography of London* (1815) describes them in considerable detail.[22]

The occasion was the restoration of the Guildhall, at which time one of the effigies – Gog – was taken down and stored in a specially constructed shed. Smith describes the statues as follows:

> I stood upright in the body of one of them. They are composed of pieces of Fir; and I am informed were the production of a ship-carver. It is also reported that they were presented to the City by the Stationers Company, which, if true, might have given rise to the [earlier] report of their being made of paper . . . [Gog . . . measures fourteen feet, six

44

inches in height, from the upper leaf of laurels to the lower point of the beard five feet, three inches, the nose is nine inches, the opening of the eyelids one inch and a half, across the shoulders about four feet, five inches and a half, from the wrist to the tip of the second finger, two feet, the feet are the length of the hands.]

This truly monumental figure accords well with the later reconstructed figures that continued to stand in the Guildhall until the Second World War, when they were finally destroyed and not replaced.

What, then, are we to make of this strange mishmash of material? Who are, or were, Gog, Magog and Corineus? Are they totally inventions of Geoffrey of Monmouth's fertile imagination? Ultimately, we cannot be certain, but we can make some educated guesses.

The antiquarian Douce, again quoted by Spence, reports reading in 'A Very Modern Edition of the Celebrated Romance of the History and Destruction of Troy' that after Brutus had captured Gog and Magog (here the brothers of the giant Albion) they were chained, as porters, to the gate of the palace built by Brutus on the present site of Guildhall. Spence adds that he has been unable to trace the reference, but traced or not, it has the ring of truth about it. If we are right in assuming that Geoffrey, as in so many other instances, was recording a genuinely ancient tradition, we should look for a possible source further back in time than the twelfth century.

It may be that such a source does exist in the shape of the 'Ancient Book in the British tongue' described by Geoffrey as his main source for the *History of the Kings of Britain*. Because no such text has ever been discovered it has generally been assumed to be a fabrication. However, it may well be that the book did exist, and that fragments of it may still be traced within the pages of Geoffrey's book, and elsewhere scattered throughout the various traditions relating to the early kings of Britain.

The very nature of the early part of the *History*, and in particular the portion dealing with Brutus, may suggest the nature of this proposed text. Whatever the true derivation of this story may be, it does, clearly, deal with a succession of incoming peoples, subjugating the native population and settling there permanently until they, in turn, are ousted. We may remember the references to Albion, of the same stock as Gogmagog, overcoming the indigenous races by his superior battle-tactics. Now again we find the Trojans overcoming the giants with a mixture of strength and cunning. Surely, what we are reading here is a kind of 'Book of Invasions', similar in many ways to the Irish *Lebor Gabála*, dating from the ninth century but recording events of a far greater antiquity.

[Figure 9: *Brutus Worshipping Diana*, from Matthew Paris, thirteenth century, Corpus Christi, Cambridge, MS 26.)

We can trace the names Gog and Magog, or Gogmagog, no further than Geoffrey, but if we look again at the evidence for the existence of the effigies at London Guildhall, we find that there were two such figures that predate the more familiar statues. These, according to an account of 1552, were called 'Hercules' and 'Sampson', an interesting detail in the light of numerous references to the former contained in the poetry of the sixth-century bard Taliesin. Earlier still, they were known by names of even greater significance for the present argument: Colebrand and Brandamore, both of which contain references to important figures in Celtic tradition.

Both names contain the name Bran, who is a character, as Caitlín Caitlin Matthews shows in Chapter 4, whose life and deeds are well documented. He is also, it should not be forgotten, one of the giants who guard the island from attack. The name Cole or Coel is also the name of an ancient British King (the 'Old King Cole' of nursery rhyme fame), father of the famous Helen or Elen of the Roads mentioned briefly by Geoffrey of Monmouth.

What we seem to have, in this account of the battle between Brutus and Gogmagog, is a distant, garbled memory of the overthrow of one set of people by another, and of their own subsequent enslavement at the hands of incomers from the fabled city of Troy. Perhaps also we may wish to consider the possibility that here we have a further reference to the mythic overlay of Julius Caesar's adventures in Britain, which in the hands of Geoffrey of Monmouth take on an epic quality of their own and contain references to an even older myth of the Goddess Fleur. Whether there is any historical foundation for any of this is doubtful, and the notion must remain purely speculative at this level. There is, however, a deeper stratum of belief, in the power of the hidden, inner guardians of the Land that accounts for the ability of these stories to move us still.

The myth of the dying god is universal, and needs no rehearsal here, beyond the statement that it entails the death, or sacrifice of the god for the sake of the people. Avatars as distant in time and space as Arthur, Adonis, and Christ match this archetype. Bran, Gog and Magog, Cadwallo and Lud, each of whom has a strong connection with London, may themselves once have fulfilled the necessary role. Bran indeed, already does so, and it may well be that Gogmagog, meeting his death at the hands of Corineus, became a similar Saviour figure to his defeated people.

Such interpretations require more space and time than the author has presently at his disposal. However, the fragmentary evidence for another London, before either history or archaeology establishes the physical city, is strong enough to recall Blake's line:

'O behold the Vision of Albion!'

3

Goddesses of London

Caroline Wise

Diana

That there stood of old time a Temple of Diana in this place some have conjec-tured, and arguments there are to make this their conjecture good.
William Camden

The Roman Goddess Diana is fundamental to the foundation legends of London. Chaste Diana of the woods, and of wild animals and hunt, was the divine guide that sent the founders of Britain to these isles. The pseudo-history of Geoffrey of Monmouth relates the tale of Brutus of Troy, who set sail in exile, with a band of loyal Trojans (see Chapter 2). Brutus and his men, numbering some 300, arrived at a deserted island in the Mediterranean where they came across a temple honouring the gods Jupiter and Mercury, and the Goddess Diana. They lit fires for all three. At the statue of the goddess, they sacrificed a white doe, and asked for an oracle to help them find a new homeland in which they could settle permanently and honour her.

> *Mighty goddess of the woodland, terror of the wild boar;*
> *Thou who art free to traverse the ethereal heavens*
> *And the mansions of hell, disclose my rights on this earth*
> *And say what lands it is your wish for us to inhabit*
> *What dwelling-place where I shall worship you all my life*
> *Where I shall dedicate temples to you with virgin choirs.*

That night, as Brutus slept on a doe's pelt, Diana appeared to him in a visionary dream, and told him to sail to a sea-girt land, beyond

Gaul, in the Western Ocean, where he would build a new Troy and start a lineage of kings.

> *Brutus, where the sun sets beyond the kingdoms of Gaul*
> *is an isle in the ocean, closed all around by the sea.*
> *Once upon a time giants lived on that isle in the ocean,*
> *But now it sits empty and fit to receive your people.*
> *Seek it out, for it shall be your homeland forever;*
> *It shall be a second Troy for your descendants*
> *There kings shall be born of your seed and to them*
> *All nations of round earth shall be subject.*[1]

The land was Albion, which became Britain, and they docked first at Totnes in Devon, where they found a race of giants whom they conquered. Brutus went on to found the city Troia Nova, or New Troy, by the Thames. In legend, Brutus built his palace where the Guildhall now stands, and his temple to Diana at the site of what is now St Paul's Cathedral, at the apex of Ludgate Hill. The Christian dedication of this London site to St Paul may be significant, since after his famous conversion, the zealous missionary Paul had preached Christianity at the great temple to Diana at Ephesus. He denounced the pagan silversmiths who made statuettes of the goddess there. A gilded statue of St Paul now stands on a tall column at his London cathedral, looking out over the city and the river, as if the missionary of old has conquered this place once sacred to the Goddess Diana.

The legend of the temple to Diana in London is persistent. The chronicler Monk John Flete, writing of the history of Westminster Abbey, imagined the time when Britain revoked to paganism in the fifth century.

> Thus belief in the old abominations returned everywhere; the Britons were driven from their homeland; London sacrificed to Diana and suburban Thorney made offerings to Apollo.[2]

The Elizabethan antiquarian William Camden wrote in his monumental work *Britannia*,[3] that he wanted 'to restore antiquity to Britaine, and Britaine to its antiquity'.

[Figure 10: Limestone altar to Diana, found on the
site of Goldsmiths' Hall, Foster Lane.]

Camden argued for the existence of a temple of Diana at the site
of St Paul's and claimed that a vaulted building had been uncovered
in the fourteenth century with the convenient inscription *Camera
Diana*, or the Chamber of Diana. Wren claims to have found no
evidence for this when the foundations were being laid for the present
cathedral, but in 1830, a stone altar was discovered during the building of Goldsmiths' Hall, 300 yards north-east in Foster Lane. It
depicted Diana iconography, complete with a figure in a tunic, with
hound, quiver and bow.[4] It was described as being:

> Though greatly corroded . . . of fine workmanship, and the outlines
> are full of grace.

This suggests it was of some significance in the area. It can be seen in
the Court Room, and a more accessible copy can be found in the
Museum of London.

The Goddess Diana is associated with stags, most famously in the
myth of Acteon, whom she turned into a stag when he was caught

spying on her bathing with her nymphs. Acteon was set upon by the hounds of his own hunting companions and killed. There are some curious reports of rituals taking place at St Paul's, which may be related to the legends of the Temple of Diana. One is the Huntsman's Festival. The Dean and Chapter of St Paul's decreed on Candlemas Day 1274 that on the feast of the Conversion of St Paul, 25 January, a doe, and on the feast of the Commemoration of St Paul, 30 June, a buck, were led around the cathedral, and the beast killed at the steps for a public feast.

John Stow's account of this festival says:

> On the feast day of the commemoration of saint Paule the bucke being brought up to the steps of the high Altar in Powls church, at the houre of procession, the Deane and chapter being apparrelled in coapes and vestmentes, with garlands of Roses on their heades, they sent the body of the Bucke to baking, and had the head fixed on a powle, borne before the Crosse in their procession, untill they issued out of the West dore, where the keeper that brought it blowed the death of the Bucke, and then the horners that were about the cittie, presently aunswered him in like manner.[5]

Camden records witnessing 'a stagges head sticking upon a speare-top, carried round about within the very Church in solemn pomp and procession, and with a great noise of Horne-blowers'. He believed it harked back to the worship of Diana: 'Surely this rite and ceremony may seeme to smell of Dianas worship and the gentiles errours, more than Christian religion.'

This particular practice originates from 1274, with a land grant agreement, between Sir William Baud of Essex and the Dean of St Paul's, with the doe and buck being offered annually for this ceremony. There is no evidence that it is based on the legends of Diana worship in the City, but the imagery of the deer ritual at this place is intriguing none the less.

In 1634, the Bishop of Norwich, seeking funds for repairs to St Paul's Cathedral, as it was then before the Great Fire, invoked the goddess in a stirring 'PR campaign'. He pointed out that the cathedral had replaced a shrine to Diana:

St Paul confuting twice the Idol: there, in person, where the cry was Great is Diana of the Ephesians! And here, by proxy, Paul installed while Diana is thrust out.

Diana's presence in Greater London can also be found in Greenwich Park in the south-east of the capital. In 1902 Roman remains were discovered here during routine works, and it was speculated that this was a Romano-Celtic temple complex, sited on the line of Watling Street. This high spot, beside a Roman road and near the Thames, would be an ideal site for a temple. The arm of a statue identified as *Diana Venatrix*, Diana of the Chase, was discovered along with Roman coins. Further excavations with the *Time Team* archaeologists in 1999 added weight to the site being a temple.[6] There is a synchronistic association with deer here, too; Greenwich Park is one of the oldest deer parks in London, the first to be enclosed for royal hunting, but home to deer long before that. There is still a deer park today near the temple foundations.

Isis

I am nature, the universal Mother, mistress of all the elements, primordial child of time, sovereign of all things spiritual . . .
Apuleius, *The Golden Ass*

In the early nineteenth century, a terracotta wine amphorae bearing the inscription *LONDONI AD FANVM ISIDIS* crudely scratched on its surface was found near London Bridge. It is one of the earliest known renderings of the word 'London'. It was discovered on the southern shore of the River Thames at Tooley Street. The inscription has been translated as 'At the Temple of Isis London' or 'To the Temple of Isis London' which could suggest a delivery address.

Isis had been a major goddess of the Ancient Egyptians. And her name means 'throne' or 'seat', suggesting she ruled the land and by extension, its productivity, or that she represented the land itself. This is reflected in the hieroglyphs of her name, which show a woman, a throne, and a loaf of bread. The symbol of an egg shows she was regarded as a mother goddess. In Egypt she was depicted with the wings of a kite, and with a headdress that displayed a solar disc between the horns of a cow, sometimes with vulture feathers at the sides. Isis played a major role in the annual myth cycle of the corn god Osiris, who, with the aid of Isis, his widow, was reborn as the child Horus. The myths concerned the yearly flooding of the Nile. The tears of the goddess, falling as she mourned the death of Osiris, caused the river to flood and fertilize the land with its rich silt deposits. The corn that rose from the fertile soil represented the god reborn.

Isis lost her animal attributes with the coming of the Alexandrian Greeks and she became important to the Romans. The Hellenized cult of Isis spread across Europe with the mystery cults of Rome, and she was paired with Serapis, the Greek form of Osiris, recognized by the corn measure on his head.[7] A beautiful marble head of Serapis was found at the site of the Temple of Mithras in London, discovered during building works in the early 1950s on the north side of the river in Queen Victoria Street.

It is fitting that the London temple dedicated to Isis, who was so entwined with the myths of the River Nile, was built on the banks of the Thames. The exact spot is debated. A third-century altar stone that had been reused in the old riverside wall bears an inscription from the local provincial governor of that time. It tells us that it is from a temple of Isis that had replaced an earlier one that had 'fallen down with age'.[8]

In 1825, a finely worked statuette of the child god Harpocrates, the Greek rendering of Horus, the son of Isis, was found in the Thames. It is from the first-to-second century and can be seen today in the British Museum. It has a heavy gold chain suggesting that it was important: a heavy amulet worn by a priest or hung in a temple. Other items with images of Isis were found in Old Dover Street, Southwark, and included hairpins and a weight. Amulets representing the God Anubis, the jackal-headed psychopomp who is closely asso- ciated with the myths of Isis, have been found there also.

Southwark Cathedral has often been suggested as the site of the Temple of Isis and there is evidence of Roman pagan observations.[9] The church stands on the site of a priory, originally dedicated to the Virgin Mary. Mary subsumed some of the iconography and titles of

Isis, when the mystery cults of Rome gave way to Christianity. Isis was associated with water, including its crossing, as Isis of the Ships, and Isis Pelagia, Isis of the Sea, and ceded the title Stella Maris, Star of the Sea to the Virgin Mary. The well-known image of Mary as a seated mother with child also comes from the depictions of Isis and the child Horus.

The church became an Augustinian priory dedicated to St Mary Overie, or Mary Over the River, in the early twelfth century. John Stow thought that there had been a nunnery on the site in the seventh century. A folktale related to him by the last prior told of a pre-conquest nunnery, paid for by the good sisters who ferried people over the river. The legend of St Mary Overie is told on a plaque by the river. A tenth-century man, a miser named Jon Overs, had become rich operating a ferry over the river. In a bid to save money, he faked his death for a day so that his household would fast. Of course his plan went awry. The plaque tells us:

> When he carried out the plan, the servants were so overjoyed at his death that they began to feast and make merry. In a rage the old man leapt out of bed to the horror of his servants, one of whom picked up a broken oar and thinking to kill the Devil at the first blow, actually struck out his brains. The ferryman's distressed daughter Mary sent for her lover, who in haste to claim the inheritance fell from his horse and broke his neck. Mary was so overcome by these misfortunes that she devoted her inheritance to founding a convent into which she retreated.

This became the priory of Saint Mary Overie, Mary having been made a saint on account of her charity. During the Reformation the church was renamed St Saviour's Church. In 1905 it became Southwark Cathedral and the collegiate church of St Saviour and St Mary Overie. Memories of a temple of Isis near this site may be responsible for the later divine feminine traditions of the Virgin Mary and the ferryman's canonized daughter. Tantalizingly, the course of the River Thames in Oxfordshire is called the Isis. This may be derived from the Ancient British name for the Thames, Tamesas, or it may be named for the memory of the goddess.

Venus and the Deae Matres

Mother of Aeneas and his race, delight of men and Gods, life-giving Venus, it is Thy doing that under the wheeling constellations of the sky all nature teems with life . . . Into the breasts of one and all Thou dost instill alluring love.
Olivia Robertson, *Urania, Ceremonial Magic of the Goddess*

Many pipeclay figurines of the goddess Venus have been found in London. These white statuettes, about 4–6 inches high, were produced from moulds in Gaul, and imported to Britain. Despite their mass production, they are exquisite, showing the naked goddess of love and fertility holding or braiding long tresses. They probably served as offerings for those looking for love and as both personal talismans and votives at a household shrine by the river. Other popular pipeclay imports showed a seated mother holding a child.

A more spectacular rendering of 'The Mothers', the Deae Matres, can be seen in the Museum of London along with some of the Venus figures. This large relief, found in the old river wall towards Blackfriars, shows four women. Each holds an emblem of fertility: a baby, bread, fruit, and a puppy. Similar groupings of two and three Mothers have been found in the Gallic lands. These may well have been from a shrine in a larger temple, perhaps the Temple of Isis, and specifically for women's concerns, especially those of pregnancy, birth, and general productivity and sustenance.

Brigid

Black the town yonder,
Black those that are in it;
I am the white Swan,
Queen of them all.
The Carmina Gadelica

St Bride's Church, the Wedding Cake Church, stands in Fleet Street, a magnificent building designed by Wren after the Great Fire. Its

[Figure 11: *The Matronae.*]

white spire resembles the tiers of a wedding cake and appears to be a play on the word Bride. The St Bride's dedication is unusual in London. St Bride, or St Bridget of Kildare in Ireland, is said to have founded the church, and it is possible that Irish Celtic Missionaries founded it. It is one of the earliest known Christian foundations in the city, with a church being on this spot for 1,500 years. St Bride or Bridget are the Christian forms of the Irish Celtic Goddess Brigid, goddess of smithcraft, poetry, healing, and light and flame. Brigid was also a goddess associated with holy wells. There is still a well at this site, although there is currently no public access. Its flow must have once been substantial, as it supplied a swimming pool for the print workers operating out of Fleet Street. Such a well was probably a place of pre-Christian worship, and it was significant to the Romans who:

> dug a mysterious extra-mural ditch on the site of the future church and built a house, which seems likely to have been one of the earliest sites of worship.[10]

During the Blitz of 1940, several London churches were deliberately targeted to break the spirit of Londoners. St Bride's was chosen, along with St Paul's. The bombing did substantial damage to the church, and cracked it open like an egg, revealing Saxon foundations and a Roman pavement, and many objects from the previous centuries. These can be seen in the crypt museum. The church was repaired and the history revealed led to St Bride's being dubbed 'The Phoenix of Fleet Street', rising from the firestorm of that night. Many go here today to connect with the goddess of water and flame, or with the saint. At the back of the crypt is a tiny chapel, which is a perfect place to sit in meditation and communion, still and peaceful beneath the hubbub of the city streets. The well lies under the south-east of the small churchyard.

Black Madonna of Willesden

The Black Madonna is mainly known in France and Southern Europe, where there are many, but London boasts its own. They are mysterious figures, sometimes statues, sometimes icons, and their origins are obscure. Some say they represent pre-Christian African goddesses such as Isis, or the Magna Mater of the black fertile earth, the underworld where all seeds quicken. In her Christian guise, she may be Mary Magdalene, or her daughter, Sarah the Egyptian. Wherever they are found, they are especially venerated.

London's Black Madonna site is in Willesden, north-west London. In legend, a holy well sprung up where the Virgin appeared. In another legend, she appeared in an oak tree, and gained the title 'Our Lady of the Oak'. The current Black Madonna statue replaced an older statue, described in 1535 as 'of woode, colour like ebon, of ancient workmanship' that was burnt at Thomas Cromwell's house in Chelsea during the Reformation. It can be seen in St Mary's Parish Church, Willesden (the Hill of Wells).

This church, which was once in the countryside, is now on a remarkably picturesque island of greenery among the traffic and urban sprawl of what is now north-west London. It was founded in 938 by King Athelstan and houses the holy well in the crypt. The church was built over the well, and medieval pilgrim badges to Our Lady of

Willesden have been found there. People came to the holy well for cures for eye ailments. The statue, which dates from 1897, is larger than the older European counterparts. She sits in the Lady Chapel, next to a container of well water that modern pilgrims can take away if they bring a container.

The cult is kept up in the local Roman Catholic church, which has a modern statue, and processions with it began in 1903, on the Feast of the Assumption of the Virgin, 15 August, a festival that absorbed the feast day of the Goddess Diana. The processions were noisily disrupted by Protestants, including the late Reverend Ian Paisley. In 1954, 'Mary's Year', thousands of pilgrims visited Willesden and a jewelled crown was placed on the head of the Roman Catholic statue by Cardinal Griffin at Wembley Stadium.[11] In April 1987, a woman claimed on BBC Radio 4 that the Blessed Virgin would appear in an oak tree in the churchyard, and 500 people turned up on the appointed day, but there was no manifestation.[12]

Cybele

There seems to have been a considerable revival of mystery religions, with their esoteric rites and doctrines, in the fourth century, in particular the Oriental cults of Cybele and Mithras, and the Egyptian rites of Isis and Serapis.
Labriolle, *La Réaction Païenne*

Lying in a display case in the Museum of London is a morbidly fascinating object. It is a bronze 'castration clamp', about a foot long and of exquisite craftsmanship. It is richly decorated with representations of the great Goddess Cybele and her son/lover Attis, plus animals including a fine horse's head, and Roman deities including Mars and Diana. Cybele's origins lie in Anatolia, at Mount Ida. She was a goddess of the mountain, and the central Phrygian goddess, wearing the mural crown symbolic of rulership and protection. She rode in a chariot drawn by lions. Cybele was assimilated with the great Greek goddesses of the earth, Gaia and Rhea. It was with the Greeks that the mystery cult of Cybele and Attis developed. Her priests castrated themselves in honour of the dying/castrated Attis.

To the Romans Cybele was the Magna Mater, the Great Mother, with Trojan origins, and she travelled with the Empire. It is not known if this clamp, which was found in the Thames near London Bridge, was actually used in castration rites, or is a symbolic item from the cult made as a votive offering to the river. It may, of course, just be a worker's tool for castrating animals, but the ornamentation and craftsmanship make this unlikely. There is little known of Cybele's cult in London, and it is possible the object was brought here by a traveller priest.

Sekhmet

Seven massive statues in grey and black granite, varying in height from seven to five feet, being of too ponderous a character for the floors of the auction room, were, with prudent caution, exposed to view in the recesses of the bridge above-mentioned. Among the singular circumstances incidental to the changes brought about by the light of Christianity will be noted the appearance of the idols of Egypt, shorn of all their honours and tutelary reputation, for several days on Waterloo Bridge.[13]
Statues of the Goddess Sekhmet, Metropolitan Museum of Art, New York

There was no ancient cult of the Egyptian lion-headed sun goddess Sekhmet in London, but her statues in the British Museum have become a place of modern pilgrimage for many with an interest in the goddess. The majestic granite statues exude quiet power. Like all the Sekhmet statues in Europe, they come from the Temple of the Vulture Goddess Mut in Karnak, built at the command of Amenhotep III, whose son Akhenaton went on to see the sun as representative of the major deity in Egypt. The life-size statues came to London in the early 1830s to be sold at auction. Due to their weight, they were left on Waterloo Bridge for prospective buyers to come and see them. There is a legend that despite the prudent caution mentioned above, one fell into the river (or was she pushed?), and lies beneath the waters to this day. An Ancient Egyptian bust of Sekhmet that was sold but not collected, sits on top of the sign of Sotheby's auction house in

Bond Street, with many Londoners passing under it every day without noticing her.

Elen

The antiquarian author Harold Bayley, writing in his book *The Lost Language of London* in the early 1930s, mentions a mysterious goddess called Elen as the primary goddess of London. He even saw her as giving her name to London, as in 'El-un-dun'. The mythic fourth-century Elen of the Hosts, St Elen of Wales, whom we meet in the medieval Welsh *Mabinogion* tales, and St Helena, the Empress and mother of Constantine the Great, became entwined with the figure proposed by Bayley. He saw Elen as one of the most ancient British goddesses and suggests that places sacred to St Helena, such as the church of St Helen's Bishopsgate in the City, may be earlier places of the Goddess Elen (see pages 219–20).

Elen is principally concerned with old roads and ancient pathways, and like the Goddess Diana, is accompanied by a greyhound. Bayley saw Elen as a guardian of London and believed that she was remembered in the legend that St Helena oversaw the building of the Roman London Wall. The church of St Helen's in Bishopsgate, founded in 1200, was a nunnery for Benedictine nuns.[14] There is a tradition that pre-conquest churches existed on the site, including a fourth-century one that St Helena's son Constantine had built and dedicated to his mother after her death. This links the site closely to St Helena's own time, and back beyond that to the elusive goddess Elen.

4

The Guardian Head: Sacred Palladia of Britain

Caitlín Matthews

Uneasy lies the head that wears a throne . . .
W.C. Sellar and R.J. Yeatman, *1066 and All That*

The Tower of London

The Tower of London is perhaps the most formidable symbol of Britain's sovereignty that tourists are ever likely to visit. Its walls are encrusted with legend, history and tradition. Housing the ultimate symbols of sovereignty – the royal regalia, including the coronation crown, it has been a national fortress and armoury, as well as a prison and place of execution. Altogether, it is an overwhelming collation of history in place.

Its fame, or rather notoriety, is represented by three places whose names and colours speak volumes: the White Tower – once the residence of sovereigns on the night before their coronation; the Bloody Tower, the place of confinement and often of violent death for many prisoners; and Tower Green, the site of execution for politically superfluous nobility or traitorously inclined commoners. The bone-white Tower has the patina of a skull, and so it is no coincidence that visitors experience a shudder or two.

Heads figure largely in the apocryphal stories surrounding the Tower. The comic song's well-known chorus refers to Anne Boleyn, the unfortunate, second wife of King Henry VIII, executed within the Tower precincts:

> *With her head tucked underneath her arm,*
> *She walks the Bloody Tower.*
> *With her head tucked underneath her arm*
> *At the midnight hour.*[1]

[Figure 12: *The White Tower* by Gustave Doré,
from *London: A Pilgrimage*, 1872.]

This hilarity is touched by more than a little fear, for on Tower Green, capital punishment was the fate of many and, on London Bridge, the sight of traitors' heads was a common sight, a salutary deterrent to the unwary.

Of course, the traditional lore which has become attached to these places gives visitors a thrilling shudder as they listen spellbound to a burly Yeoman of the Guard rehearsing the gory details with considerable relish. But yet, there is no smoke without fire. That same shudder of horror is akin to the atavistic frisson that attends the coronation of a British monarch with all its pomp and ceremony.

The Tower of London is a kind of time machine or rather a time-condenser, where the layered traditions and their attendant ghosts rise up to seize the visitor's sleeve. Some sensitives cannot visit it all without feeling decidedly unwell and even stolidly unpsychic people get disoriented. That it is a place of power is unquestioned, but it is to get to the roots of that tradition that this essay is concerned, rather than with ghost-hunting or psychic phenomena.

The history of the Tower, according to the guidebooks, starts with William the Conqueror but this piece of information, like the edited versions of national chronology that are repeated in many old English history books, is not the whole story. The Norman Conquest built upon the foundations an existent Anglo-Saxon economy that in turn built upon and incorporated Romano-British and Celtic frameworks. The site of the Tower has ever been of great importance, deeply connected with the sovereignty of the land, and has served as a royal fortress, and symbolic stronghold of the land's potency.

Part of the site of the Tower of London was built upon the Romans, who discerned its strategic position, but it was the indigenous population of Britain – the Celts – for whom this site became a focus of mystical awe. This tradition goes totally unacknowledged in official guidebooks, which proffer a cleaned-up, tourist version of English history that ignores the wider chronology and influence of the indigenous Celtic nations, who have been subsumed into the homogeneity of Great Britain.

Bran the Blessed

For the Cymru (the name by which the Welsh call themselves), the Tower is more than a national armoury or stronghold; it is associated with one of the great legendary palladia of Britain – the guardian head of Bran the Blessed, which was interred at the Gwynbryn or White Hill, as the Tower is known in Welsh lore.

This legend appears in *The Mabinogion* in the story of Branwen, Daughter of Llyr,[2] and is further corroborated by the Welsh Triads.[3] It describes the troubled times of the legendary Bran, King of Britain; the unfortunate marriage of his sister, Branwen, to the King of Ireland; and the subsequent fall of the British in Ireland. At the end of this story Bran, mortally wounded, charges the seven men who are the remnant of his army:

> 'And take you my head,' said he, 'and bear it even unto the White Mount, in London, and bury it there, with the face towards French. And a long time will you be upon the road. In Harlech you will be feasting seven years, the birds of Rhiannon singing unto you the while. And all that time the head will be to you as pleasant company as it ever

was when on my body. And at Gwales in Penfro you will be fourscore years, and you may remain there, and the head with you uncorrupted, until you open the door that looks towards Aber Henvelen, and towards Cornwall. And after you have open that door, there you may no longer tarry, set forth then to London to bury the head, and go straight forward.'[4]

Needless to say, the forbidden door is opened, the head begins to decay and the seven men recall the sorrow of the tragic events in Ireland. This Otherworldly sojourn in which the natural processes are suspended is called 'The Entertainment of the Noble Head' and was one of the prime stories told by bardic storytellers. What is significant for our purposes is the fact that Bran is voluntarily beheaded in order to become a sacred palladium for Britain.

Goddess of the City

Before we proceed, it is probably wise to discover the origins of the concept of a palladium. In British terms, as we shall see, sacred palladia draw from a tradition of sacrificial kingship. In classical terms, the idea of a palladium (Greek: *palladion*) springs from the goddess, Pallas Athene.

In one myth, Athene acquired her epithet, Pallas, from her father who was a winged, goatish giant. She added his name to her own after having flayed him of his skin to make the aegis, taking his wings for her own shoulders. This tradition is at odds with the myth that tells of how it was the skin of Medusa, the Gorgon, which formed the aegis. The aegis was the strong shield of Zeus over which this skin was placed.

Interestingly, the priestess of Athene visited newly married women dressed in the aegis from the cult statue in order to mediate the protection of Athene.[5] It is described as being Athene's armour in Euripides's *Ion* (lines 989–93). Athene is also credited with beheading Medusa and taking her head for a defensive mask: this was the *gorgoneion* or gorgon's head, which is sometimes shown on Athene's breast. She is the strong, unvanquished, virginal goddess, and her image, the

[Figure 13: Figurehead of HMS *London* built in 1840. Personifying London she is crowned with a representation of the White Tower.]

Palladium, guarantees security for the city and for the besieged a sacred place of refuge whose desecration by force is fiercely punished by her fierce anger.[6]

The original *palladion* was a statue of Pallas Athene, three cubits tall; it had a spear in its right hand and distaff and spindle in the left. 'The continuance of the city depended on the possession of the Palladion: if it fell into the hands of the enemy, Ilion fell.'[7] It was stolen by Odysseus, with the connivance of Helen, who showed him the way to the shrine. Pausanias concluded that Aeneas must have taken it to Italy.[8]

The City of London has no goddess parallel to Athene's protection of Athens, unless it be the Celtic goddess, Fflur, over whom the native British Caswallawn (Cassivelaunus) and the Roman invader, Julius Caesar, fought.

This mythic tradition may well conceal the known historical facts. For Julius Caesar did encounter Cassivelaunus, son of Beli, the elected war-leader of the southern British tribes, when he attempted to invade Britain in 54 BC. Cassivelaunus put up a considerable fight, pulling up his troops behind a fence of stakes on the northern side of the Thames – the only fordable point of the river.[9] He was overcome and continued to clear the land of people, in order to hide from Caesar the location of his stronghold, as well as to harry the Roman troops with devastating onslaughts of chariots. But, eventually, Cassivelaunus was forced to capitulate and Caesar granted him terms, requesting an annual tribute payable to Rome as well as hostages. (It is likely that Cassivelaunus received moderately favourable terms, seeing as Caesar was considerably overextended from his base in Gaul and the campaigning season was at an end.)

There is a tradition of Caesar's Tower being supposedly built on or near the site of the present Tower, but it is unlikely that Julius Caesar did much to fortify London.

It is interesting to speculate whether Fflur was really taken by Caesar as a hostage, in this deal, or whether she symbolically represents the sovereignty of Britain and that Cassivelaunus's loss of her reflects his inability to maintain the land free of invasion.

Elements of this tradition are preserved in both Branwen, daughter of Llyr and Manawyddan, son of Llyr, where Cassivelaunus is cast as Caswallawn, the usurper of Bran's kingdom.[10] *The Mabinogion* says that after the debacle in Ireland, Caswallawn is subsequently crowned King of London. The transparent figure of Fflur, preserved in Triad 67 as the one for whom Caswallawn went to Rome to seek, appears also in twelfth-century Welsh poetry:

> There has been Julius Caesar, he had sought out Fflur
> From the lord of Britain, costly his care for her.[11]

From this scanty evidence, we can only posit the name 'Fflur', which means 'flower', as a symbolic title for the land of Britain.

As I have written elsewhere, the concept of the goddess of the land was strong in Celtic myth.[12] This figures even within the story of Bran where, at the beginning of the tale, Bran's sister, Branwen, is sought in marriage by Matholwch, King of Ireland. The family confer and agree to this match; all, that is, except Efnissien, Branwen's brother. He grievously insults Celtic hospitality by mutilating Matholwch's horses so that, in compensation, Bran is forced to gift Matholwch with the cauldron of rebirth. The chief property of this hallowed object is that it can revive dead men, though it denies them speech.

Branwen sails to Ireland with her husband, but Efnissien's insult rankles deeply and he is forced to cast her off, even though she has born him a son, Gwern. Branwen suffers humiliation in Matholwch's kitchens and trains a starling to take a message to Bran, warning him of her plight. Bran and his men make a foray into Ireland to rescue Branwen. A truce is agreed, by dint of deposing Matholwch and substituting his son, Gwern. At the inaugural feast, Efnissien, on the pretext of hugging his nephew, casts him on to the fire. There ensues a terrible carnage, during which Bran receives his mortal wounding and the cauldron ruthlessly reprocesses dead Irish warriors until Efnissien gets into it as a living man and breaks it in pieces. Branwen dies of grief and Bran is beheaded as stated above.[13]

The most puzzling thing about this story is the role of Efnissien. For without the back-up knowledge of Celtic kingship and sovereignty lore, his position is untenable. Efnissien actually represents the role of 'Provoker of Strife' and, more importantly, the champion of the Goddess of Sovereignty, represented by his sister, Branwen.[14]

Branwen represents the land of Britain in her own person. By marrying her to Matholwch, Bran virtually gives away the sovereignty of Britain. Only Efnissien combats this – a purist to the end, even down to killing Gwern, the child of mixed British and Irish blood.

In giving away the cauldron, Bran leaves his land vulnerable to attack, for the cauldron of rebirth is one of the sacred Hallows – the symbolic empowerment of the King by the land. He pays for this piece of generosity with his own life, becoming the kingly sacrifice that will keep the land safe in future.

The fate of Bran and Branwen is deeply allied with the sacred relationship that should be between the monarch and the land. Anciently, when a Celtic king was inaugurated, the ceremonial included a symbolic or actual marriage to the land, represented by the priestess or royal woman of the clan.

The Goddess of the Land is specifically linked to London in Geoffrey of Monmouth's *Prophecies of Merlin*:

A girl shall be sent to remedy these matters by her healing art . . . She shall carry the Forest of Caledon in her right hand and in her left the buttressed forts of the walls of London . . . Tears of compassion shall flow from her eyes and she will fill the island with her dreadful cries.[15]

Branwen's role is a mysterious and little-understood one. But her fate, so closely allied to the guardianship of the land exercised by her brother, Bran, cannot be coincidental. The patterns of Celtic kingship discount the incestuous marriage of brother and sister as practised by Egyptian dynasties, but, in death, Branwen and Bran represent the Goddess of the Land and its inner guardian.

The Hidden God

The palladium of Britain, associated with its chief city, is the head of Bran, although, as we shall see, it is not the only sacred defence. In British tradition, it is the body, or more particularly, the head of the king that fulfils this role. As long as the king's head is buried at a certain point, then the land cannot be conquered.

The Welsh Triads present us with weighty evidence for this tradition. Triads are terse mnemonic sentences, arranged in groups of three; they are the remnant of an extensive oral tradition in which bardic poets, storytellers and druids preserved ancestral lore. Triad 37 records a tripartite British tradition about its sacred palladiums:

Three Fortunate Concealments of the Island of Britain
The Head of Bran the Blessed, son of Llyr, which was buried in the White Hill in London.
And as long as it was there in that position, no Oppression would ever come to this island.
The second: the Bones of Gwerthefyr the Blessed, which were buried in the Chief Ports of this Island.
The third: the Dragons which Lludd, son of Beli, buried in Dinas Emrys in Eryri.[16]

These are juxtaposed by:

Three Unfortunate Disclosures of the Island of Britain

Gwrtheyrn the Thin disclosed the bones of Gwerthfyr the Blessed
    for the love of a woman; that was Ronnwen the pagan woman.
And it was he who disclosed the dragons.
And Arthur disclosed the Head of Bran the Blessed from the White
    Hill, because it did not seem right to him that this Island should
    be defended by the strength of anyone, but by his own.[17]

Gwerthfyr is none other than Vortimer, son of Vortigern – the
Gwrtheyrn the Thin of the triad. Vortimer predeceased his father,
having spent his energies on repelling the invading Saxons.

Geoffrey of Monmouth writes of Vortimer's dying wish:

He commanded that a brazen pyramid should be wrought for him,
and set in the haven wherein the Saxons were wont to land, and that
after his death his body should be buried on the top of it, so that when
the barbarians should behold his image on it they should sail back and
return to Germany . . . And after his death the Britons did otherwise,
for they buried his body in the city of Trinovantum.[18]

Although the triad and Geoffrey are at slight variance, we note that
the fifth-century prince, Vortimer, is credited with the same protective powers as Bran – even to the extent of being classed with him in
the same triad.

The last tradition of fortunate concealment is told about the dragons that troubled the reign of Lludd ap Beli, Geoffrey of Monmouth's
King Lud, the founder of London or Troia Nova. Lludd is troubled
by three different kinds of Otherworldly interference, one of which is
a great shriek that is heard over the country on May Eve. It strikes
terror into the hearts of warriors, makes women and fields barren,
and kills the old and young. Lludd discovers the cause: the national
dragon and a foreign dragon do battle on this night. He is instructed
to find the exact centre of his realm – discovered to be Oxford – and
there place a chest full of mead. The dragons sink down from their
labours, drink the mead and are imprisoned in Snowdonia.[19]

The story of their disclosure is well known from Geoffrey of
Monmouth's story about the coming of Merlin. Vortigern, after a

70

disastrous reign in which he invites the Saxons into Britain, retreats to Wales and attempts to build a stronghold. It keeps falling down and his druids say that this can only be remedied by the foundations being smeared by the blood of a boy who has no father.

Young Merlin Emrys' mother was visited by a daimon and Vortigern's men overhear some boys taunting Merlin with this and so bring him to Vortigern's tower on Dinas Emrys. The wondrous child challenges the druids, in the manner of Christ debating with the elders in the temple, to tell him what lies under the foundations. They are unable, and so Merlin Emrys reveals the tradition of the dragons to be a true one. Men are sent to dig and they uncover the dragons that resume their eternal combat. At this point, Merlin is moved to utter a series of brilliant and obscure prophecies related to the history and destiny of Britain.[20]

Thus Vortigern is indirectly responsible for uncovering the dragons. Their concealment, like the Otherworldly sojourn of the Entertainment of the Noble Head, seems to impose the suspension of time and normal activity. Vortigern's reign is marred by the Saxon invasion and, as we have seen, he is roundly accused of two unfortunate disclosures – the dragons and the body of his son Vortimer (a prototype of Bran).

The fact that the dragons were originally buried due to the intervention of the founder of London, Lludd, shows the close interrelation of these stories with the central tradition of the king as palladium. For these are stories about the safeguarding of Britain and all, to some extent, reflect the importance – political or mythic – that the City of London has in this role.

The last story, of Bran's disinterment by Arthur, presents us with a facet of the Arthurian legend that is seldom considered. The Welsh Triads, together with *The Mabinogion* present the native character of King Arthur before it was developed by the chivalric, medieval romances. Instead of a heraldic, cut-out king, whose knights perform all his significant actions for him, the early British Arthur is a figure of courageous vigour, one who goes out on quest and fights in his own person. A reading of Culhwch and Olwen or The Dream of Rhonabwy immediately testify to this understanding of Arthur as a powerful protector of his people, as Arthur himself remarks to Cai:

It is an honour to us to be resorted to, and the greater our courtesy the greater will be our renown, and our fame, and our glory.[21]

The fact that Arthur wishes no other palladium but himself may seem indicative of hubris, but perhaps there is a more mystical explanation for the unfortunate disinterment.

The Succession of the Pendragons

In my book, *Mabon and the Guardians of Celtic Britain*, I speculated that, within the native British tradition, there could be discerned a mythic pattern of sovereignty which I termed 'The Succession of the Pendragons'.[22] Within one or more generations there seemed to be present three mythic personas:

Mabon – the innocent youth, who acts as the candidate king, or bardic adjudicator, whose function is to reveal injustice and establish peace.

Pendragon – the king or battle-lord whose function is to hold the land in balance by the exercise of his authority.

Pen Annwn – the elder, who may be either a disincarnate king, or a restrictive ruler whose reign has come to its close or has deteriorated into chaos, whose function is either to impart wisdom or else to be overcome and replaced by Mabon.

There is a successive pattern to this schema, in that the person representing the Mabon function succeeds to the office of Pendragon and thereafter to that of Pen Annwn (a title that is derived from the Welsh for 'Lord of the Underworld'). The person in the position of Pen Annwn is understood to be either overcome or else to retire to an Otherworldly state, during which he renews himself, to take up the office of Mabon in another age.

This long explanation is necessary if we are to proceed. Using the Succession of the Pendragons, we see that the characters from this article can all be placed upon this schema:

72

MABON – Merlin Emrys, Vortimer
PENDRAGON – Arthur, Lludd
PEN ANNWN – Bran, Vortigern

As we have seen, it is Lludd who protects his kingdom by burying the dragons and Vortigern who disinters them. The unsuccessful attempt by Vortimer to fend off the Saxons is balanced by the successful over-coming of Vortigern – the causer of chaos – by the young Merlin Emrys (who later becomes the chief adviser of Uther, Arthur's father). Bran's attempt to rescue his sister Branwen is unsuccessful and he relinquishes the sovereignty of Britain, becoming a withdrawn King. He literally becomes a Lord of the Underworld, a source of great power, under the White Mount.

Arthur himself passes through all three functions in the Succession of the Pendragons in a clearly defined way. There is room to discuss one such metamorphosis. A ninth-century poem, 'Preiddeu Annwn' or 'The Spoils of Annwn', relates how Arthur, in an incident paralleling Bran's foray into Ireland, went to retrieve the cauldron of Pen Annwn.[23] Of his company, only seven returned. One of these was the poet Taliesin, who also figures as one of the survivors of Bran's foray.

Now Bran was also the possessor of a cauldron. Later Welsh tradition also refers to it as 'the horn of Bran the Niggard'. This object appears, with twelve other items, in a list known as 'The Thirteen Treasures of Britain'.[24] These are said, in some traditions, to be guarded by Merlin in his Otherworldly observatory on Bardsey Island. But there is an alternative tradition that speaks of Taliesin as being their guardian.

It is said of Taliesin that 'he transformed Bran the Niggard into one better than the three generous men'.[25] This curious statement helps us make the link between Bran and Arthur, for 'the three generous men' is a reference to a triad, which speaks of three British rulers famed for their generosity. But, says the triad, Arthur himself was more generous than the three.[26]

The implication of Taliesin's mysterious action is that he is responsible for translating the role of Bran into that of Arthur.[27] This obscure tradition seems bent on replacing Bran by Arthur in much the same way that Triad 37 implies. Arthur, with the typical economy of mythology, takes on the attributes and powers of Bran, becoming the palladium for Britain. The subsequent legends surrounding the passing of Arthur – like Bran, mortally wounded but undying – merely reinforce the likeness between the two figures. Arthur is withdrawn to Avalon, from whence he is popularly supposed to be available in the time of Britain's need. This belief draws upon the mythos of Bran in the enduring tradition of the king as national palladium. Arthur, like Bran, is the hidden god who will return and whose wise guidance is available when chaos and invasion threaten.

The Abiding Raven

The sole remaining trace of Bran's legend at the Tower of London are the ravens, about which a significant tradition is preserved. If the ravens should leave the Tower precincts, runs the saying, then Britain shall lose her sovereignty. This is truncated legend derived from the Bran story for, in Welsh, Bran means 'raven'.

These mythic traditions have a political underpinning, for they undoubtedly reinforced the embattled national identity of the Welsh during a time when Norman monarchy was overcoming the Cymric dynastic rule that had existed since the times of Arthur.

The names of Bran and Arthur had been talismans to ward off the evils of Saxon incursion. They were used again in order to rally the Cymru against the encroachment of Norman rule.

There have been numerous attempts to snatch back the sovereignty of Britain by the Welsh – the original British people. Chief and most lamented of these many leaders is Llywellyn II, whose own father, Gruffydd, was killed in attempting to escape from the Tower. Llywellyn proclaimed himself the Pendragon of Wales – a notable title in the light of his subsequent demise. After the defeat and death of Llywellyn on 11 December 1282:

> The skull of Saint David went with the Crown of Arthur to Westminster as part of the loot. The Prince's severed head crowned with ivy, was carried on the end of a pole through the city in derisory fulfilment of a Merlin prophecy that a Welsh king would ride crowned through London.[28]

It was then placed on the battlements of the Tower of London in unconscious imitation of a more ancient palladium. It was in such a climate that stories of Bran the Blessed would have circulated and been written down, since the date of *The Mabinogion*'s transmission is shortly after this time in the early fourteenth century. Geoffrey of Monmouth, writing some hundred and forty years before the demise of Llywellyn II, recorded the following prophecy of Merlin:

> Then shall a Tree spring up on the top of the Tower of London. It will be content with only three branches and yet it will overshadow the whole length and breadth of the land with the spread of its leaves. The North Wind will come as the Tree's enemy and with its noxious breath it will tear away the third of the branches. The two branches which are left will occupy the place of the one ripped off; this until one of them destroys the other by the very abundance of its leaves. This last branch will fill the place of the other two and it will offer a roosting place to birds come from foreign parts. To birds native to the country it will seem harmful, for through their dread of its shadow they will lose their power of free flight.[29]

This obscure prophecy has been seen as referring to the Hanoverian monarchy. The last branch refers, of course, to Queen Victoria, whose numerous offspring intermarried with every royal house in Europe. The last reference seems to refer perhaps to the clipping of the ravens' wings at the Tower of London, which only took place at the turn of the century, to stop the birds flying off. (They rarely strayed beyond St James's Park, upriver.) This piece of self-deception was entirely to prop up the sovereignty of the British Empire, since it was perhaps felt expedient to insure against the fateful day when the ravens might indeed leave the Tower and Britain's greatness be toppled.

And so the ravens remain the last vestiges of the sacred palladium of Britain at the Tower of London, traditionally fulfilling the role of Bran. They are still present, cared for by a Yeoman Warder rejoicing under the name of the Master Raven Keeper, who houses them in their lodgings at the base of the Wakefield Tower.

The Island Enclosure

Britain has been called by many names, but the one most calculated to provoke response is Clas Merddin or Merlin's Enclosure. This expression is found in a list of names given in an appendix to the Welsh Triads.[30] The word *clas* has the overtones of 'monastic community' or 'druidic enclosure' – a sacred enclave upon which the profane may not tread.[31]

The tradition that Merlin stills guards the island of Britain enjoys a new lease of life in the continuing popularity of the Matter of Britain, as the Arthurian legends are known. For just as Arthur will come again at the nation's need, so Merlin rings the island round with a protective barrier. It is within this enclosure that the palladium of the guardian head remains.

And though the Tower of London may now seem bereft of its ultimate power, a symbolic stronghold only, suitable for tourists and cranky national traditions, it nevertheless provides a microcosm of this very Clas Merddin: its walls enclosing the bodies of kings and sacrificial maidens, preserving the empowering treasures of the monarchy, its precincts redolent with the overwhelming potency of sovereignty.

5

Templar London

Nigel Pennick

T HE KNIGHTS TEMPLAR remain the most enigmatic of the knightly orders that came into being during the Crusades. Because the order was suppressed and the leading Templars executed, controversy still rages over the spiritual meaning of Templarism. In the twelfth and thirteenth centuries, London was an important centre of the Templars, and even today, their influence is present in that part of London called 'The Temple'.

The origin of the Knights Templar lies in the genesis of the First Crusade. In 1095, Pope Urban II called for a military expedition to Palestine to recover Jerusalem, occupied by the Moslems since the year 638. Persecution of Christianity had become institutionalized there, culminating in the early part of the eleventh century in the deliberate extirpation of the holiest of Christ's shrines. So this first crusade was presented as a summons by God to pious military men to overthrow unbelievers and punish the enemies of Christ. Many saw it also as an opportunity for colonization of new lands, and a means for personal aggrandizement in both wealth and renown.

In a short time, the crusade was a remarkable success. Jerusalem was captured in July 1099, with the massacre of the entire population. Seventy thousand people were put to the sword, the same number killed by the atomic bombing of Nagasaki in 1945. When the massacre finally ceased, the leaders of the crusade put on fresh clothing and went to the church of the Holy Sepulchre for a service of thanksgiving. Jerusalem was repopulated with Christians, and then became the major object of Christian pilgrimage.

After the Christian conquest, increasingly large numbers of pilgrims journeyed to the Holy Land to visit the sacred places of the Christian faith. But when their ships reached the port of Joppa, the pilgrims had to make a two-days journey to reach Jerusalem. Travelling the mountainous, rocky road, the scantily armed pilgrims were easy targets for bandits and the marauding Saracen soldiery, who had not been driven out of Palestine. The German Abbot Ekkehard, writing at that time, recorded that robberies, kidnappings into slavery and 'martyrdoms' of pilgrims had become an everyday occurrence. But help was at hand. In 1118, a group of eight religious warriors, led by the French knights Hugues de Payens and Godfrey de S. Audomaro, swore an oath before the Patriarch of Jerusalem that they would live as monks in the manner of the Canons Regular. Unlike the Canons Regular, whose rule they took, these men were of the warrior class, who undertook to protect pilgrims on the road to Jerusalem from Saracen attacks.

King Baldwin gave the monk-knights part of his palace and the former mosque of Al-Aksa. At this time, the great mosque Al-Aksa was known as Templum Solomonis, for, as an example of sacred site-evolution, it overlay the site of Solomon's and later temples. Archbishop William of Tyre, described the event as follows:

> Certain pious and God-fearing knightly noblemen, devotees of The Lord, expressed the desire to live in poverty, chastity and obedience in perpetuity. They vowed before the Patriarch to serve God as Regular Canons . . . Because they had neither a church nor a fixed dwelling-place, the king granted them a temporary home in his own palace, to the north side of the Lord's temple . . . [he] also gave them a square belonging to the canons near his palace in which the new Order could carry out the duties of its profession.[1]

The new Order took the name of 'The Military Order of the Knights of the Temple of Solomon', known shortly as the Knights Templar.

Christian military orders like the Templars, the Knights of St John and the Teutonic Knights were a Christian development of the older northern martial arts warrior tradition. In tenth-century Scandinavia, only a century earlier, the pagan military order known as the Jomsvikings had been founded. This was a model for later chivalric orders. Only warriors of proven valour were admitted to the brother-hood. They lived in barracks without women, being under a strict discipline very similar to that later adopted by military religious orders like the Templars. The Jomsvikings were warriors dedicated to Odin, and, like the Templars, warriors dedicated to Christ, they were sworn to die in battle if necessary.

Shortly before the founding of the Templars, there were also other military orders in the northern martial arts tradition such as King Sweyn Forkbeard's feared Huscarles. The Norse Varangian Guard of Harald Hardrada, bodyguards of the Emperor of Constantinople, was the direct model for the Templars, Hospitallers and Teutonic Knights. The traditions of the northern martial arts, vitally alive at the battles of Stamford Bridge and Hastings in 1066, only forty-five years before the foundation of the Templars, were continued in a new form in the twelfth century.

Having been founded in Jerusalem, the Knights Templar took to building their churches circular in emulation of that erected over the reputed tomb of Christ. Churches (or 'temples') were modelled after the round Holy Sepulchre church at Jerusalem. More specifically, the circular portion of these churches imitates the round *anastasis*, which enclosed the supposed site of the tomb of Christ, the Holy Sepulchre itself. Attached to this was the *martyrium*, the apsidal choir that stood above the reputed site of the crucifixion. Effectively, the crusades were concerned with sacred places, restoring those sites of the Christian faith that had been captured by Islam. Of these sacred places, the Holy Sepulchre was the most important. Being in Jerusalem, it had been built at a major sacred place over which Jews, Moslems and Christians claimed mutually exclusive possession, a certain formula for conflict.

At first, the Islamic governments had respected the churches. The Holy Sepulchre's Christian Arabic name, Al Qiyàmah (The Resurrection), was popularly altered to *Al Qumameh* (The Shit-heap), but it was not until around the year 935 that a mosque was built in the atrium of the Holy Sepulchre. But things took a turn for the worse in 967, when Moslems, aided by Jews, burned the *anastasis*, the remaining Christian part of the Holy Sepulchre, and with it, the Patriarch, John. This occasioned a Byzantine crusade that led, paradoxically, to the establishment of a Shiite fundamentalist government in Jerusalem.

In the year 1008 the Caliph, Al Hakem bi-Amr Illah, began to perse-
cute the Christians, a campaign that resulted the next year in the
destruction of the Holy Sepulchre church. Yahya, the historian of
Antioch, wrote:

> He . . . ordered them to destroy the Church of the resurrection to the
> very roots, and to pull up its illustrious foundations . . . They took
> possession of the church and its ancillary buildings and completely
> demolished it . . . They destroyed Golgotha, and the Church of St
> Constantine and everything that stood within the churchyard, and
> caused the dispersal of the sacred relics.

Ibn Abi Daher persisted in the demolition of the Holy Tomb, even to
the last trace, and he did, in fact, cut out a large part of the foundation, which was taken away. For this act of religious intolerance, Al
Hakem bi-Amr Illah was subsequently canonized, becoming a saint
in the Lebanese Druze denomination of Islam.

However, the site of the church of the Holy Sepulchre was too
important to be abandoned by Christian believers, and so, when the
outburst of Islamic fundamentalism had subsided, it was rebuilt in
1047. After the successful capture of Jerusalem by the Christian forces,
it was sumptuously refurbished. Because it was the reputed tomb of
Christ, and also because it had suffered at the hands of anti-Chris-
tians, the Holy Sepulchre then became a symbol of the faith, to be
defended against the infidel at all costs.

There was another reason, too – the geomantic one. According to
medieval cosmology, the Holy Sepulchre at Jerusalem stood at the
exact centre of the (flat) Earth. To possess the Compas, as this point
was known, was to exercise dominion over all of the Earth. To the
Christians, the Holy Sepulchre at Jerusalem was the Compas. This
can be seen in surviving medieval maps, such as the Mappa Mundi at
Hereford. In addition, each round church built in imitation of the
Holy Sepulchre, such as the London Temple, was seen itself as the
world in microcosm. The ruined round church at Orphir, Orkney, is
still called the 'Girth House' in recognition of its microcosmic nature.

In this emulation of the conceptual form of the Earth, the Orkney
and London churches also followed the fortresses of the pagan

military orders that had been built in Denmark a few years earlier. These circular earthen and wood castles, such as those that still exist at Trelleborg, Aggersborg and Fyrkat, reproduced the quartered 'holy city' plan, which was ascribed to Jerusalem and the world by medieval mapmakers. Their precise layout and accurate measurements demonstrate the presence of highly competent *locators* and surveyors in the ranks of the military orders. This is present, too, in the Masonic elements of Templarism. The knightly connection with the round table of King Arthur also comes to mind, for the Templar age was the time when chivalric legend saw its fullest flowering. But Jerusalem was recaptured by the Saracens in 1187, and the Christian Latin Kingdom which had given rise to the Knights Templar came to an end.

The first English preceptory of the Templars was established soon after 1128 in Holborn on a site on the north-east corner of what is now Chancery Lane. The ruins of this settlement, complete with the foundations of a round church, were found during redevelopment in 1875. The round consisted of a central circular area of 20 feet in diameter. This used the medieval masons' scheme of sacred geometry known as *ad triangulum*, having six pillars supporting the roof. This church seems to have been very similar to the still-existing Hospitaller round church at Little Maplestead, Essex.

Later, the London Templars removed their house to a new site near the Strand. The reason for this is not known. The new location to which they moved was the present site, which is still known as the Temple. This new Templar foundation dates from around 1160. The round church known as the New Temple was consecrated by Heraclius, the Patriarch of Jerusalem, on 10 February 1185, probably in the presence of King Henry II. An inscription above the inside of the entrance records this event.

The importance of the London Temple is emphasized by the fact that it was considered necessary for the Patriarch to travel to England from Palestine to consecrate the church. It is thought that originally this church had a short nave and apse similar to several other circular churches such as those at Little Maplestead, Temple Bruer in Lincolnshire and Drüggelte in Germany. This apsidal end was swept away in reconstruction that was consecrated on Ascension Day in

1240 in the presence of the king, Henry III. Subsequent alterations are of little primary geomantic interest, though they will have altered somewhat the character of the site.

Like the Old Temple at Holborn, the round of the New Temple, the present Temple church, is also built *ad triangulum* though much larger, being 59 feet in diameter. The other major round church in London, the Knights Hospitallers' church at St John at Clerkenwell, had eight pillars, making it *ad quadratum*. The extant Round Church at Cambridge has eight pillars, too. Although it is often stated to be a Templar church, it was actually built by the Fraternity of the Holy Sepulchre, a lay guild. Unusually for an imitation of the Jerusalem Holy Sepulchre, the New Temple does not bear that dedication, but is dedicated to St Mary. Paradoxically, the Holy Sepulchre dedication in London, at Holborn, is for a church with a standard (for London) rectangular form.

The circular form, emblematical of the world in microcosm, was a common form for Templar churches, many of which once existed in Europe and the Near East. Now, only six round churches of medieval date survive in the British Isles: the Temple, London; Little Maplestead, Essex (Knights Hospitaller); the Holy Sepulchre, Cambridge (lay guild); the Holy Sepulchre, Northampton (possibly Templar, nearby was a small street called Temple Bar); a ruined chapel dedicated to St Mary Magdalene in Ludlow Castle; and the Round Church, also ruined, at Orphir on Orkney mainland.

The existing Temple church is the major surviving Templar site in Britain, and the best-preserved Templar site in northern Europe. According to the Rev. Professor T.G. Bonney:

Its rotunda was built about the year 1185 . . . the rest of the church appears to have been completed during the next half-century. Thus the latter is a beautiful example of the best period of the 'first Pointed' or 'Early English' style, while the rotunda marks the transition from the Norman. The entrance door and windows are round-headed, the triforium has similar arches interlacing, while the supporting arches are pointed. It thus exhibits a peculiarly felicitous combination of Norman solidity and Early English grace – the fruit of a happy union of styles, essentially masculine and feminine. The effect also of this dome-like structure, with its circular ambulatory and elevated central 'drum', is peculiarly good. Whether we look into the body of the church from it, or into it from the other part, the contrast of the two plans and the novel grouping of the pillars may well cause us to regret that this arrangement has been so rarely adopted by English architects.[2]

The church has several unusual features dating from Templar times, which give some indication of its former uses. For example, an annexe to the round church, the Chapel of St Anne, is thought to have been the place where the secret initiation ceremonies of the knights took place. Part of it can still be seen through a grille on the crypt stairway. The church also has the 'Penitential Cell' or 'Little Ease', which has slit windows looking into the church itself. This cell is accessible through a door in the north-west corner of the choir. In Northern Tradition geomancy, the north-west is the direction of death. Knights who had broken the Order's rules, or who had disobeyed the Master, were imprisoned here. Walther de Bacheler, ex-Grand Preceptor of Ireland, was imprisoned here for offences against the Order, and starved to death in this cell.

The Temple church is known for the twelfth- and thirteenth-century effigies of knights that, until they were damaged in the Second World War, were recognized as some of the finest in existence. These effigies have been moved around the church on several occasions, and the remains of the warriors they commemorate are now lost. There is also a thirteenth-century effigy of a bishop, standing with his feet upon a dragon. Various theories as to his identity suggest that he represents Heraclius, the Patriarch of Jerusalem, Bishop Hugh of Lincoln, who lived close to the Temple, or the Bishop of Carlisle, Sylvester de Everdon, who was, rather inexplicably, buried in the Temple Church in 1255. But, being a microcosmic representation of both the tomb of Christ and the centre of the world, the temple may have had an attraction as an especially sacred burial place. According to Dugdale's *Monasticon*, 'King *Henry* III by a solemn and formal Deed of Grant dated the nineteenth year of his reign gave his Body to be buried . . . at the *New Temple* in *London*, The like did Queen *Alianour* [*sic*].' These wishes were not carried out.

[Figure 14: Interior of the Temple church, 1870, from *Old and New London,* Walter Thornbury, first published 1872–8.]

Unlike many monasteries in the capital, the London Temple played an important part in the life of the nation, both politically and financially. The Templars were known for their financial acumen, being early capitalists, and bankers to European royalty. As in other countries, the Templars in England were very industrious, and excellent managers of their estates. At the time of their suppression, the annual income from Templar lands in England was £4,720. Everywhere they went, the Templars were known as bankers and moneylenders, even though this was contrary to the Christian teaching of the period.

St Bernard of Clairvaux, patron of the Templars, and fanatically anti-Semitic, condemned 'the Jews' for inventing the sin of money-lending, and Christian bankers for copying them and outdoing them with even more exorbitant interest rates. The Third Lateran Council of 1179 condemned moneylending as a form of moral decadence. But then, as now, there was need for credit, and where there is a need, someone will fill it. In England, the Knights Templar fulfilled the need for financial services. In the twelfth century, as today, the Royal Exchequer of England was at Westminster, but there were also a number of treasuries. There were royal treasuries at Winchester and in the Tower of London. But also the New Temple in London served as a national bank, just as the Temple at Jerusalem did for the Christian Kingdom there. In 1204, King John had the Crown Jewels entrusted to the Templar treasury for safe-keeping. Taxes were collected at the Temple, which played a major part in the nation's financial system.

In 1259, during the reign of King Henry III, Parliament met at the London Temple while discussing the 'Provisions of Westminster', a major legal revision. Perhaps the later occupation of the site by the legal profession, still extant, dates from this period. Two years later, during the Baron's Revolt, Henry III deposited the Crown Jewels with the Templars again. But in 1283, King Edward I, respecter of no one, gained entry to the treasury of the Temple on the pretext of wishing to see his mother's jewels, which the Templars held. Having gained admission, the King helped himself to whatever he fancied. A subterranean crypt of the Temple church cleared of coffins and skeletons in 1950 during postwar restoration work is believed to be the site of the treasury.

The story of the Templars' suppression is well known. They were accused of all sorts of offences, from sodomy to idolatry, and, under torture, many confessed to anything their accusers wanted. In turn, these 'confessions' were used as a means to attack other Templars, and the whole process culminated in the suppression of the Order, and the confiscation of their property by greedy monarchs and other religious orders. After the suppression of the Templars in France, in 1309, Pope Clement sent his Bull to the Archbishop of Canterbury and other bishops, ordering them to investigate the Templars in England, who were next in line for dissolution.

In October 1309, the Inquisition sat in the Bishop of London's Hall, and 'divers Knights of the order' were questioned, but nothing was admitted that was out of order. Unlike that of many other countries, English law at this period prohibited the torture of prisoners, and the expected confessions did not materialize. The Inquisitors then sat at York, to investigate the northern ecclesiastical province of England. The Templars were suppressed officially in April 1312. The order was condemned and perpetually annulled by the Council of Vienne in 1312. The Grand Preceptor of the Templars in England, William de la More, died imprisoned in the Tower of London. English Hospitallers always referred to him thereafter as 'the Martyr'. The Templars' property in London then passed into the possession of the Order of St John of Jerusalem, which profited greatly by it.

In 1381, the leaders of the Peasants' Revolt gained entry to the Temple, which, by then, was occupied by lawyers, tenants of the Order of St John. As in Cambridge, where the 1381 revolutionaries destroyed the university charters and records, the Londoners took out 'the books and records that were in closets of the law apprentices, carried them out into the street, and then burnt them'. When all monastic orders were suppressed at the Reformation, the New Temple passed to the Crown. The Temple church was damaged on 6 April 1580 in an earthquake, but was repaired subsequently. The lawyers, whose rents were a good source of income for the new landlord, were allowed to remain in the Temple, and, in 1608, King James I granted them the freehold to the property. The round church then officially became the lawyers' chapel, remaining separate and not subject to the jurisdiction of the Bishop of London.

The Great Fire of London of 1666 did not get as far as the Temple, but that did not stop Sir Christopher Wren from refurbishing it in 1682. It was 'repaired and beautified' once more in 1706, when it was whitewashed. It underwent three further reconstructions or refurbishments before, between the years 1839 and 1842, the church suffered a major rebuilding at the hands of Victorian 'restorers', who, under the architect Blore, altered many features and lowered the chancel floor by 16 inches. Many of the early features, which today would have given Templar researchers valuable information, were obliterated by this early 'Gothic Revival' architect. But the worst destruction was occasioned by the second major war of the twentieth century, when, during an air-raid on 10 May 1941, the church suffered catastrophic damage by bombing. The nave roof was burnt out, and fell into the church, severely damaging the famous stone effigies of the knights there. After the war, it was restored, and rededicated in 1954.

One of the most significant medieval prescriptions concerning the London Templars was the right of sanctuary in their property. Long before their suppression, Pope Innocent II made the order that the houses of the Templars should be a sanctuary, and that those who broke the sanctuary were to be excommunicated. This seems to have been a direct continuation of the ancient Jewish tradition that the Temple of Solomon in Jerusalem and its successors were a sanctuary. Customarily, the New Temple offered sanctuary. The other London sanctuaries were not Templar, being at St Martin's Le Grand and Westminster. But a second Templar sanctuary existed on the other side of the river at Parysh Garden, otherwise known as Wideflete, in Southwark.

In medieval times, any criminal who reached sanctuary could not be arrested, but had two choices as to his future (women sanctuary-seekers were rare). The miscreant could live there in monkish poverty for the rest of his life, relying on alms given by passers-by for support. Or he could 'abjure the realm'. This entailed leaving England for another country – usually Scotland or France – travelling on a prescribed route and staying at designated inns until he reached the port or the Scottish border.

As already mentioned, London had three major sanctuaries in medieval times: the Temple, St Martin's Le Grand and Westminster

Abbey. According to tradition, the sanctuary of St Martin's Le Grand was originally a college, founded in the year 700 by Wythred, King of Kent. It was confirmed as a sanctuary in 1068 by William the Conqueror, being made independent of all other ecclesiastical juris- diction, including that of the monarch and the Pope. Because of its right of sanctuary it was, according to Pennant, 'the resort of every species of profligates, from the murderer to the pickpocket; and was most tenaceously [*sic*] vindicated by its holy rulers.' When the king's justices held their sessions in St Martin's Gate, the accused were brought before them on the other side of the street, and guarded to prevent them from advancing forward. If they had done so, and crossed the water-channel in the middle of the street, they would have entered the precinct of sanctuary, and have had the proceedings against them annulled. The St Martin's jurisdiction contained a church, which was in use until the college was suppressed in 1548. It was then pulled down, and a tavern was erected on its site.

The Temple's status as sanctuary was gradually reduced. In the time of King Edward III, a statute was made, affirming only St Martin's and Westminster Abbey as sanctuaries for treason, felony or debt.

As at St Martin's, even after the fall of the monastic orders and the accession of the land to the legal corporation, remnants of the former sacred, sanctuary nature of the ground remained. An entry in the *Inner Temple Manuscript Miscellania* (No. 32, f. 12 v) states that in 1601, the fields there were 'large and lovely walks . . . ornyfied with beauti- ful banks, sundry scentes and sortes', surrounded by 'strong and stately rayles of carved timbe worke' with posts bearing 'the twelve celestiall signes, verie lively and artificially cutt'.

In England, the right of sanctuary was finally abolished in 1623. But even today, the realm of the Templars in London still retains a special character, being the location of two of the Inns of Court – the Inner Temple and the Middle Temple. The Inns of Court are not included in any church parish, being extra-parochial *peculiars*, self- governing autonomies in ecclesiastical matters. Among the Inns of Court, only the Master of the Temple enjoyed security of tenure, as the incumbent of an 'impropriated benefice in the crown's gift'. In the fifteenth century, the legal corporation known then as The Temple was subdivided into two. The church is now part of the Inner

Temple, while the rest of the property became the Middle Temple. There is no Outer Temple any longer. The Outer Temple consisted of lands that lay just outside the boundary of the City of London. The Outer Temple was also known as Stapleton Inn (or Exeter Inn). Today some of the site forms part of the Middle Temple, while the rest now has no connection with the legal profession.

Temple Bar, close to the gatehouse of the Temple sanctuary, was the outer westward limit of the City of London towards Westminster, and so symbolized the boundary of the municipal power as against the power of the monarch and Parliament. Kings and other dignitaries were forced to stop at the bar and ask permission (always granted, of course) to enter the municipality of the City. As a magic boundary, its power was reinforced by the dismembered parts of miscreants. The westward orientation of the gate may have had something to do with it, as that direction was the way of the dead in ancient pagan tradition. Parts of human beings adorned the gateway until late into the eighteenth century. The other site for the grisly display of heads, etc., was the south gate-tower of Old London Bridge, the other major entry-point to the City.

Like many monasteries, in its day the London Temple owned considerable property. Next to the River Fleet (now an underground sewer) was a swampy area known as the London Fen. This was part of the lands of the Knights Templar, who drained it making it into usable land. The Temple owned the advowsons (i.e. patronage) of the Chapel of Holy Innocents in the Strand, as well as that of the church of St Clement Danes, also in the Strand, close to the Temple itself. In addition, the Temple owned houses in Holborn, and mills on the River Fleet. It seems that, like military men of all lands and periods, the Templars had scant regard for the law or their neighbours. In 1307, a petition by Henry Lacy, Earl of Lincoln, concerning the Fleet River complained that it had been interfered with by the Templars, who had raised the quay and diverted the waters to drive their own mills near Baynard Castle along the Thames shore. Other Templar mills were at Southwark, and Loughton.

The suppression of the Templars in London, as elsewhere, did not obliterate their monuments or their memory. More than other monastic orders, the Templars caught people's imagination. Their heroic military prowess, the very essence of chivalry, their wealth, their mysterious initiations, and the unfair manner of their demise, has led to a perennial interest in their mysteries. Even in the medieval period, they were considered the epitome of the chivalric ideal. In his *Parzival*, Wolfram von Eschenbach, who visited Jerusalem on pilgrimage in 1218, used Templar knights to guard Muntsalvasche, the Castle of the Grail. The tradition that the Holy Grail was in the possession of the Knights Templar, or perhaps also the Ark of the Covenant, is a persistent legend in Templar lore. According to Louis Charpentier (*The Mysteries of Chartres Cathedral*), the mission of the Templars was not just to police the highways of Palestine for the protection of pilgrims, but was to obtain the Jewish Ark and perhaps the Tables of the Law from the underground parts of the Jerusalem Temple, which, Charpentier claims, still survived in their day.

Whether or not they did find the physical remains of these sacred relics, the Templars are believed to have been responsible for bringing back to Europe certain information and techniques in architecture, which led to the creation of the so-called Gothic style. Their secret may have been the knowledge of the Islamic sacred geometry, obliquely referred to in 'the square' given to the Templars for their observances by Baldwin at Jerusalem. It is certain that the pointed arch, hallmark of Gothic architecture, was brought to Europe from Islamic sources. Perhaps architect members of the Templar Order were responsible. The special forms of architecture adopted by the Templars, for their churches, and their sacred flag, signify considerable symbolic knowledge in that direction. The banner of the Templars, Beauséant, was a black-and-white chequered flag, like that now used to signify the completion of motor races. This emblem, it is said, was symbolic of the chequered pavement of the Temple of Solomon, and still plays a major part in the mysteries of Freemasonry.

The influence of the Knights Templar can still be seen in modern Freemasonry, where one of the degrees relates to the knightly Order. Knight Templar Freemasonry is considered part of the *Chivalric* orders, for which, unlike the three degrees of the Craft, members have to be Christian. Membership is restricted to Companions of Royal Arch Masonry. This distinction seems to date from the eighteenth century. In 1780, the Grand Lodge of York sanctioned the working of five Masonic degrees, the three degrees of the Craft, the Royal Arch, and the Knight Templar. These *Five Degrees or Orders of Masonry* were: Entered Apprentice, Fellow Craft, Master Mason, Knight Templar and Sublime Degree of Royal Arch.

Like the Rose Croix degree, the Knight Templar is said to occupy an 'honoured and exceptional place' in modern Freemasonry.

Today, Knight Templar masons use the calendar known as AO (*Anno Ordinis* – in the Year of the Order), which begins in the year 1118. Thus, for instance the year 1990 CE (*Common Era*) or AD (*Anno Domini* – The Year of Our Lord) becomes the year 872 AO (*Anno Ordinis*). There is also the more esoteric 'Year of Strict Observance', dating from the year of the suppression of the Templars, 1314, which makes 1990 equivalent to 676.

6

Wise Women of London:
Witchcraft and Magic Before 1736

Carol Clancy

THE HISTORY OF magic and witchcraft is older than the city itself. Until modern times, witchcraft was an oral tradition and witches seldom left personal records of their beliefs and experiences. We have to rely on the records of the Church and the courts for information about them, since the background of illegality, lasting from the rise of Christianity until 1951, forced magic and witchcraft underground. This is a history of London witchcraft cases, from the earliest written records in Anglo-Saxon times, until 1736 when the death penalty for witchcraft was abolished.

The Earliest Witchcraft Cases in London

A series of statutes against magic were passed in Anglo-Saxon times, but the penalties were not harsh. Unless magical murder was committed it was not a capital offence, and prosecutions were few. A London case is mentioned in a charter of about AD 963 when a nail-studded effigy of Aelsi, father of Wulfstan, was found in the room of a widow. She and her son were charged with witchcraft, the son fled and was outlawed and the widow was drowned at London Bridge, her land at Ailesworth in Northamptonshire being forfeited.

After the Norman Conquest, a witch had to be proved to have committed a definite act of evil, and the penalties varied from court to court. Again, examples are rare, one of the few taking place in London in 1209, during the reign of King John. Agnes, the wife of a wealthy merchant, accused a woman called Galiena of witchcraft, and she was forced to undergo ordeal by hot irons. This was believed to be an extremely accurate way of probing the conscience of the accused, but Galiena succeeded in the ordeal, which involved walking a set distance holding a red-hot piece of iron in both hands, and was acquitted.

In 1331, in the reign of Edward III, a Winchester goldsmith was found guilty by a Southwark court of attempting to kill two people by making magical images. The court considered that, as no one had died, the case was outside the jurisdiction of the King's Bench, and the man was sent to the Tower of London, for charges to be brought by the King or the Bishop of Winchester. In 1371, a Southwark man was brought before Justice of the Peace John Knivet, charged with possessing a grimoire and a human head. Such heads were used for oracular purposes, the spirit of the dead person being recalled from the other side and consulted on various matters. The man swore never to practise sorcery again, and was released. The head and the book of spells were burnt on Tothill Fields, a vast, marshy area below Westminster Abbey, now covered by Victoria and Pimlico.

Although magical murder was not tolerated, the authorities were less concerned with the activities of the poor, who were seen as having a narrow sphere of influence. Throughout the Middle Ages, a series of accusations were made against people of high rank. Many of these accusations had a purely political motivation, but in changeable and troubled times people did turn to magic to maintain or further their interests. When Adam de Stratton, Chancellor of the Exchequer, was arrested for fraud in 1289, he was found to possess a silk bag containing human hair and nail parings, and the feet of toads and moles. De Stratton managed to destroy the evidence before charges of sorcery could be brought.

The Trial of Eleanor Cobham

The trial of Eleanor Cobham, Duchess of Gloucester, is one of the most famous of the medieval period. Bold and ambitious, Eleanor had a strong faith in magic, and consulted Margery Jourdemaine, who lived in the manor of Eye-next-Westminster, close to the great

Abbey, and was known as the Witch of Eye. Margery helped her out with love philters and charms, and Eleanor married Humphrey, Duke of Gloucester. The Duke was Henry VI's uncle and was Regent during his minority, so Eleanor became a woman of great power and influence. Not content to let her future rest on the uncertain whims of fate during a period of unrest that was to culminate in the Wars of the Roses, she decided to take charge of the future herself. This resulted, in 1441, in her being tried for conspiring with others to murder Henry VI by magical means, a charge of high treason.

Having employed her successfully in the past, Eleanor had turned again to Margery Jourdemaine. Margery had brushed with the law in 1430, but after two years' imprisonment she returned to Westminster, practising witchcraft without attracting attention until she became embroiled in Eleanor Cobham's political intrigues.

At the trial, it emerged that Eleanor had conspired with Margery, Sir Roger Bolingbroke, a priest and necromancer, and Thomas Southwell, the Canon of St Stephen's, Westminster. They had enquired into Eleanor's political future, and had made a wax figure of Henry, to be placed in front of the fire so that his strength ebbed as the wax melted. Bolingbroke and Southwell chose the deserted Bishop of London's hunting lodge, at the highest point in Hornsey Park, as the scene for their rituals, a site later occupied by the Highgate Golf Club. Southwell's task was to say mass over Bolingbroke's magical regalia, and to say a mass for the dead for the living King Henry. Renegade priests brought terror to the hearts of God-fearing people – a priest saying mass for the dead while the person was living was thought certain to dispatch them to the grave within days.

Roger Bolingbroke's magical instruments were discovered on his arrest, and displayed with him in St Paul's churchyard, where he did penance dressed in his magical robes. They included a chair 'wherein he was wont to sit when he wrought his necromancie', painted with curious designs and hung at the four corners with swords and copper images dangling from the points, a ceremonial sword and sceptre, and a wax image, declared to be the one intended for use against the King.

On Bolingbroke's exposure, Eleanor fled for sanctuary at Westminster, but was forced to appear before Henry Chicheley, Archbishop of Canterbury at St Stephen's Chapel on twenty-eight charges of necromancy, sorcery, witchcraft, heresy and treason. She claimed as her defence that she had been desperate to get pregnant, and that the wax image, far from being a weapon to harm the King, was merely a magical way of ensuring conception. Eleanor was a powerful, well-connected woman, related to the royal family. The court chose to believe this tale.

Eleanor was condemned to carry out three sets of public penance, barefoot and bareheaded and carrying a two-pound candle. She was then banished for life, ending up at Peel Castle, Isle of Man, which she is said to haunt. She is also said to have founded an Isle of Man witch coven that still meets today.

At his trial held at the Guildhall, Bolingbroke denied using sorcery against the King, but confessed that he had, at Eleanor's instigation, looked into her future. This was construed as an inquiry into the length of the King's life and the possibility of the Duke succeeding him. Bolingbroke, along with Margery Jourdemaine and Canon Southwell, was condemned to death for treason.

Southwell was fortunate enough to die in the Tower, on the date he had predicted, but Bolingbroke was drawn through the street from the Tower to Tyburn, where he was hanged and quartered. To the last, he denied any treason against the King's person, but regretted that he had 'presumed too far in his cunning'. His head was pickled and put on London Bridge, the rest of him being sent to Oxford, Cambridge, Hereford and York, a dire and dreadful warning to any learned priests and clerics who were tempted to dabble in the occult arts.

Margery, who seems to have been a genuine witch, and may well have lived to old age if she had not consorted with the Duchess, was burnt at Smithfield. It is important to remember that she was burnt for treason, not for witchcraft. Unlike Scotland and the Continent, witches were never burnt in England, unless their crimes constituted high treason against the King or murdering their husbands, that being held as 'petty treason'. It is interesting to note that the most sure-fire way of disposing of husbands was said to be to offer a peck of oats to the statue of St Wilgerfort, better known as St Uncumber, in St Paul's Cathedral, eliminating unwanted husbands being one of her attributes.

Witchcraft, Law and Punishment

In the popular imagination, the Middle Ages are a time of numerous witch trials and executions, but the facts do not bear this out. Some medieval records have been destroyed, others remain unresearched, but before 1500 the sum total of witchcraft cases seems to amount to 'two or three deaths, a broken leg, a withered arm, several destructive tempests and some bewitched genitals'. During the period from the Norman Conquest to the Reformation, only half a dozen people seem to have suffered severe penalties in the whole of England, including Jourdemaine, Bolingbroke and Mabel Brigge of York, who was executed for holding a 'Black Fast' against Henry VIII and the Duke of Norfolk in 1538. Neither is there any evidence for an organized witch cult in London – all the known cases involve people working alone or with a few others, never in fully fledged covens.

By the late fifteenth century, opinion in Europe was hardening against witchcraft. The Roman Catholic Church had originally founded the Inquisition to deal with the Cathar heresy, and later used it against the spread of Protestant Christianity. At the same time, it waged war against old pagan beliefs that had survived the medieval period, identifying the Horned God of pre-Christian Europe with the Christian Devil. Witchcraft now became a Christian heresy, and witches were seen as renouncing their allegiance to God, in order to align themselves with his enemy. This new idea spread among witches, who began to see themselves as the enemies of God and the worshippers of the Devil. In 1493, Elena Dalok of St Mary Abchurch appeared before the Commissary of London, having made malevolent threats. She was quite unrepentant, boasting that everyone she cursed died, if she 'bid the rain to rain, it rained at her command' and that while there was a God in heaven, she was content to remain in hell.

The Reverends Kramer and Sprenger published the *Malleus Maleficarum* or *Hammer of the Witches* in 1486, an extremely misogynistic book that blamed women and their sexuality for most of the ills of the world, and rested on the bench of every judge on the Continent for three centuries, the unquestioned authority on how to conduct a witch hunt. Detailed instructions were given on the most effective means of torture and execution was to be carried out by burning the victims alive. This was backed up by Pope Innocent VIII's Papal Bull of 1484, condemning witches as the allies of Satan. Fortunately, the *Malleus* was not translated into English until modern times, and although copies made their way into the libraries of intellectuals, the book never gained a hold on the popular imagination.

The English trials seldom had the twisted sexual aspect of the Continental trials, although they were undoubtedly based on misogynistic, patriarchal attitudes, and England was also spared the horrors of the Inquisition. Estimates of the numbers who died in the Continental witch hunts run from a conservative 200,000 upwards. England did not experience wholesale slaughter, as Germany did, and it has been estimated that fewer than 1,000 executions took place between 1542, when Henry VIII widened the death penalty to include invoking evil spirits, using magic for treasure-seeking and the recovery of stolen goods and 'to provoke any person to unlawful love', to 1736, when the death penalty for witchcraft was finally abolished. The 1542 Act itself was seldom used, and was repealed under Edward VI.

Elizabethan London

There were many magical attempts made on Elizabeth I's life and although she laughed them off in public, in private she took them more seriously. She had already employed John Dee, the famous occultist and astrologer, to find the most propitious date for her coronation, and she turned to him again when Elizabeth Style confessed to burying a spiked image of her somewhere in Lincoln's Inn Fields. Removing the Court to Greenwich, Elizabeth dispatched Dr Dee to find and dispose of the image, which he did, taking Mr Secretary

Wilson along with him as a witness. Dee had been imprisoned under Mary I, but Elizabeth's patronage protected him from the authorities. However, she could not save him from the mob that ransacked his house at Mortlake, Richmond, while he was abroad, burning or stealing many of his books. When James I introduced stringent anti-witchcraft laws, Dee was so concerned about his safety that he petitioned the King. He was left alone, and died peacefully at Mortlake. Some of his magical instruments can be seen on display at the British Museum and in the Museum of the History of Science in Oxford.

In 1563 another Witchcraft Act was passed, reinforcing the death penalty for magical murder, with lesser penalties for lesser offences. People were very afraid of malevolent magic, and increasingly turned to practitioners of popular magic, known as 'cunning women and men', to find out how to remove bewitchment, and to discover the identity of the witch responsible. Most victims of witchcraft were poor, but prominent citizens were also attacked. A tablet was found in Lincoln's Inn in modern times, bearing magical symbols and the words: 'That nothing may prosper or go forward that Ralph Scrope taketh in hand.' Scrope was Treasurer of the Inn from 1564–5. Neither were public figures exempt from gossip about their own magical dabblings. According to *The Ingoldsby Legends*, Lady Hatton, wife of the Lord Chancellor, Sir Christopher Hatton, made a pact with the Devil. When the contract expired, he appeared and tore her heart out. The place where this is said to have happened became known as Bleeding Heart Yard, near Leather Lane, EC1.

As interest in the occult took an upturn, it was possible to make a good living, and many cunning women and men practised popular magic in London. Although their activities were illegal, they tended to escape prosecution unless they harmed or deceived people. As well as healing, they specialized in finding lost objects, discovering thieves, scrying with crystals, divination, removing curses, and charms to awaken and keep love, prevent drunkenness and win at gambling. This could sometimes backfire – spells to outdo a business rival or transfer sickness to another person could result in accusations of witchcraft from the injured party. Neither was it wise to go too far. Judith Philips, a London cunning woman, was whipped through the streets of the city in 1595 for extracting large sums from the gullible, whom she promised to introduce to the Queen of the Fairies.

A new view of bewitchment was gaining ground. Previously, it had been considered necessary to carry out elaborate rituals, using curses, image magic and spells. Now it was considered possible to 'overlook' people, to give them the 'evil eye', just through a glance. Margaret Hacket, a widow from Stanmore, Middlesex, was hanged at Tyburn in 1585 because she had 'consumed a young man to death' and had 'rotted his bowells and back bone asunder'. She had also stopped butter and cheese from turning, blighted a field so no crops would grow, dried up a brewing-stand, and made a man mad after he struck her. A man who had refused to pay her the agreed price for a pair of shoes also died. Tyburn had become the traditional place to hang witches. Anne Kerke of Broken Wharf died there in 1599, having vented her magical spite against a family who refused her share of the doles for the poor at a funeral, as they believed she had caused the death.

Jacobean London

James I had a keen interest in witchcraft and some experience of it; his cousin, Francis, Earl of Bothwell, having conspired against him with the North Berwick witches in 1590. James published his *Demonology* in 1597 and the first of several anti-witchcraft acts of his reign was passed in 1604. James has been regarded as the driving force behind the seventeenth-century witch craze, but this is unfair. He had a scholarly interest in the matter, and as time went on, became more sceptical about the motives of those who brought complaints. However, his legislation did pave the way for the excesses of the Commonwealth period.

James I's scepticism was shared by others, as is apparent from the trial of Elizabeth Jackson in 1602. She was accused of bewitching a fourteen-year-old girl, Mary Glover, who told her mistress that Elizabeth, begging at the door, had wished 'an evil death to light on her'. In fact, Elizabeth had not spoken to her, merely passing back and forth, hoping for a share of the newly baked bread Mary was eating. After Elizabeth left, Mary had a fit.

Medical opinion was divided over the case. Two members of the College of Physicians, Dr John Argent and Dr Edward Jorden, argued that the fits had natural causes, but three members of the college supported the prosecution, including Thomas Moundeford, subsequently seven times president. The judge, Lord Anderson, ruled that since medical expertise could not cure the fits, they could not have a natural origin, and Elizabeth Jackson was condemned.

Frances Howard and Robert Carr

The most famous London witchcraft trial of this period involved Frances Howard, Countess of Essex, and Robert Carr, Earl of Somerset, a favourite of James I. Frances had been married off at thirteen to Robert Devereux, Earl of Essex. She was beautiful, wild and uncontrollable, and when Essex returned from abroad three years later, she was already in love with Robert Carr. She was a close friend of Anne Turner, a court dressmaker who ran a sideline in supplying love potions, drugs to procure abortion and the like, which she obtained from Simon Forman, the Lambeth astrologer and magician. Frances and Anne visited Forman to win the love of Robert Carr and Sir Christopher Maynwaring, and Forman's methods worked, for in 1613, having used further potions to make her husband impotent, Frances gained an annulment on the ground of non-consummation and married Carr. Anne became Maynwaring's mistress.

Simon Forman made a fortune running one of the most fashionable astrology practices in London, averaging over 1,000 charts a year. Frances was among his wealthy clients, and she often consulted such people, including Anne Taylor, a Southwark astrologer, and the witch, Mary Woods, who gave her a powder to hang around her neck to help her conceive after her marriage to Carr.

Problems soon arose for the newly married couple. Carr's patron, Sir Thomas Overbury, had at first encouraged the affair, but he objected to the divorce and said so. The couple decided he had to be got rid of. Contriving that James offered Overbury a post abroad, Carr advised him to refuse it, and then turned James against him. Overbury was sent to the Tower. By this time, Simon Forman had died untroubled by the authorities, and Anne Turner found an apothecary and magician, Dr Franklin, to supply a vial of red arsenic. The first attempt to poison Overbury failed as they had forgotten to bribe the Lieutenant of the Tower, so they began to send poisoned delicacies to him, using a combination of 'aquafortis, white arsenic, mercury, powder of diamonds, lapis cortilus, great spiders, and cantharides'. When he became ill, it was attributed to prison food, and more delicacies flooded in. A doctor was finally called, but this time the Lieutenant was properly bribed, and mercury sublimate was put in Overbury's enema. Not surprisingly, he died.

Too many people were involved to keep the murder quiet, and Franklin, in particular, boasted of his part in the affair. James was forced to hold an inquiry, and when Anne Turner was arrested, magical images, parchment scrolls with spells and a piece of human skin were found. Frances and Carr were sent to the Tower, where they put her into the room where Overbury had died. She became hysterical and had to be moved. They were tried for murder, and found guilty.

Anne Turner was hanged at Tyburn. Both she and the hangman wore the yellow, starched ruffs and cuffs she had made fashionable, a fashion that died with her. Frances and Carr escaped execution by virtue of their high rank, and were imprisoned in the Tower until their release in 1621, a surprisingly light sentence in view of the seriousness of their crime.

Magic under Crown and Commonwealth

High rank protected some, but others were less fortunate. Dr John Lambe enjoyed the protection of Charles I's favourite, the Duke of Buckingham, but was hated by the London crowd. He had a fashionable practice, often charging forty or fifty pounds a case, although the College of Physicians had found him ignorant of medicine and astrology in 1627. He appeared before the King's Bench for witchcraft, but was acquitted, and carried on with such practices as fortune telling and recovering stolen goods. On the day that Buckingham was denounced in the House of Commons, a mob attacked Lambe as he left the Fortune Theatre in Maiden Lane, Cripplegate, cornering him in Wood Street, and stoning him to death at St Paul's Cross, with cries of 'Kill the wizard'. The next day, placards appeared warning Buckingham of the same fate, and a few weeks later he was assassinated.

Although the Puritans condemned all forms of magic, popular interest grew during the Commonwealth period. There were more books on alchemy published from 1650–80 than before or since. Works by Agrippa, 'Hermes' and Paracelsus were translated into English for the first time, along with reprints of the works of Roger Bacon, Dee and Elias Ashmole. Witch trials were frequent events, and in the eastern counties the professional witch-finder, Matthew Hopkins, claimed over 200 victims, using the confusion of civil war to employ torture, which had always been illegal under English law without royal assent.

Wild stories were believed true. A woman was caught sailing on a board on the River Fleet, beside St Pancras Old Church, by Parliamentary troops, who claimed she caught and chewed their bullets. She was rendered harmless by slashing her forehead, for drawing a witch's blood was believed to negate her powers.

Joan Peterson was a wise woman, known as the Witch of Wapping, who practised healing and love spells and lived on Spruce Island, near Shadwell. Christopher Wilson had come to her for remedies, but then refused to pay. When Joan threatened that his illness would get ten times worse if he didn't pay up, he began to have 'very strange fits' and 'for twelve hours together would slabber out his tongue and walk up and down like a mere changeling'. She was charged with witchcraft.

Witnesses were bribed against Joan, and others were intimidated against speaking in support of her. She was accused of causing fits in a neighbour's child, her former employee stated she had a squirrel as a familiar and Joan's eight-year-old son was coerced into giving evidence against her. The presiding judge was Sir John Danvers, a member of Oliver Cromwell's council, who had been instructed to find her guilty. She was hanged the day after her trial, in 1652.

[Figure 15: The Witch of St Pancras shown crossing the River
Fleet with St Pancras Old Church in the background. From
a pamphlet printed by John Hammond in 1643 entitled, 'A
Most Certain, Strange and True Discovery of a Witch'.]

After her death, it was found that the case had been rigged against
her and there was a public outcry. Some wealthy gentlemen in Oliver
Cromwell's favour had approached Joan, seeking to get rid of an heiress who stood between them and a fortune, and Joan had refused.
Unwilling to risk the danger of her talking they had trumped up
charges, to the extent of men standing at the entrance of the court on
the day of the trial, offering money to anyone prepared to turn hostile
witness. By the time the truth emerged, Cromwell was out of office
and it was too late to do anything more.

Mother Red Cap or Mother Damnable

A more successful witch of this period lived in Camden Town. Jinny
Bingham, known as Mother Red Cap, or Mother Damnable, lost her
lover, Gypsy George, at Tyburn for stealing sheep at Holloway, and

her parents for magical murder. She then lived with a man who disappeared suddenly after quarrels. A third lover, a man called Picher, was found in her oven, burnt to a crisp. At the trial, witnesses claimed that Picher often hid from Jinny in the oven when they quarrelled, and must have been burnt by accident. She was acquitted.

Jinny became a recluse, with a reputation as a witch, as she was often seen at night collecting berries and herbs. During the Civil War she hid a fugitive, who stayed with her for several years. When he died, the rumours she had poisoned him could never be proved, and he left her a considerable fortune. From then on, she lived alone, visited by clients who wanted remedies and spells, or to have their fortunes told. She was a friend of Moll Cutpurse, the highwaywoman, who always wore men's clothes and about whom Dekker wrote his play *The Roaring Girl*.

When Mother Red Cap was found dead, she was still holding a teapot, and it is said that when its contents were fed to her cat, its hair fell out and it was dead within two hours. Another woman took over the site, calling herself Mother Red Cap, and opened a tavern where

[Figure 16: Mother Red Cap, also known as Mother Damnable, of Camden Town. Based on a 1676 print published in 1793, now in the Guildhall.]

she brewed exceptionally strong ale. There has been a pub on the site ever since, formerly called the Mother Red Cap, now called The World's End.

The Decline of Magic

With the Restoration of the monarchy, belief in magic declined among educated people, and it came to be seen as a mixture of Catholic superstition and the ignorance of the 'lower orders'. Reginald Scot's *Discoverie of Witchcraft* (1584), which divided witches into the innocent, the deluded, the fraudulent, and the genuine article, who, however, harmed by poison rather than supernatural powers, was reprinted in 1651, and made a great impression on the clergy and judiciary. Sir John Holt presided over eleven sorcery trials, and acquitted every case.

[Figure 17: Bellarmine jar. Witch-bottles, these were stuffed with nails, pins, hair and sometimes a cloth heart and were meant to cause harm to witches. Found buried near the Walbrook. Now in the Museum of London.]

One of his trials concerned Richard Hathaway, a blacksmith's assistant from Southwark. He had accused Sarah Murdock, a local waterman's wife, of bewitching him, causing fits. He attacked her, drawing blood, later going to her home with a crowd of friends to again draw blood. She was tried, and acquitted on the evidence of a minister. This verdict was extremely unpopular, and there was talk that the judge and jury had been bribed. A mob attacked Sarah's house, threatening to duck her in the Thames. Hathaway's fits became worse, and he began to vomit pins. Witnesses noticed that some of the pins were quite dry, and, when searched, more pins were found in his pockets. When he was brought before John Holt for trial, many of his neighbours stood by him, but broke down under cross-examining, and Hathaway was imprisoned for a year for fraud and perjury.

In the same year, 1702, William Woodehouse presided over a St Pancras murder trial. A man accused an elderly couple, the Osburns, of bewitching him, and when word spread around the neighbouring parishes that a ducking was to be held, a crowd of a thousand strong turned up. The officers of the parish had hidden the couple in St Pancras Old Church the previous night, and the mob, believing them to be inside the nearby workhouse, rioted, wrecking the workhouse and threatening to set fire to it. The mob caught the couple and, stripping them and tying their toes and thumbs together, they threw them in the River Fleet. The woman died, and the man was seriously injured. The main ringleader was hanged on the spot where the murder took place, his body left there, hanging in chains. Woodehouse, who had no belief in witchcraft, recorded local reactions in his diary, writing, 'The infatuation of the people is such that they will not be seen near the place of execution, insisting that it was a hard case to hang a man for destroying an old woman that had done so much injury by her witchcraft.'

The last execution for witchcraft in England took place in 1684, with a woman reprieved by Royal Pardon in 1712. In 1736, the 1604 Act was repealed, to be replaced by legislation that removed witchcraft as a hanging offence, but made it illegal to *pretend* to practise magic. After 1736 it was at least possible to practise magic without fear of the gallows, but witchcraft went underground. Beliefs and traditions were passed down from generation to generation within families that had become very secretive, often regularly attending church to draw attention away from their true beliefs.

The last half of the nineteenth century saw a great revival of interest in the occult, and women in particular were drawn to the Spiritualist Movement, which had the advantage of being Christian, and therefore respectable. By the turn of the century the two most influential non-Christian occult groups were the Theosophical Society and the Order of the Golden Dawn. However, interest in the occult tended more towards ceremonial magic rather than witchcraft, which was still illegal. This trend continued into the twentieth century, when the work developed by the Order of the Golden Dawn was continued through Dion Fortune and the Society of the Inner Light, and Aleister Crowley and the Ordo Templi Orientis.

Modern Witchcraft

The 1736 Act was last used in 1944, when a medium, Helen Duncan, was tried at the Old Bailey for communicating with spirits. She had held a series of séances in Portsmouth during the war, and received messages from sailors who had gone down with HMS *Barham*. The authorities had not, at that time, released news of the disaster, and reacted by prosecuting Helen Duncan, who was sent to prison for nine months. This led to a campaign to repeal the legislation, which was finally removed in 1951, to be replaced by the Fraudulent Mediums Act. The concept of genuine mediumship is now enshrined in British law.

Once the 1736 Witchcraft Act was repealed, witchcraft slowly began to come out into the open, influenced by Gerald Gardner, who had been initiated into a New Forest coven in the late 1930s, but had found traditional witchcraft beliefs fragmentary and put together his own version of 'Gardnerian Witchcraft' or Wicca. In the 1960s, Alex Sanders, who had an eye for publicity and did a lot to spread interest in witchcraft, developed Alexandrian Wicca, an offshoot of Gardnerian Wicca. By the later part of the twentieth century a wide range of neo-pagan forms had proliferated, many focusing on worship of the Goddess, the re-emergence of which has been central to all modern forms of witchcraft. Today, anyone curious about witchcraft has only to consult the Internet and books of spells are freely available. It is to be hoped that the days of witch hunts are well and truly over and that modern witches will be left in peace.

7

Merlin in London

R.J. Stewart

T HERE ARE A number of stories concerning Merlin and London, but very little convincing evidence. As with all matters connected to Merlin, we should exercise common sense and discretion in preference to wild imaginings and romantic fantasies. Having done so, we will find that the amount of powerful and inspiring material concerning Merlin that remains to us is both extensive and coherent. To approach the complex, frequently romanticized presence of Merlin in London, we need to work our way through several strata, a process of mythic, magical, and literary archaeology, which deals, despite its elusive quality, with substantial matters. It is not, unfortunately, possible to progress through the strata in a chronological order from the present to the earliest levels, as one might in an idealized archaeological dig. The analogy holds good, for archaeological evidence is often jumbled and juxtaposed, sometimes by accidents of time and cultural activity upon any site, and too often by previous efforts at digging. This is certainly the case when we examine any information concerning Merlin.

We should begin with a leap into the distant past, with a brief summary of what is known concerning Merlin himself. Without this early foundation we cannot possibly arrive at the truth of his presence in, or absence from, London. If you, the reader, feel that you know about Merlin already, kindly be patient and please read this short summary anyway; the true background to the legends of Merlin will always bear restating. If you wish to know more of Britain's premier prophet and guardian, there are several titles listed at the end of this book for further reading.

The earliest sources that describe Merlin are medieval, though they unquestionably draw upon earlier traditions, and compare favourably with known aspects of Celtic myth and legend. In these sources, Merlin is described as semi-human and semi-spirit, a child of two worlds, human mother and Otherworld father.

His father was, we are told, a *daemone* or advisory spirit. This is a classical Greek term, not connected in any way to the much later Judeo-Christian *demon*, though it seems likely that the word was deliberately given a negative meaning by the early Church Fathers to correspond to their developing definition of an evil entity. This significant change was part of the evolving propaganda of the early Church as it sought to supplant paganism and absorb or discredit all pre-Christian beliefs, practices, and philosophical or metaphysical concepts. The nature of *daemones* was particularly embarrassing to the Church, as belief in their existence was fundamental to the ancient world-view, and widely employed in inspirational and prophetic arts in paganism. Socrates, we should remember, was advised by such a spirit.

Scholars see this dual parentage of Merlin in medieval literature as an echo, a partial rationalization, of an even earlier legend. In brief, the story is of a divine child, gifted with prophecy and spiritual power, mediating between the human and the Otherworld. This child may appear in Celtic tradition as Mabon, the child of light, obliquely referred to in *The Mabinogion*, and known in Romano-Celtic inscription as a type of young Apollo, a child-deity of prophecy, therapy, and possibly of redemption or spiritual transformation.

The connection between Mabon and Apollo is further reinforced by a famous classical reference (originally in Hecateus's lost *Geography or Circuit of the Earth* (written in approximately 500 BC but subsequently quoted by Diodorus Siculus), linking Britain and Apollo. The Greeks, as Diodorus writes, believed that Apollo was originally a Hyperborean deity (from the north), and that his home was a triangular island off the coast of Gaul (France and Belgium), where a circular temple of stone was built in his honour. There he returned every nineteen years and was worshipped with dance and the music of harps (lyres or kitharas, to be more exact). Commentators have often suggested that this passage refers to Britain and to the ancient, well-established cult of a prophetic deity, known in various forms in Celtic tradition, mythology, and through archaeological evidence.

Geoffrey Ashe, in his 'Merlin in the Earliest Records', in the Merlin Conference anthology *The Book of Merlin*[1] reminds us that Britain was known to the Welsh bards as Clas Myrddin or 'Merlin's Enclosure', and suggests that this ancient tradition, found in the collection known as *The White Book of Rhydderch*[2] coheres with that quoted by Diodorus concerning Hyperborean Apollo and that Mabon, the prophetic Celtic deity, and Merlin, the traditional prophet, may have much in common.[3] In short, the child Merlin of medieval legend is a reworking of a British 'Apollonian' myth, which revolved around a deity whose name we now do not know for certain, but seems very likely to have been Mabon, the Son of Light. Myrddin, or Merlin, was probably a title rather than a name, given to inspired prophets and poets who were filled with the power of the native god, the Hyperborean Apollo.

Culturally we find Merlin legends in Wales, particularly in the north, and in mid and lowland Scotland. This suggests that Merlin was connected to the ancient kingdoms such as Strathclyde, which were, in modern terminology, Welsh-speaking confederacies under powerful kings during the Dark Ages. In terms of folklore, tradition, and early literature, Merlin hardly appears at all in England. He is first and foremost a character of Wales and southern Scotland, and all the firm evidence points to these areas and away from England.

Even Cornwall, which claims a Merlin's cave at Tintagel, has no deep connection to Merlin other than through his legendary visit to that land in Geoffrey of Monmouth's *History of the British Kings*.[4] This was, of course, for the purpose of magically inducing Ygerna (Igraine) to make love to Uther Pendragon and so bring the child Arthur into the world. It is worth adding at this stage that in Geoffrey's books Merlin has very little to do with Arthur – he aids in his begetting (*History*) and carries the wounded king to the Fortunate Isle for healing (*Vita Merlini*). Stories concerning Merlin advising the ruling Arthur at his court, be it Camelot, Caerleon or London, are later developments moving away from primal bardic tradition.

Many of the bardic traditions concerning Merlin are preserved – and admittedly expanded upon – in Geoffrey's long poetic biography, the *Vita Merlini*.[5] Here the adult Merlin is dealt with as a prince in the prime of life. He is located primarily in North Wales and connected to a known historical battle, that of Arthuret (not connected in any way to King Arthur, for the name is an Anglicization of Ardyrdd) in lowland Scotland, near Carlisle in approximately AD 575. At this battle he was driven mad with grief at the death of so many fine men, and fled to live alone close to essential nature in the wild woods. The remainder of the *Vita* describes prophetic and shamanistic traditions, bardic cosmology, and Merlin's eventual growth towards spiritual illumination. He does not go to London.

Despite all of the foregoing, which is drawn from an extensive body of literature, our common image of Merlin is as a wise old mage who assists King Arthur. Through this connection of wise elder and Crown (Druid advising an elected King in Celtic terms, a relationship well established by both classical and native Irish evidence) we feel that Merlin should be present in London, the seat of power. Are our intuitions right, or are they merely the victim of increasingly romantic and politically inspired literature? As we shall find later, there was no shortage of political capitalizing on the Merlin and Arthur legends; indeed, there is so much of this political capitalizing, propagandizing and, in extreme cases, blatant nationalistic lying, that we cannot possibly present more than a few directly pertinent examples in a short chapter such as this.

Perhaps we can approach the subject by considering London as a capital, a seat of power. Then we may examine literature, place names and Merlin legends, and discover how these elements fit together. It must be clearly understood that at the time of the assembly of the Merlin legends in literature, which mainly occurred during and after the twelfth century (though there are earlier sources such as the chronicles of Nennius), London was not a place of importance, and had been of minor significance for several centuries. The seat of power was Winchester, and much of the land was devastated by repeated civil wars, roving armies and robber barons. We are not likely, therefore, to find much that coherently connects Merlin with London during the literature of this period, and certainly not in the context of Arthurian legend, kingship, or nationalistic politics. Indeed, to reach a period in which London was significant, we need to go back to Roman times, when the site was a small but significant trading and route centre.

In the twelfth century the revival of Welsh and Breton tradition in medieval literature had not quite been fully linked to contemporary politics. Geoffrey of Monmouth more or less began this long-lasting connection in his 'Prophecies of Merlin', a text inserted into the centre of his vast *History of the Kings of Britain* to which we shall return later, as London features in several of the prophecies.

We also find some obscure but important references to London in late medieval Welsh literature, such as *The Mabinogion*,[6] deriving in turn from older oral traditions. London is cited as the location of a sacred head, the severed head of Bran the Blessed, which acts as one of the guardians of the Isle of Britain. We have noted above that one such guardian in Welsh tradition was also Merlin, whose enclosure (Clas Myrddin) is said, in the Triads, to be one of the oldest names for the island of Britain. The sacred head of Bran – sacred heads being a venerable pagan tradition and of considerable importance to the Celts – was buried within the White Hill, on the site of the Tower of London today.

Here we find a resonance of an ancient Celtic tradition concerning a place of power in what is now London, but Merlin is not directly connected to it. His sacred hill is Dinas Emrys in North Wales, where, tradition asserts, he declared his enigmatic prophecies to the usurping King Vortigern in the presence of two dragons aroused from within the earth. So although early tradition from the regions truly associated with Merlin, such as Wales, states that he is both a guardian and a prophet of the land of Britain, it does not locate him in London . . . any such locations are solely the properties of later literature, expansions upon primal traditions and early sources.

Bran, however, is set as a guardian in London, and his totem bird, the raven, is associated with the Tower of London to this day, though the ravens may have been originally brought to the site to reinforce certain legendary aspects, rather than having any truly ancient connection. Bran is a gigantic figure, a type of titanic, yet orphic, being, concerned with guardianship, music, the passage of time and memory, and the sanctity of the land. He is, in fact, a late legendary and poetic storyteller's or bard's representation of a primal god of the underworld, of the sun or light hidden within the earth. So we must assume that he is connected in some way to similar deities such as Apollo,

Mabon, and therefore to the prophet Merlin. All are involved in matters of time, underworld forces, prophecy, and therapy (though in the case of Bran the magical power of his severed head prevents ageing, rather than cures ills).

We can assume, therefore, that the tradition of the guardian head and the White Hill is genuine in essence, stemming as it does from pagan Celtic religion and ceremonial practices, with persistent resonance in the folklore and tradition of many centuries into the Christian era. But this is the sole primal connective between the prophetic powers and deities, and the possible presence of Merlin, the national prophet (as a person or as a title), in what is now London.

Most important in this context is that although Bran, as a primal god or titanic ancestral figure, and Merlin as a prophet, are both guardians of the land, Merlin is not associated with the emblem of a severed head. This is, in fact, a major difference between the Merlin traditions and other Celtic prophetic or mythic sources: whereas Merlin in the earliest sources in Wales and Scotland is associated with ritual sacrifice, a Celtic ceremony known as the 'Threefold Death' (usually but not inevitably in the form of hanging, falling and drowning), his head is not severed. Bran, however, is wounded near to death, a motif also found in the Grail legends in connection with kingship, and orders his followers to cut off his head. There is an implication, therefore, of two distinct streams of tradition, myth, and possible ceremonial practice.

If Merlin is not connected to London, or even to England, in early literature and legend, or in the Celtic traditions from which he springs, where else might we look? One of the most important and, regrettably, most confused and abused areas of potential insight into ancient traditions is through place names.

It is possible, by analysis of place names, to establish general historical facts, as the names reflect the language and customs of the people who dwelt in the location. In the case of Merlin there is a small but potentially admissible body of evidence deriving from place-names within London. Unfortunately this has been greatly coloured by events in the eighteenth century, when a fashionable revival of Merlin occurred in London, to which we shall return shortly.

Place and Street Names

An interesting pattern appears when we examine locations in London, which are, through their name at any rate, connected to Merlin. As is often the case with British tradition, we begin in a public house, the New Merlin's Cave in Margery Street. This building is supposed to be connected to a Merlin's Cave associated with the Islington area, and several authors have perpetuated a connection between Merlin, Pentonville and adjacent Islington. This connection involves the existence of a sealed cave or tunnel under or within a building, supposedly dating back to ancient times. Margery Street, in Finsbury, is parallel to Merlin Street, in which there are the (now closed) Merlin Street Baths. This seems a promising start to an exploration, and has certainly generated an argument that Merlin may have had an ancient connection with this part of London. Let us examine this argument in brief, and reassess it, bearing firmly in mind that some of the romantic antiquarian sources are dubious by modern standards of research.

In Harold Bayley's *Archaic England*[7] we find:

From the cavern at Pentonville, known as Merlin's Cave, used to run a subterranean passage: modern Pentonville takes its title from a ground landlord named Penton, a tenant who presumably derived his patronymic either from that particular penton or from one elsewhere.

In George Daniel's *Merrie England in the Olden Time*[8] we find, in a passage concerning North London (pages 21–2):

. . . proceeding in almost a straight line towards 'Old Isledon' were the London Spa, originally built in 1206; Phillip's New Wells; the New Red Lion Cockpit; the Shakespeare's Head Tavern and Jubilee Gardens; the New Tunbridge Wells, a fashionable morning lounge of the nobility and gentry during the early part of the eighteenth century; the Sir Hugh Middleton's Head; the Farthing Pie House; and Sadler's Music House and Sweet Wells. A little to the left were Merlin's Cave, Bagnigge Wells, the English Grotto (which stood near the New River

Waterworks in the fields) and further in advance, White Conduit
House . . . we enter Islington, described by Goldsmith as a pretty and
neat town . . .

Pentonville is likely to be derived from the word *penton*, which incor-
porates the genuine Celtic element *pen* meaning head. It has been
assumed, therefore, that the Pentonville area, or Penton, was originally sited around a sacred hill, with a possible buried head connection, similar to that stated by tradition at the White Hill and Tower of
London. Furthermore, a 'Merlin's Cave' formed part of the busy
collection of Islington spas in the eighteenth century. From this
connection – Penton = head, Merlin's Cave = springs – it has been
suggested that the spa and the later public house are on an ancient
sacred site connected to Merlin.

The tale, sometimes a persistent urban legend, of mysterious
bricked-up caves and tunnels, it must be stated, is found all over
Britain in connection with various historic sites, and popular folklore.[9] It is not so much suggestive of true ancient subterranean works
as of the deeply rooted emblem of such tunnels and caves in the
popular imagination.

As we have seen above Merlin is not connected to the severed head
motif in British tradition or Celtic legend. He is, however, certainly
connected to therapeutic springs, which form a major theme in both
the 'Prophecies' and especially in the *Vita Merlini*. The Penton or
Pentonville area may indeed be connected, if we read Brythonic
language sources into the place-names, to the concept of a head; it
may also simply mean a head-place or the dwelling of a chieftain, as
in the famous name of Uther Pen-Dragon.

The link to Merlin, springs and spas, caves and public houses,
is of a quite different kind. For it is not a matter of a public
house, the New Merlin's Cave, replacing an old public house or
– no pun intended – watering place, the Merlin's Cave, upon an
ancient site holding caves or tunnels. The suggestion of continuity in this case is almost certainly mistaken, for during the eighteenth century the name Merlin's Cave became very fashionable,
especially for watering holes, spas, entertainment houses and
coffee houses. The present public house known as New Merlin's

Cave, close to Merlin Street and Merlin Street Baths, therefore, is more likely to be the last of those eighteenth-century commercial ventures rather than the venerable inheritance of ancient locations or traditions.

Queen Caroline and Merlin

We now leap into the eighteenth century, that most un-mythic of times, and consider Queen Caroline, wife of George II. Hardly, we might think, a person to have connections to Merlin, Celtic tradition, or similar matters. In 1732, for instance, she ordered the building of a monument, or rather an ornament, called The Hermitage, in Richmond Gardens. This was a type of shrine to science and reason, with busts of Newton, Locke, other worthies of the period, and a central place occupied by a bust of Robert Boyle. This edifice received popular support and enthusiasm.

[Figure 18: *Merlin's Cave*, engraving by T. Bonles
from *Merlin: or The British Inchanter and King Arthur,
The British Worthy*, London, 1736.]

However, in 1735 Queen Caroline went on to order the building of a Merlin's Cave, originally planned as a partially subterranean structure, but finally finished as an odd building in a mixture of styles, including conical thatched roofs of the type much beloved by romantic primitivists in theoretical sketches of Celtic times. This contained fanciful images of Merlin and was duly inhabited by a rustic poet or bard, Stephen Duck and his wife. There was from this time onwards, it should be said, a developing fashion for rustic poets in follies, a whim increasingly but briefly indulged in by wealthy patrons. Merlin's Cave, however, was received with contempt, amusement, and much ridicule and satire.

It was in imitation of this folly (and here a pun is apt) that various taverns, coffee houses, baths and other public buildings in London were named. But this was not the sole evidence of a slightly bizarre Merlin revival in London. In 1724 and 1731 a spectacular comedy entitled *Merlin the British Enchanter* had been staged successfully, and it was revived in 1736 and 1738. This was nothing less than a reworking of *The Birth of Merlin* by William Rowley, with a dubious attribution to William Shakespeare as co-author. The original play was published by Kirkman and Marsh in 1620 and was written by Rowley, one of the great Jacobean comic actors, as a vehicle for himself, the main role being that of the Clown, Merlin's uncle.[10]

It might be worth mentioning that this is a very romantically pro-British and anti-German or Saxon play. The plot is paraphrased from Geoffrey of Monmouth's *History*, Holinshed's *Chronicles*, and other semi-historical sources generally available during the Elizabethan and Jacobean periods. The play deals with the heroics of Uther Pendragon, the treachery of Vortigern, and, of course, the birth of Merlin and his prophesies. Invading Saxons are described as 'lousy slaves', 'the offal of barren Germany' and 'pernicious rats', who try, unsuccessfully, to usurp the Crown. Such a theme would have been delightful to any fashionable audience, or even the general populace, in the light of the Hanoverian succession, even if some of the overtly anti-German lines were prudently removed from the eighteenth-century performances.

London saw a veritable flood of Merlin dramas at this time, including John Dryden's opera *King Arthur*, also revived, a Covent Garden fantasy called *Merlin's Hermitage*, and a pantomime entitled *Merlin in*

Labour. The pantomime theme developed with a number of later productions, which we need not detail here, but as late as 1814 we find the Royal Amphitheatre presenting *Merlin's Cave, or The Harlequin's Masquerade.* These were not mystical or even truly patriotic, as their original writers from a previous century might have intended. The aim was entertainment, satire, and pantomime. As an aside we should add that the modern pantomime owes much to these Merlin plays or revivals of the eighteenth century.

Merlin's Prophecies Concerning London

Let us now leap back to the medieval period, and examine those prophecies of Merlin which relate to London.[11] The text of 'The Prophecies' was assembled by Geoffrey of Monmouth in the middle of the twelfth century, drawing upon Welsh or Breton bardic tradition, i.e. prophetic verses ascribed to Merlin that were preserved and circulated by word of mouth among the Welsh-speaking peoples.

Geoffrey did not, of course, simply report these verses in the manner of a modern scholar; like all medieval writers he expanded, edited, modified, and to a limited extent correlated certain aspects of the verses to his own contemporary history. The bulk of the material, however, remains true to certain specific prophetic cosmological and mythic patterns that certainly predate Geoffrey by many centuries, and are likely to be at the core of the old oral traditions concerning Merlin. Let's see what Geoffrey's text tells us concerning London, and how such verses might be interpreted.

In the following examples, the numbers are merely for convenience in our present context, and do not refer to translations, editions, or original manuscript numberings.

1. *The dignity of London shall adorn Dobernia, and the seventh pastor of York shall be visited in the kingdom of Armorica.*

This refers to the removal of the Bishopric of London to Canterbury, possibly during the sixth century. The second part refers to the removal of authority of the old British or Celtic Church to Brittany during the same period, traditionally said to be as a result of the increasing Saxon invasions.

2. . . . *the Man of Bronze upon a Brazen Horse shall guard for long the gates of London.*

In the *History* (XII, 13) we find that the British king Cadwallo was embalmed 'and placed with wonderful art in a brazen statue . . . over the Western Gate of London . . . to be a terror to the Saxons.' This is not likely to be accurate history in the modern sense, but seems resonant of the old concept of magical guardianship, which we have already observed as associated with the White Hill, the Tower of London and Bran.

3. *The river Thames shall encompass London, and the fame of this work shall pass beyond the Alps. The Hedgehog shall hide his apples within it, and shall make subterranean passages. At that time shall stones speak, and the area towards the Gallic coast be contracted into a narrow space. On each bank (of the English Channel) shall one man hear another, and the soil of the island (of Britain) shall be enlarged. The secrets of the deep shall be revealed, and Gaul shall tremble for fear.*

It is tempting to refer this passage to the twentieth century when London has a major tidal barrier scheme to stop the Thames flooding the city, is permeated with subterranean passages, and is a great world centre for finance. The image of the hedgehog and his apples was a standard symbol for accumulation and preservation of goods and wealth, in the medieval period. The speaking stones are curiously suggestive of modern quartz crystal technology, by which the distance between Britain and Europe is greatly reduced, and people in France and England can indeed speak easily and instantly to one another.

4. *After this shall be produced a Tree upon the Tower of London. Having no more than three branches it shall overshadow the whole Island (of Britain) with the breadth of its leaves . . .*

The use of tree symbolism and the Tower of London implies a royal lineage, and it is tempting to ascribe this verse to the three branches of George IV, William IV, and Victoria, especially when we learn that one branch was to be snatched away (William died without heirs) and that one branch 'shall destroy the other by the multitude of its leaves and fill the place of the other two, and shall give sustenance to birds of foreign nations'. As we know, Victoria's branch married into all the royal families of Europe (German, Spanish, Prussian, Russian, Swedish, etc.)

> 5. *All these things shall Three Ages see, till the buried kings shall be exposed to public view in the city of London.*

Once again, this verse, coming toward the conclusion of the historic flow of prophecies, is resonant of the present day, when the buried kings in Westminster Abbey are no longer hallowed or sacred interments, but commercial tourist attractions.

The last verse of possible future-history relating to London is somber:

> 6. . . . *London shall mourn for the death of twenty thousand, and the river Thames shall be turned to blood . . .*

The reader will of course form his or her own opinions regarding these verses, which are merely offered here in addition to the varied evidence concerning Merlin and London. It is significant in our present context that nowhere in the 'Prophecies' is Merlin himself connected to London.

Conclusions

To conclude this brief survey of Merlin's presence in London, which has taken the form of comic drama, public entertainment, inns and spas, follies and prophecies, we can return to primal legends. London is associated, as a locus or place of power, with the ancient cult of the severed head. This connects to a very early form of Celtic religion, and may suggest that the location of what is now London was an early Celtic settlement of some importance. There is not sufficient space here to go into the historical and archaeological evidence for this, as we are concerned mainly with legendary matters, but any good text books on Romano-Celtic archaeology (such as Anne Ross's *Pagan Celtic Britain*) will give the reader a great deal of material on this subject.

The cult of the sacred severed head is not, however, associated with Merlin. Geographically and culturally we find Merlin in Wales and Scotland, not England. It is not surprising, therefore, that there is little in the way of solid evidence to connect him with London, other than by several removes and lines of association.

There might be some fruitful research to be done in London archives concerning the exact locations and histories of buildings bearing his name; much of this has been summarized in this chapter, but there is still an element of uncertainty over the original Merlin's Cave in Penton or Islington. If this could be firmly dated in sources earlier than the eighteenth century as an actual cave site still traceable under the modern streets, we might have a potential key to a tradition of Merlin in London. On the available evidence, however, this seems unlikely.

8

William Blake's Spiritual Four-Fold City

Bernard Nesfield-Cookson

B LAKE SEES THE London of his day[1] as being ruled by a rigid
system of oppression, as a manifestation of a closed system in
which every aspect of life is codified. No freedom of expression, creative energy, individual feeling, thought and will, is permitted. Thus, for
instance, the priest of organized religion in Blake's poem, 'A Little Boy
Lost',[2] makes a martyr of a child who cannot comprehend and accept
an abstract God somewhere above the clouds, but sees the divine both
within himself and in 'the little bird / That picks up crumbs around the
door'. Any attempt to break through the rigid boundaries of dogma
and tradition is regarded by the Establishment as being dangerous.

Similarly, the King's power depends on a preservation of the status
quo. Regardless of personal suffering, the soldier must fight and the
child must labour under dire physical conditions. In his poem,
'London', Blake denounces a society which sustains its hierarchical
stratifications at the expense of individual fulfilment:

> *I wander thro' each charter'd street,*
> *Near where the charter'd Thames does flow,*
> *And mark in every face I meet*
> *Marks of weakness, marks of woe.*
>
> *In every cry of every Man,*
> *In every Infant's cry of fear,*
> *In every voice, in every ban,*
> *The mind-forg'd manacles I hear.*
>
> *How the Chimney-sweeper's cry*
> *Every black'ning Church appalls;*

And the hapless Soldier's sigh
Runs in blood down Palace walls.

But most thro' midnight streets I hear
How the youthful Harlot's curse
Blasts the new born Infant's tear,
And blights with plagues the Marriage hearse.[3]

'London' is not an expression of simple despair but a profound analysis of human misery in cities. The London Blake describes here is created by men with 'Selfish Centres',[4] selfish, contracted, hardened hearts, in which 'False Holiness / is / hid'.[5] It is a spiritual void. Blake sees London 'petrified' under the yoke of prohibitions, rigid social codes, inflexible moral laws, and so on. In his view, the city he sees is impermeable to creative imagination[6] and 'become barren mountains of Moral Virtue; and every Minute Particular hardened into grains of sand'.[7] Instances of such degraded and petrified 'Particulars' are the Tower, Court, and the New Bethlehem Insane Asylum.[8] Forming the fallen version of immortal London, such institutions of repression (prison, Court, mental hospital) demonstrate, for Blake, the consequences of spiritually blind (Urizenic)[9] abstract, analytical reasoning and religious error.

When Blake looks into the dark shops and den-like hovels in the shadow of London's spires and towers, into the 'caves of solitude & dark despair', 'among Albion's rocks & precipices', he sees that individuals, 'every Minute Particular of Albion', are 'degraded & murder'd' as by cruel pyramid-builders who 'take up / The articulations of a man's soul and laughing throw it down / Into the frame, then kick it out upon the plank'[10] – in the same way that brickbuilders in the London kilns threw clay into a mould and knocked the moulded brick out on to a board to be baked.[11] In his walks through the 'darkness & horrid solitude'[12] Blake finds humans in the crowded alleys of the poor, he sees individuals, 'The jewels of Albion, running down / The kennels[13] of the streets & lanes as if they were abhorr'd.'[14]

The reversal here is typical of Blake: the oppressors talk of casting pearls before the swinish populace. Blake, in contrast, sees that the people are the pearls, the jewels, and that they have been 'Harden'd into grains of sand' by the contempt of those in power who treat them like swine, and who cast forth 'all the tenderness of the soul . . . as filth & mire'.[15] Blake cannot but help 'looking on Albion's City with many tears'.[16]

When we are considering Blake's attitude towards and view of life we need to recall that in his lifetime the mechanical model of the Newtonian system made its influence felt in all spheres of human activity. Newton's mechanistic science was used to close and enclose the world in a rigid system. A typical example of this influence is reflected in the fact that Richard Bentley, a divine, sought to prove that the world was held in a God-given order. It was, in truth, an age of systematizers,[17] or, in Blakean terms, Urizen's Age. Blake repeatedly shows his dislike of the heritage of such a system, not solely because it is rigid, but because it is abstract and has, in his view, no relation to real life.

Blake's criticism of philosophical, scientific[18] and religious thought is inseparable from his social criticism. The intellectual and philosophical atmosphere of the eighteenth century and early nineteenth century strengthened the class structure in which everyone had his/her allotted place. John Locke[19] had gone so far as to say, 'Knowledge and science in general are the business only of those who are at ease and leisure.' Such a view is anathema to Blake. The universe became increasingly regarded as the 'Great Machine' working by rigidly determined laws. Blake's 'dark Satanic Mills'[20] may be understood as being, *inter alia*, a symbol of a mechanical social order in which each institution such as Church, university[21] and industry is like a grinding mill within the mechanical social system which suppresses Man. Everyone, according to such a system, has his/her predestined place and there can be no outlet for creative, imaginative activity.

Such a system is abhorrent, indeed, 'Satanic', to Blake, who notes that all these institutions teach passive obedience to the ruling interests and regard silence and obedience as wisdom and virtue. In 'Public Address' he writes: 'Obedience to the Will of the Monopolist is call'd Virtue, and the really Industrious, Virtuous & Independent . . . is driven out.'[22] Blake also makes the point, however, that those who adopt passivity towards the violators of human rights — be it physical exploitation or mental suppression – do, in fact, accept and approve the system and are part of it.[23]

Throughout his life, Blake's anger was directed against the social, philosophical and religious atmosphere that suffocated and suppressed human individuality and imagination. Let us now, in the light of all this, look a little more closely at the poem quoted in full above – 'London'.

This poem is a concise social history of the time. When Blake was born (1757) it was a year of dearth. From that year onwards, for many years to come, scarcity of food was common – nowhere more so than in London. Malnutrition was most marked in the capital city where rickets, the 'English Disease', also prevailed and cheap gin was the 'principal sustenance . . . of more than 100,000 people'.[24] Weakness and woe were indeed etched on every face.

'London' is a prophetic cry in which Blake turns upon George III and William Pitt's city of oppression.[25] It is 'a dark picture of a city whose inhabitants, then as now, come and go, for the most part, unlit by the light of eternity.'[26] The sixteen lines of this poem give a succinct picture of man's inhumanity to man. The 'mind-forg'd manacles' of the second stanza show that Blake is concerned with a mental state symbolized by the social injustices he sees every day in a society which is dominated by the financial interests of a privileged few – be they individuals or monopolies. The term 'charter'd' here applies specifically to the streets and the Thames, and signifies the restrictive, suppressive and exploitative effects of the charters and corporations of the world of high finance upon the individual. Despite the old Charters of Liberty, the city is enslaved by the new, commercial, charters. In more general terms Blake is also saying that the 'streets', or, rather, men in the street, are 'chartered' by laws and social attitudes and conventions, which function in such a one-sided way as to stifle and manacle individual and original action and thought.

We should note, however (as has been suggested already), that such 'manacles' are not applied solely by some higher authority, but also by man upon himself, for, as Blake says, there are 'marks of woe', but also 'marks of weakness'. Blake indicts the Church with grim puns as he hears the sweep's cry that 'Every black'ning Church appalls'. The building's funeral cloth of soot is emblematic: the institution is morally blackened because it has failed to be properly appalled at the young chimney-sweeper's situation. On the contrary, as the child sweep tells us,[27] it is a situation that the clergy's complicity with political and economic power has actively promoted. In another poem, entitled 'Holy Thursday',[28] Blake expressed strong indignation that children should be reduced to being fed by 'cold and usurous hand' in a land that is rich and fruitful. The Church's false position makes for a zealous and 'cold' hypocrisy. No wonder the little vagabond of London's streets cries out:

> Dear Mother, dear Mother, the Church is cold,
> But the Ale-house is healthy & pleasant & warm;
> Besides I can tell where I am used well . . .[29]

Blake's reaction to Bishop Richard Watson's published sermon on 'The Wisdom and Goodness of God, in having made both Rich and Poor' (1797) is equally vehement: 'God made Man happy & Rich, but the Subtil made the innocent Poor. This must be a most wicked & blasphemous book.'[30] 'Watson', Blake comments, 'has defended Antichrist.'[31]

'The Subtil made the innocent Poor'! Blake does not make such a statement without justification. He could make it also in response to Samuel Johnson's contention that a man with money 'cannot make a bad use of his money, so far as regards society', and that it would be misguided to improve the conditions of the poor without 'raising the wages of day-labourers is wrong; for it does not make them live better, but only makes them idler, and idleness is a very bad thing for human nature.'[32]

In mockery of such a view – and with particular reference to T.R. Malthus's *Essay on the Principle of Population* (1798) – Blake writes:

> . . . when a man looks pale
> With labour & abstinence, say he looks healthy & happy;
> And when his children sicken, let them die; there are enough
> Born, even too many, & our Earth will be overrun
> Without these arts. If you would make the poor live with temper[33]

With pomp give every crust of bread you give; with gracious cunning
Magnify small gifts; reduce the man to want a gift, & then give with pomp.

Say he smiles if you hear him sigh. If pale, say he is ruddy.
Preach temperance: say he is overgorg'd & drowns his wit
In strong drink, tho' you know that bread & water are all
He can afford.[34]

A more devastating criticism of the social conditions to be found in London (and elsewhere, of course) and of the manner in which those in power treated the underprivileged would be difficult to imagine.

Social inequality of inhuman proportions forced poor parents to sell their young children's labour. They were cheap labour and could easily be replaced and were therefore constantly exploited. Some parents were 'ready to dispose of their children under the influence of a glass of gin'.[35] Blake's chimney sweeper is a typical example of a child labourer. In 'The Chimney Sweeper', a poem composed three or four years before 'London', Blake writes:

When my mother died I was very young,
And my father sold me while yet my tongue
Could scarcely cry 'Weep! Weep! Weep!'[36]

In another poem, also entitled 'The Chimney Sweeper', published together with 'London', the small boy tells of his exploitation by his parents, who imagine they are not wronging him because his spirit is not completely subdued:

A little black thing among the snow,
Crying 'Weep! Weep!' in notes of woe!
'Where are thy father & mother? Say?'
'They are both gone up to the church to pray.

'And because I am happy & dance & sing,
'They think they have done me no injury,
'And are gone to praise God & his Priest & King,
'Who make up a heaven of our misery.'[37]

It is not only poor labourers, men and women and small boys who suffer misery in Blake's London, but also, we learn from the poem of that name, babies, young girls and soldiers.

Poverty and lack of opportunity drove young girls on to the streets where they soon became infected and in turn passed on their 'blight' to others, including their own children. These infants were often abandoned in the streets by mothers to whom they meant only expense and shame.

During the reign of Hanoverian George III (1738–1820) England repeatedly suffered the 'dislocating change from peace to war and war to peace'.[38] In peace time the soldiers themselves were 'hapless'. Wounded or discharged, they were sent penniless to swell the ranks of the starving unemployed.

The London Blake sees as he wanders through her streets is, to express it somewhat dramatically, the city of the slave-owning tyrant who affirms the oppressive 'Selfish Centre'.[39] It is a city built and ruled by what Blake called 'single vision',[40] a vision which is so narrow and blinkered that the 'viewer' stands outside, apart from things. Such a closed, self-centred person is a lifeless, feelingless observer and confines himself to cold analysis. In the words of William Wordsworth (1770–1850):

> *Our meddling intellect*
> *Destroys the beauteous form of things*
> *We murder to dissect.*[41]

This single, rationalizing vision (on the part of Church, King and Parliament) is specifically depicted in 'The Human Abstract'[42] which Blake published together with 'London'. This poem articulates a mental state of selfishness and mental cruelty, which the illustration visually personifies: an old man, white-haired and white-bearded, crouches beneath a net of heavy ropes on a rocky shore, hemmed in by dark waves and a barren tree – all of which, in Blake, are symbols of spiritually blind and heartless materialism and rationalism.

It is of interest to note the changes Blake makes to his first draft of the poem 'London'. In his manuscript notebook (1793)[43] he describes

London with pejorative adjectives: 'dirty street', 'dirty Thames', 'dismal streets'. But in the final version he substitutes adjectives which, as well as being more neutral, are more symbolically weighted ('charter'd street', 'charter'd Thames', 'midnight streets'), thereby indicating that London's evils are not to be seen as being exclusively the fault of the city *per se*, or of those who wield power in the city, but also of the ordinary man and woman of the street.

The most telling of these changes is from 'German forg'd links' to 'mind-forg'd manacles'. The chimney-sweeper, the conscripted soldier and the prostitute are undeniably victims, but the changes which Blake makes highlight his conviction that repression is not simply the result of 'bans' issued by higher authority. Blake knows, of course, that German George III and William Pitt issue the bans, but even they cannot forge the manacles with which men and women shackle their spirits into obeying them. As we have noted already, 'marks of weakness' are partially the cause of 'marks of woe'. Blake is saying, in other words, that he finds among his fellow citizens a willingness to be tyrannized.

The cities men build are both metaphorically and literally the form of their being. They are both geo-political units and the states of mind which create them. We have seen that, for Blake, any attempt by the Establishment to thwart the fulfilment of ordinary men and women in London's streets is evil:

> Some say that Happiness is not Good for Mortals, & they ought to be answer'd that Sorrow is not fit for Immortals & is utterly useless to any one; a blight never does good to a tree, & if a blight kill not a tree but it still bear fruit, let none say that the fruit was in consequence of the blight.[44]

Blake knows that the blight must be fought within society, and that it is the responsibility of individual men and women and not of the Establishment, nor of a metaphysical God, to change evil into good and an oppressive society into a humane one. In his great epic poem, *Jerusalem*, calling on people to rally their own creative power and rise against the social tyranny, Blake/Los,[45] the man of creative imagination and spiritual energy, angrily asks:

Why stand we here trembling around
Calling on God for help, and not ourselves, in whom God dwells,
Stretching a hand to save the falling Man?[46]

Blake is saying here that we must be true to our own creative imagination which alone can hold a true vision of social reality.

We saw earlier on that the city described in 'London' is constructed
by men with 'Selfish Centres', and that their construction is a spiritual void. Man can emerge from this void, Blake contends, by following the promptings of Los, his own creative imagination, by 'opening
the Centre'. With opened heart and 'cleans'd' organs, 'doors of
perception',[47] Man can perceive the potential harmony between
himself and his fellow-men and between himself and the city. The
city Blake envisages should be an environment and outer embodiment of Man's imaginative vision; it should be the 'garment' of Man,
the material substance which manifests his creative energy and vision;
it should be a manifestation of his love for his fellow-men. It is clear
that imagination places greater emphasis on human values than on
any of the laws devised by ruling interests and is therefore regarded by
the law-givers as a dangerous weapon against established dogma,
tradition and order.[48]

Imagination/Blake/Los knows that through love one expands
rather than divides oneself – division, of course, being a principal
tool in the hands of analytical reasoning. When the creative imagination perceives that the material world and self-centredness are but
passing manifestations of the all-permeating divine life, then Man
can give up his encapsulated ego and his sense of physical imprisonment to participate actively in this divinity. Inspired by such regen-
erative awareness Los, imaginative, creative Man, can turn to artistic
creation. By 'fabricating forms sublime',[49] by creating ideal outlines,
the artist can provide fallen man with a spiritual image of the human
form which he can emulate (to reiterate: the cities men build are
literally the form of their being). The man of imagination, Los,
therefore sets to work to build a heavenly city on earth, a 'spiritual
Four-fold London',[50] which Blake calls 'Golgonooza', to replace
abstract, analytical reason's anti-utopia. *As Man perceives himself, so he
creates.*

When, in Blake's view Man – life on earth – begins to emulate the sublime form of divinely inspired art, then the process of psychic reintegration and social renewal and cooperation has truly begun. The building of Golgonooza, the city of imaginative labour as well as that of art,[51] is the decisive preparatory step taken towards the building of the New Jerusalem. The creative and loving, true relationship between Man and God, between man and woman, between people and city, will be realized most completely, of course, in the New Jerusalem.

Blake insists that true vision does not function haphazardly, thus it does not haphazardly build a fictitious city but is grounded in and works through the sensually perceived 'Particulars', through reality as we encounter it. In short, Blake disagrees with the neoclassical attempt to get at the principles of things by discarding the details. These very details – each individual human being, each and every one in a unique situation in life, for instance – these very details, he insists, are the key to perception whatever the subject may be. 'Sacrifice the Parts, What becomes of the Whole?'[52]

Blake expresses his vision of London in which there 'is a completer harmony of all things with each other'[53] in the lyric which forms a prelude to the second chapter of *Jerusalem*:

> *The fields from Islington to Marybone,*
> *To Primrose Hill and Saint John's Wood,*
> *Were builded over with pillars of gold,*
> *And there Jerusalem's pillars stood.*
>
> *Her Little-ones ran on the fields,*
> *The Lamb of God among them seen,*
> *And fair Jerusalem his Bride,*
> *Among the little meadows green.*
>
> *Pancrass & Kentish-town repose*
> *Among her golden pillars high,*
> *Among her golden arches which*
> *Shine upon the starry sky.*

The Jew's-harp-house & the Green Man,
The Ponds where Boys to bathe delight,
The fields of Cows by Willan's farm,
Shine in Jerusalem's pleasant sight.[54]

Here we need to recall that in Blake's childhood, when he lived in Broad Street, Golden Square, most of the area north of Tyburn Road or Oxford Street was meadowland dotted with warm and hospitable inns; it was a paradise 'from Islington to . . . Saint John's Wood'.[55] When Blake moved to South Molton Street in September 1803, new residences were being built half a mile or so further into the northern fields, but the Jew's Harp, the Green Man, and other inns were still in open countryside.

Blake's song should not be misconstrued. It is not a lament over the departure of some of the countryside. On the contrary, the boom of dwelling-house building at the time of the Peace of Amiens (1802) represented for him a victory of the arts of peace over the Establishment's call for human sacrifice. Rather than for the past, Blake is here expressing a nostalgia for the future.

Besides this 'innocent' landscape, however, Blake, as we have seen already, is only too well aware of the London of his day with all its visionlessness and inhumanity. Hints of human sacrifice are brought to bear upon the London of the day in the following lines in the same lyric just quoted:

They groan'd aloud on London Stone,
They groan'd aloud on Tyburn's Brook,
Albion gave his deadly groan . . .[56]

The images refer to familiar themes in Blake. The tyranny and oppression exerted by those in power is suggested by 'London Stone', a Roman milestone (see pages 214–16). For Blake this stone symbolizes the cold and rigid 'rock' of anti-vision, for from it all distances were measured and it was therefore a central point of reference for a conception of the world rooted in Newtonian abstract calculation. Tyburn was the place where criminals were hanged. Most of the hanging crimes in Blake's day (there were well over 150 of them) were crimes against wealth and property (five shillings' worth of goods from a shop, for instance). For Blake, Tyburn is the site where men and women are sacrificed to an abstract and rigid moral law. He relates Tyburn to Golgotha, the place of spiritual martyrs, 'Victims of Justice'.[57] 'The law was not merely savage for lack of a police force; it was vicious, because it was irresponsible.'[58]

Such a London, for Blake, has become, or is becoming, Babylon. The 'materials' with which it is built are misery, destruction (of soul and body) and death, because, he claims, Man has turned his back on the 'Creative Imagination' (which, for Blake, means on Christ)[59] 'into the Wastes of Moral Law':

> . . . Babylon is builded in the Waste, founded in Human desolation.
> . . . The Walls of Babylon are Souls of Men, her Gates are Groans
> Of Nations, her Towers are the Miseries of once happy Families,
> Her Streets are paved with Destruction, her Houses built with Death,
> Her Palaces with Hell & the Grave, her Synagogues with Torments
> Of ever-hardening Despair, squar'd & polish'd with cruel skill.[60]

It is against the building of Babylon, the city of death, that Imagination (Los) builds Golgonooza, in which the destruction and death of the unholy city, where the God of this world (Urizen/ Reason) is worshipped, are answered by brotherhood and forgiveness, by love. As we shall soon see, in the City of Art, of Imagination, 'The stones are pity, and the bricks, well wrought affections' and 'The mortar and cement of the work, tears of honesty'. In the city Los creates it is recognized, just as it will be when Jerusalem is rebuilt in 'England's green & pleasant Land':[61]

> That Man subsists by Brotherhood & Universal Love.
> Not for ourselves but for the Eternal family we live.
> Man liveth not by Self alone . . .[62]

In contrast to this stands the London Blake sees around him; a London peopled by isolated and inflated selfhoods, egotists, antagonistic to one another, 'Is this', he asks:

Is this thy soft Family-love,
Thy cruel Patriarchal pride,
Planting thy Family alone,
Destroying all the World beside?[63]

In such a London, Jerusalem is driven 'far away from / its / spires.'[64] But Jerusalem was not always so remote. Blake recalls the days of primal concord of all peoples:

In the Exchanges of London every Nation walk'd,
And London walk'd in every Nation, mutual in love & harmony.[65]

And, in a regenerated London, it would be so again. Commerce would no longer be fiendish but a mutual exchange of love and labour:

In my Exchanges every Land
Shall walk, & mine in every Land,
Mutual shall build Jerusalem,
Both heart in heart, & hand in hand.[66]

It should be so again, Blake proclaims, for the spiritual blindness, psychic and physical foulness and misery which he sees around him is not the true, essential London. The process of regeneration has to be set in train by the poet, the artist in each and every one of us, by the Imagination, only then will 'the spiritual Four-fold London' be built – and, eventually, Jerusalem rebuilt in England.

In Golgonooza, the City of Art, 'spiritual Four-fold London',[67] created by Imagination, people no longer selfishly and aggressively assert their individual 'selfhoods'[68] against one another, for each man and woman is free to express his or her inner creative energies in brother- and sisterhood. The builders of Golgonooza know 'not of self in / their / supreme joy'.[69] In a Babylonian London where personal gain, prestige and position are of paramount importance, self is ultimately the only real thing.

Whereas Babylon is built of groans and miseries, Golgonooza is built of virtues, of real human values. Golgonooza is, of course, no more than the urban form of the New Jerusalem. It is not to be equated with the Edenic state that Blake envisages should, eventually, replace it.

The vision of Eden, of the New Jerusalem, is not a peculiar possession of the artist as such, for Imagination exists in all men and women regardless of their vocation. It exists, in Blake's view, as the original, universal, and highest phase of human consciousness.[70] It is through holding the vision of perfection, of Eden, that Man can build Golgonooza, which, nevertheless, is but an imperfect reflection of Eden. It is the artist in Man, the Imagination, which strives to make the invisible, ideal world, visible in physical form, knowing full well that what is created and recreated could always be better. 'Go on, builders in hope, tho' Jerusalem wanders far away.'[71] Los (Imagination) builds the 'spiritual Four-fold London' to nurture Man's creative capacities and to protect them against the oppressive and repressive power hostile to processes of spiritual regeneration. Golgonooza is generally characterized by Blake as being a place wherein spiritual forces are centred. In *Jerusalem*, Golgonooza's mathematical symmetry is clearly based on Ezekiel (41–3) and on the related vision of the New Jerusalem in Revelation (21). But this symmetry is not rigid and sterile, 'squar'd & polish'd with cruel skill' as in Babylon, for Golgonooza is 'continually building & continually decaying'.[72] It is 'ever building, ever falling'.[73]

True to the process of artistic creation, it is a perpetually evolving structure which changes constantly to meet new expressive needs and new developments of ideas. Not, of course, Babylonian needs of greater commercial and selfish profits, and so forth, but evolving needs and ideas of selfless love. In such a city of spiritual activity and freedom Man is no longer a victim of 'mind-forg'd manacles', nor is he imprisoned in the dark blindness of 'soft Family-Love'. 'Love that seeketh not Itself to please'[74] is the key to the release of Man from his prison of spiritual darkness. Unselfish love, Blake stresses again and again, is crucial to Man's spiritual activity and freedom.

The point and essence of Los's (Imagination's) building is its moral and spiritual effect. Typically with Blake this depends on the building process as well as on the finished product, and, as we have just seen, the process is never-ending; it is 'eternal labour!'[75]

We have previously noted that the city Blake envisages should be the 'garment' of Man, the 'material substance' which manifests his creative energy and vision exercised in freedom and love; that it should be a manifestation of selfless love. This Blake makes quite clear in the image of Golgonooza, the golden City of Art, the 'building of pity and compassion' created by 'golden builders'.

Before looking more closely at Blake's 'spiritual Four-fold London', the urban form of Jerusalem, let us consider another of his pictures describing a metropolis devoid of spiritual life.

He speaks of those who dwell in a modern city in the following terms:

> . . . *many stood silent, & busied in their families.*
> *And many said, 'We see no Vision in the darksom air.*
> *Measure the course of that sulphur orb that lights the darksom day;*
> *Set stations on this breeding Earth & let us buy & sell.'*[76]

These are, in a nutshell, the conditions of life without Imagination, of those whose minds are cast in the mould of 'single vision', who, defying Imagination, see only the material world. Nature is 'denatured', reduced to scientific measurement; marriage and sexual relationships debased to mere breeding contracts; and, significantly, attention is powerfully focused on commerce. The city constructed by such minds has a fitting rigid, geometric, concrete form devoid of creative imagination:

> *In right lined paths outmeasure'd by proportions of number, weight*
> *And measure, mathematic motion wondrous along the deep,*
> *In fiery pyramid, or Cube, or unornamented pillar square*
> *. . . Such the period of many worlds.*
> *Others triangular, right angled course maintain. Others obtuse,*
> *Acute, Scalene, in simple paths; but others move*
> *In intricate ways, biquardrate, Trapeziums, Rhombs, Rhomboids,*
> *Paralellograms triple & quadruple, polygonic*
> *In their amazing hard subdu'd course in the vast deep.*[77]

Such a city is a far cry from the ideal of imaginative vision. Nevertheless, Blake does not neglect to give Urizen, the calculating mind, credit for the crystalline beauty of his construction, despite its mechanical rationalism. 'Infinitely beautiful the wondrous work arose . . .'[78] Blake knows that the process of spiritual regeneration can only take place when Man is fully integrated. Urizen's rational skills are therefore also necessary to Man's full redemption, though destructive when set to work in isolation.

Blake gives us an even more vivid picture of an inhuman city than that which we have just seen constructed in an orderly fashion by mechanistic rationalism. This is the Urizenic city in which order is achieved by falsehood, reflected in a religion based on mystery, by an economy based on slavery, and politics based on militarism – reminding us, of course, of the poem 'London':

> First Trades & Commerce, ships & armed vessels he builded laborious
> To swim the deep; & on the land, children are sold to trades
> Of dire necessity, still laboring day & night till all
> Their life extinct they took the spectre form in dark despair;
> And slaves in myriads, in ship loads, burden the hoarse sounding deep,
> Rattling with clanking chains; the Universal Empire groans.
>
> And Urizen laid the first Stone, & all his myriads
> Builded a temple . . .
> And in the inner part of the Temple . . .
> They form'd the Secret place, reversing all the order of delight,
> That whosoever enter'd into the temple might not behold
> The hidden wonders . . .[79]

As the mind, so the temple, city, and empire.

In Blake's mythology the complete contrast to Urizen's coldly inhuman, 'dry-cleaned' and sterile city is the humanized creation described in *Jerusalem*:

> What are those golden builders doing? . . .
> . . . near Tyburn's fatal Tree?
> . . . near mournful
> Ever weeping Paddington? Is that Calvary and Golgotha
> Becoming a building of pity and compassion? Lo!

> *The stones are pity, and the bricks, well wrought affections*
> *Enamel'd with love & kindness, & the tiles engraven gold,*
> *Labour of merciful hands: the beams & rafters are forgiveness:*
> *The mortar & cement of the work, tears of honesty: the nails*
> *And the screws & iron braces are well wrought blandishments*
> *And well contrived words, firm fixing, never forgotten,*
> *Always comforting the remembrance: the floors, humility:*
> *The ceilings, devotion: the hearths, thanksgiving.*[80]

Los, Imagination, the architect of this city, knows the intimate relationship between Man and city. Whereas Urizen's city is a mere utilitarian construction, a 'substance' without soul and spirit, Los's city is a spirit- and soul-imbued living organism. Imagination gives form to a city which breathes and pulsates with creative life. Rationalism, unless it works in harmony with Imagination, remains cold and abstract and constructs a form that reduces Man to the existence of a heartless robot. In Los's city, Golgonooza, selfishness, intolerance and oppression have no place.

What Blake does in the passage just quoted is a typical instance of the way his imagination works: he embeds the allegory in actual building projects going on in early nineteenth-century London – the excavation for new dwelling-houses in Paddington, the consequent digging up of the bones of criminals hanged at Tyburn, the construction of a house of mercy, and so on. The phrase 'near mournful / Ever weeping Paddington' is a poetic expression based on fact. At the time Blake was writing, St George's burying-ground occupied a large portion of the Paddington area near the intersection of Edgware, Bayswater, and Oxford roads. This was also the location of the Tyburn gallows. Moreover, in 1812, Paddington was a slum area inhabited by poverty-stricken Irish labourers.[81]

In another passage in *Jerusalem*, London, 'a Human awful wonder of God', speaking through Blake, says:

> *My Streets are my Ideas of Imagination.*
> *Awake Albion, awake! and let us awake up together.*
> *My Houses are Thoughts: my Inhabitants, Affections,*
> *The children of my thoughts walking within my blood-vessels . . .*[82]

Here, as in the earlier passage quoted from *Jerusalem*, Blake presents us with a humanized city created from unorthodox materials – ideas, imagination, thoughts, and affections. London is both a city and 'a Human awful wonder of God', creation and creator, material, human, and divine. In this it resembles Jerusalem, its prototype, described in the Old Testament prophets as both city and human, nation and woman. 'By repeating identical images in both individuals and collective constructions such as cities,[83] Blake demonstrates that consciousness or vision is not solely an internal matter, but is reflected in outer circumstances.'[84] Cities and landscapes 'are also Men; every thing is Human',[85] while all individuals contain 'a Universe'.[86] 'Renewed consciousness thus renews its world just as fallen consciousness degenerates its world. The imaginative individual and city are thus identified, as are inner consciousness and outer being.'[87]

Urban renewal, 'continually building & continually decaying' is a central metaphor for Blake's ongoing theme of ceaseless 'Mental Fight / Till we have built Jerusalem / In England's green & pleasant Land.'[88]

It was mentioned earlier on that Golgonooza is not to be equated with the New Jerusalem, but Blake would have us recognize that this City of Art, of Imagination, can offer us the foundation, through the experience of Golgotha (Blake clearly locates Golgonooza within the world of suffering, of Calvary and Golgotha), through the experience of death and resurrection, of inner renewal, upon which, eventually, the New Jerusalem can be realized. William Blake is a man of the modern world. Far from destroying the city, the factory, commerce and industry, he would transform them, through the 'Creative Imagination', from oppressive 'tyrants', depriving individual men and women of free expression and initiative, to creative havens in which they can find inspiration and new life.

The form of life in the metropolis is the form of a nation's consciousness. The vital question Blake raises is this: is it abstract Reason or Creative Imagination which is the forming agent? If the former, then spiritual 'death' is the keynote; if the latter, then creative life is the 'expanding centre' of the city.

9

Towers of Sound and Light

Gareth Knight

A LL CITIES BEGIN as a meeting place of ways. At a crossroads, or often, as in the case of London, where there is a crossing of river and of road. Two different elements, land and water, meeting. Thus the actual site of a city is determined by the natural lie of the land; the configuration of the Earth itself. Human activity then shapes itself around this nexus.

From the crossway, a vortex of trade and human interchange springs up. Soon a stockade or wall is thrown up to mark its boundaries, its 'ring-pass-not', to protect the little human cosmos that lies within its bounds. Within that circle, surrounding a cross, there springs up a system of fair-trading and of local law which binds all that dwell within it. And eventually towers begin to rise, set above places of worship, to show that man's true origin, and that of the city, lies in another dimension, signified by their pointing to the heavens.

Thus in river, road, bridge, wall, tower and spire, we see the first principles of cosmic manifestation being re-expressed on Earth in the little works of man.

Thus is the city a focus, a chakrum, a psychic and spiritual centre, a whirling vortex of force within the etheric body of the planet. Capital cities especially form a focus for each nation, although the principle applies not only to other major cities of the world, but also to every town and to the smallest village. Each in their way are nodes within the network of human life on Earth.

As such, towns and cities, and the links between them, are as important in their way as the network energies between mountains, lakes and rivers; and also between ancient megaliths, sacred sites and stone circles. Each is another type or mode of interchange, or network.

All are different dimensions of an inner web upon which they form like crystals of shining dew.

One could indeed fill an encyclopedia with detailed explanation of all of this, for it is as extensive in its ramifications as life itself. However, let us, as a small case study, examine one or two of the more important focal points of talismanic London. We use the world 'talismanic' in a deliberate sense, and in what we consider to be the deepest and truest meaning of the word. That is, a talisman is an expression in the substance of the Earth of an inner or spiritual reality or force. So although the word is generally used to refer to lucky charms, it also applies in a profounder sense to man's buildings and whatever of a higher nature is contained within them.

A reliable indication of the presence of an inner power source is the growth of legend about a place. This can occur to historical and semi-historical characters as well as to places. A particular focus of legend are the bells of St Mary-le-Bow. It is well worth our examining this building and its symbolic connections in some detail.

In popular legend the essential qualification for being a true citizen of the city of London, or a 'cockney', is to have been born within the sound of Bow bells. It is these bells also that are recalled in the old tale of Dick Whittington who, as a dispirited apprentice returning home to Gloucestershire, having failed to find the streets of London paved with gold, was stopped at the foot of Highgate Hill by the sound of the bells that seemed to be saying, 'Turn again Whittington, Lord Mayor of London!'

So he did, and a commemorative stone and a hospital near the site mark the occasion. He became Lord Mayor of London no less than four times and was a benefactor and creditor to no less than three kings, one of them Henry V, the great victor of Agincourt.

London bells are indeed a force to be reckoned with, as are bells throughout the country. In a sense they are the tongues of angels. Monstrous clanging tongues that tell of joy and celebration, warn of invasion, mourn the passing of the dead, and, as in the case of Dick Whittington, may have much to say of personal destiny to those who know how to listen to them aright. Even the custom of change ringing is a form of perfect patterning that has its links with symbolic magic squares – expressed directly in sound.

To return to St Mary-le-Bow, however, which is in the City itself, not in the more recent eastern suburb of Bow, when we approach it down Cheapside we can turn first into its old churchyard, which is now paved over. Here City workers can sit in the shade of shrubs and trees overlooked by a very striking statue of an Elizabethan adventurer by the name of John Smith.

It is difficult to know why his statue should stand here when his bones lie under the choir of St Sepulchre outside the City walls. However, he is a fitting introductor to the mysteries of the church of St Mary-le-Bow in a somewhat unlikely way. John Smith has an important global connection in that he was Governor of Virginia in its earliest days. He was one of those hardy spirits who heeded the words and active encouragement of men of vision such as Sir Walter Raleigh and Dr John Dee to seek new lands and treasures to the West.

What makes him particularly important for us is that, in a time when it is becoming realized that we need to come to terms with the mysteries of the Earth, and also that much of these mysteries are in the custody of the American Indian, we find that John Smith was actually initiated into the mysteries of the Algonquin Indians.

Bluff, brave John Smith may well have had little appreciation of the finer points of this initiation, but what befell him marks him out as a key talismanic figure in the sense that we have described the term, together with the other protagonist of the story, the Indian princess Pocahontas.

As with all events that have an inner significance, the tale has become the focus of legend and romance. The story is, and it is true, that when John Smith was simply one of a band of inquisitive Englishmen who had planted a tent village on the shores of Chesapeake Bay in what they called Virginia (after Elizabeth, the Virgin Queen), he was captured by Indian hunters who took him to their chief, Powhatan.

Here all the assembled elders of the tribe gave a great shout as he was ushered in to them. He was invited to ceremonially wash his hands and then a feast was spread before him. No sooner had he finished eating than two great stones were brought in and John Smith was forcibly stretched over them and two executioners stood over him with clubs raised as if to beat his brains out. A tense silence descended upon the company, which was broken, not by the order for execution but by a young Indian girl, the chief's daughter Pocahontas, who threw herself upon John Smith's body and interposed her head between his own and the clubs of the executioners. John Smith was then released, treated well and cordially, and a few days later returned safely to his camp.

He and Pocahontas acted for some time as intermediaries between the colonizing Englishmen and the local Indian tribes. The story has come down as one of romantic love, wherein the Indian girl saved the life of one whom she loved. However, it bears the hallmarks of an initiation ceremony. In fact, in the end, Pocahontas married another Englishman, John Rolfe. She was received into the Christian faith under the baptismal name of Rebecca, and came to visit England, where she was presented at the court of James I but tragically caught an infection on the ship that was taking her back to Virginia. She was taken ashore and died at Gravesend, where her body still rests in the church of St George, which has become a focal point for transatlantic accord, and is well worth a visit by those who take talismanic pilgrimage seriously. Other focal points of this story are a statue of her in London's Red Lion Square, and Powhatan's mantle, which is to be seen in the Ashmolean Museum, Oxford, with a replica in the church of St Mary's, Lambeth.

So let us return to the churchyard of St Mary-le-Bow with all this in mind when we look upon the statue of Captain John Smith, and we can, if we are so minded, imagine that it is he who conducts us on our tour of the crypt and the various symbolic levels of the church outside which he stands.

Descending a spiral stair to the crypt we should remind ourselves that there is no ascent to the spiritual heights without first a grounding in the depths of the good Earth. It was not simply a search for a place of refuge that guided the early Christians to worship in the catacombs. We find here too that the holiest place of the church of St Mary is in the crypt, for here communion is celebrated underground, in the chapel of the Holy Spirit, which is a place of great spiritual serenity and power.

Here also are to be seen the bows from which the church gains its name. They are Norman arches, built in the midst of the roughly constructed Saxon stonework, and using nearly two-thousand-year-old Roman bricks. This was also the seat of the Court of Arches of the Archbishop of Canterbury, and a link with the great English martyr Thomas à Becket is also to be found in the fact that he, too, was a true cockney, born and bred in the streets around Cheapside.

As a link with this powerful spiritual source one can visualize St Thomas standing under one of the arches. Visualize the pillars of the arches being of two shades of alchemical gold, one of lemon yellow, the other of orange, with the arch above being like a rainbow with a keystone of brilliant white light. This gives a hint of a profound initiatory tradition that has come down in the nursery rhyme about the bells of London that commences 'Oranges and lemons, say the bells of St Clements' and finishes with a sequence about 'Here comes the candle to light you to bed. Here comes the chopper to chop off your head.' Within these childish rhymes is contained a mystery as deep as that which befell the unsuspecting Captain John Smith.

The original St Clements stood in Eastcheap, which was the main trading thoroughfare of old London, and the sale of oranges and lemons – exotic fruits from faraway places brought to the port of London up the river – emphasize the trading that was the very origination of the city.

The sequence of rhyming couplets, as commonly sung in school playgrounds, those great repositories of the folk imagination, runs:

> *Oranges and lemons, say the bells of St Clements.*
> *You owe me five farthings, say the bells of St Martin's.*
> *When will you pay me, say the bells of Old Bailey.*
> *When I grow rich, say the bells of Shoreditch.*
> *When will that be, say the bells of Stepney.*
> *I'm sure I don't know, says the great bell at Bow.*
>
> *Here comes the candle to light you to bed.*
> *Here comes the chopper to chop off your head.*

To those who have played the game in childhood, the final couplet has a frisson quite out of proportion to its apparent doggerel simplicity, as the line of children passes under the extended arms of two elder children who move them up and down with a final 'Chop! Chop! Chop!' and on the third chop capture some child in the cage of their arms to be 'out' or 'it'.

The farthings of St Martin's were originally 'four-things', for an old silver penny was marked with a cross so that it could be easily cut into two or four pieces to make 'ha' pennies' and 'farthings'. The five 'four-things' we all owe, then refer to the cross and the five wounds of Christ, by which fallen mankind was redeemed.

When will mankind be able to repay such a debt, is asked by those great overseers of justice, the bells of the Old Bailey. That will not be until the last days, when at the sound of the last trump all shall be changed as in the twinkling of an eye, and the heavens will roll back to reveal the spiritual glory of the enthroned lamb in the bejewelled heavenly city. This is referred to by the bells of Shoreditch but the time of its coming is unknown to any man, which is all the more emphatic in coming from the great bell at Bow, for it is this bell that through the centuries rang the curfew and regulated the days of Londoners, from calling the apprentices from bed in the morning to sending them packing indoors at night.

However, in the meantime, we have the candle to light us to bed, the 'Light of the World' whose evocative picture by Holman Hunt is now one of the additional features of St Paul's Cathedral, and the chopper, that handy instrument of practical politics of an earlier day, which is an especial instrument of martyrdom, particularly as related to the dynastic and religious problems of the nation.

The blood of the martyrs is the seed of the Church and also of all other movements within the group soul of the race. And so 'beheading' in particular carries an esoteric significance that not only goes back to the most ancient mysteries of, for instance, Bran the Blessed, Orpheus, John the Baptist and certain imagery of the Holy Grail, but carries forward into history to become the stuff of hagiography and legend as with St Alban, Britain's first Christian martyr, Sir Thomas More, Anne Boleyn, Mary Queen of Scots, Sir Walter Raleigh, King Charles I, or Oliver Cromwell (struck off after his death). Indeed it could be said that many famous figures that met their end in this way did so because they embodied a particular archetype in the racial soul that expressed itself as a minority interest or movement of the day.

And it is for this reason that such figures attract about themselves popular legend, for they are gateways to particular power points in the ancestral memory of the race.

The candle also has its place in these particular mysteries, for there is another evocative little couplet:

> *Wee Willy Winky runs through the town,*
> *Upstairs and downstairs in his night gown,*
> *Shouting down the chimney, calling through the lock,*
> *Are all the children safe in bed, it's past 8 o'clock.*

Who is this strange figure, dressed in what appear to be night robes, but which might also be angelic draperies, or even a shroud, running around calling the curfew for children? In many illustrations to be found in nursery rhyme books he, too, is often invested with a candle. This little being of light has connections with the 'Light of the World', and also with that other line of martyrs who have been human candles in the pyres of religious intolerance at Smithfield, whose light has nonetheless continued to shine through the subsequent ages to Catholic and Protestant alike.

The 'oranges and lemons' sequence also has other couplets that have become attached to it throughout time, as the temptation for some is to include all the church, or at any rate their own. The symbolic value of these will vary according to the depth of imagination from which they come, but even the apparently most arbitrary should not be dismissed out of hand in any consideration of this kind of manifestation of the group mind.

The exemplar in this is the great modern prophet of London, William Blake, who made no bones about constructing a personal iconography and mythology to embody his visionary insights. Thus in delineating particular powers of evil he listed the names of particular adversaries of his, such as Schofield, the drunken soldier who accused him of treason. He also chose particular towns of England or districts of London to represent particular inner powers. This is an exemplification of a perfectly valid magical use of images, for it is what they mean to us within our deepest selves that is all important, for we ourselves are each the centre of our own universe. We interpret what we see without by the light of the reality that we are within.

While taken to extremes this can degenerate into arbitrary subjectivism, when allied to objective inner insights it demonstrates the importance of tradition and legend and popular imagination over the so-called 'objective facts' of academic history – if indeed this is anything but a particular form of subjectivism that sets great store by 'objective facts'. We all live in a magical universe, if truth were told!

So let us now pass back up the spiral stair from the crypt of St Mary-le-Bow to the normal level of human interchange, where we can profitably examine what is contained in the main body of the building. It is, as a whole, modelled upon the Basilica Maxentius in Rome, as part of our native Renaissance tradition bequeathed to us by Sir Christopher Wren, about whom more anon.

The interior, with a main colour scheme of white and gold, is dominated by a rood cross that is unusual in that it is surrounded by four figures instead of two. To the traditional images of the Blessed Virgin, and the beloved disciple St John, there are added Mary Magdalene and the centurion Longinus, which give special emphasis to the morning of the resurrection and the symbolism of the Grail. This is truly a divine pentagram of potent iconography.

It also contains within its very substance the principle of international reconciliation in that it was a gift from the people of Germany, whose bombs a generation ago destroyed all but the walls and tower of the church, and it was carved by a craftsman from the Passion play village of Oberammergau, and painted by a German prisoner-of-war.

To the south there is a chapel reserved for the Blessed Sacrament, which is kept in an aumbry shaped like a bell tower that is surmounted by a pelican, a symbol of great significance to every Rosicrucian. To the north, the quarter traditionally of greatest symbolic darkness, there is a chapel dedicated to those who gave their lives in the resistance to that hideous strength that engulfed Europe in the years culminating in the Second World War.

This is a gift from the people of Norway in recognition of the fact that it was the sound of Bow bells, acting as a radio call-sign over the airwaves from the BBC, that brought hope to the afflicted in the darkest days of war and oppression. And to the east there are high windows showing Christ in majesty surrounded by the Holy City of the Book of Revelation, and beside him St Paul, the patron saint of the city, and also the Virgin Mary with the church cradled in her arms.

From this place of congregation we may now, accompanied by our guide John Smith if we will, ascend another spiral stairway into the tower. Partway up the tower there is a balcony, just under the clock that projects over the street below. It is the replica of a tower that stood near here from which the kings and queens of England could watch the jousting in the tournaments held in the lists below. It can be a useful spiritual exercise in visualization to imagine ourselves as kings or queens of our own projected kingdom in the world. Each one of us as a spiritual evolutionary being looking down upon the activities of our projected personalities below.

Above our heads is the clock that indicates that all that is below it is subject to the laws of time in the worlds of form. And as we look down in vision upon the street below we can see it at any period of linear time and watch the boisterous life below that is the projection in Earth of the spiritual beings among whom we number ourselves. This can give a profound conscious contact with our own Higher Self or Holy Guardian Angel. It is a locally based version of the vision of 'the secret watcher in the tower'.

From this high point of vision we can ascend yet further, if we so will, to the chamber of the bells, four-square, with the twelve bells arrayed about us, five of them dating from very ancient times. There is also a symbolism of the harmonies of the scale in all of this, from our present twelve-toned scale to the ancient pentatonic scale of our forebears. These are the bells that have been called the most famous chime in Christendom.

We would do well while we are here to contemplate the message of the bells to each and every one of us, for they speak not only to Dick Whittington. 'Send not to ask for whom the bell tolls,' said another, 'it tolls for thee.' The change ringing of the bells can hold the pattern of the perfect plan, the plan that is read and administered by angels, and which is above words and lowly human understanding, but which can come to the awakened man as a pattern of sound that forms the woof and warp of the fabric of life. A fabric that is invisible but immeasurably strong within the ether; spun, woven and

[Figure 19: St Mary holding St Mary-le-Bow Church, surrounded by the bombed churches of London, and their saints. From the stained-glass window in St Mary-le-Bow Church, designed by John Hayward.]

formed by the pattern of sound that is sung by the bell-tongued angels. Upon this fabric do we embroider the pattern of our lives below.

This tower is also, like so many others, a beacon tower, for a watch tower can radiate many forms of energy, be it sound or light or the spiritual energies that cannot be recorded by the physical instruments of mortal man – the wave and quantum theory of a truly spiritual science. We ourselves can take our part in this raying forth of light and sound by adding the keynote of our own spirit, if we visualize ourselves as columns in the circular temple form that is constructed over the bell tower.

Directly above us there is the shaft of the steeple upon which is balanced a golden ball, and upon this the mighty emblem of a golden dragon. It is the emblem of the guilds of the City of London but it has its analogue in the skies above us in the constellation of the Dragon about the northern celestial pole. This dragon also has its equivalent polar complement in the fiery dragon power that lies deep in the heart of the Earth itself. That is why the crypt is also, like the steeple, a very holy place. 'Visit the interior of the Earth to find the Rectifying Stone,' says the old alchemical adage. We do not gain wisdom by denying our roots in the Earth.

[Figure 20: The seal of Bow Church, from *Old and New London*, Walter Thornbury, first published 1872–8.]

This high steeple beneath which we stand is one of the most famous of those designed by Christopher Wren. It is said that he set it to act as a foil to the great dark dome of the cathedral of St Paul that stands, a mighty inverted hemisphere, beyond it.

We would do well to reflect upon the vision and example of Christopher Wren. If anyone can lay claim to be a human representative of the Great Architect of the Universe, it is he. For he it was who was commissioned by King and Parliament to rebuild the new city after the years of pestilence and fire of 1665 and 1666. It is all the more remarkable, and esoterically significant, that he was an astronomer rather than an architect by profession. But if anyone was a man marked out by destiny then it was surely he. Even his name has an inner significance – Christopher pertaining to the god-man-saviour, Wren being the totem emblem of the divine king.

We live in a fallen and corrupt world and so all of his designs, for city or for churches, could not be carried out according to his vision. However, much remains, and the spires he raised above the city retain their splendour and their magic despite the monstrous growths of corporate greed that seek to overpower them, towers of a modern Mordor indeed.

The bones of Christopher Wren lie in the crypt of the great cathedral which he built and his son placed there a simple epitaph: *Si monumentum requiris circumspice*, 'If you require a monument, look around you.' However, greater by far than the actual stone edifice of the cathedral itself is another version of it that stands within the crypt. This is a fantastic example of seventeenth-century joinery, 15 feet long and large enough for a man to get inside. It is known as the Great Model and was an earlier conception of the cathedral conceived by Wren.

It is said that when it was rejected by the ecclesiastical authorities that Christopher Wren wept, and never again publicly displayed his designs or constructed a model in advance of an actual building. Although those who rejected the design did so because they felt it was not traditional enough, in fact it contains ancient traditions indeed, such as were beyond their understanding.

It is built on the principle of an equal-armed cross, in the centre of which is a great circular vault upon which is a dome surmounted by

[Figure 21: John Dee's *Hieroglyphic Monad*.]

a steeple. Much of this is retained in the actual modern design that
was altered to conform more to medieval conceptions of what a
cathedral should look like. However, the original equal-armed form
is one that is of profound esoteric spiritual significance. Whether or
not Christopher Wren had this in mind intellectually is difficult to
determine. He probably drew inspiration directly from spiritual
sources. However, there are similarities between this original design
and the principles of construction of Dr John Dee's *Hieroglyphic
Monad*.

Dee considered this particular symbol, upon which he wrote a
treatise, to represent the height of his contribution to human wisdom
– this from a man who was one of the foremost mathematicians and
scientific investigators of his day. It consists of a crescent with horns
upward over a circle with a dot in the centre all surmounting a cross,
which is in turn over a double curve representing fire. The parallels
with the Great Model are that of the cruciform figure (which is a
level of gathering elemental energy), the circle and central point
(which are represented in three dimensions by tower, dome and
central steeple), and above and below, the crescent-shaped receptors,

153

which can gather higher or lower energies. These energies are the higher and lower 'dragon' power, which are associated respectively with steeple and crypt, having links with angels and ancestors, or over-world and underworld powers.

This may sound a little far-fetched until one constructs such an edifice in the imagination and starts to work magically with it. In fact the complete magical diagram is a version of the universal image of the mysterious abbey that is found in many legend cycles. One may visualize it as an equal-armed cross-shaped building with a drum-shaped tower in the centre surmounted by dome and steeple. Below the tower and dome, however, is a mirror reflection of them, so to speak, in the form of a circular pool, which in fact is an inverted dome or cauldron of healing and inspirational waters, in the very nadir of which is a deep shaft going down to the interior of the Earth, as the antithesis of the steeple that points up to the heavens.

(Those who seek a more detailed treatment of these dynamics would do well to refer to R.J. Stewart's *Underworld Initiation*,[1] *Living Magical Arts*[2] and *Advanced Magical Arts*,[3] although I have given some coverage to them myself in *The Rose Cross and the Goddess*.[4])

Whether Christopher Wren was consciously aware of all this is a moot point. It is, however, interesting to note that on an extension to the Great Model that was requested by the authorities of the time to provide a library and office facilities at the western end, there is a figure of St Paul, who stands on a cubic stone on the summit of a seven-stepped pyramid.

This certainly suggests some conscious esoteric intention.

In his historical thriller *Hawksmoor*,[5] Peter Ackroyd depicted Wren as someone to whom the esoteric deeps were either unknown or an anathema. Entertaining though this treatment might be, there seems to be much to indicate that Wren knew a great deal more than his rather morbid assistant in the novel realized. Although if the latter was motivated by Satanic powers his spleen towards his master can be all the better understood. However, the original Hawksmoor, who was an assistant to Christopher Wren, seems to have been one more oriented toward the light than to spiritual darkness, and his church of St Mary Woolnoth, for instance, sited over the Bank Tube station and upon an ancient Roman temple of Concord, in later years became a centre for anti-slavery. Here William Wilberforce was inspired by a vicar who was a reformed sea dog and African slave-trader, and today it is used as a centre for relaxation and meditation for city workers.

Many of the churches of Wren and his colleagues are four square, and originally designed to have plain glass, as temples of balanced and temperate light. The later Victorian taste for putting stained glass in them is not an aid to the original conception.

The Wren churches remain as a standing symbol of hope and human aspiration on the city skyline, and each in their way has something to teach those who care to visit them. We have spoken of talismanic significance, and this is augmented in many minor ways. For instance, in the church of St Sepulchre, where the bones of Captain John Smith repose, there is another model, of the Holy Sepulchre itself in Jerusalem, and also an actual stone from that most holy of places. Again, a stone from the body of the church of St Mary-le-Bow is lodged in the church of Holy Trinity in New York, where George Washington used to worship, and where are interred the bones of many of the original emigrants to the New England colonies.

Thus there are many international connections in the study of this subject that have many unexpected facets. For instance, the obelisk on the Thames Embankment that we know as Cleopatra's Needle has its twin in Central Park, New York. Originally they stood as a pair outside the Temple of the Sun in Heliopolis in the time of the Pharaoh Thotmes III. It is a sobering thought to recall that Moses himself would have known them as a pair *in situ*.

In the case of Christopher Wren himself, it seems fitting that he should also have been concerned with the design of the Naval Hospital at Greenwich and the old Royal Observatory there. Thus we have a living link with both the sea and the stars. Greenwich was the birthplace of Elizabeth I, the Virgin of the Stars, Astraea, under whose domination the sea power of England established sufficient strength, in spite of the might of Hapsburg Europe, that North America speaks English rather than Spanish, Portuguese, Dutch or French.

It is not nostalgic nationalism, neo-imperialism or jingoistic fervour to reflect with pride upon these matters. There are deeper things to human destiny than are dreamed of by those who judge by well-intentioned superficialities. The Islands of Albion are, in tradition, the holy islands of the West, and they hold a double destiny. On the one hand to preserve traditions from the most ancient past, some say from Atlantis, which are encapsulated in what has been recast as the Arthurian, Grail and Merlin legends. The other is to hold in trust a heritage for the future, which is somehow bound within the secret power of speech. Hence the importance of language. This seems likely to be the passing on of the language which will one day become the root of a universal tongue, when the results of the Fall of the Tower of Babel and the resultant confusion of tongues has become eliminated from the karma of the world.

10

A Long Tradition: Old Customs of London

Robert Stephenson

E NGLAND AS A whole may be world-renowned for her pageantry
and traditions, but her capital city is outstanding in the number
of its surviving ancient customs – in fact, no other city can claim so
many. It has taken long centuries to amass this unequalled body of
rights, liberties and customs, some of which have a continuity unbro-
ken since medieval times and others with origins far earlier.

London's remarkable position in this respect has been recognized
and reinforced by several monarchs. William I respected the existing
legal system enough not to impose continental laws after his conquest,
and granted a charter of rights in which London, unlike the rest of
the country, was allowed to keep its ancient privileges – 'I will not
suffer any person to do you wrong.' Henry I (1100–35) also granted a
charter of rights respecting London's exceptional standing, and the
Magna Carta, signed in 1215 by King John under pressure from the
City-backed barons, contains a special clause protecting the rights and
liberties of the City of London. Later Edward I (1272–1307) confirmed
Magna Carta saying, 'The City of London should have all the old
liberties and customs which it hath been used to have.' All these
monarchs conceded the independence and autonomy achieved by
this virtual state within a state.

At the heart of the now vast metropolis still lies the famous and
perennially influential Square Mile of the City of London. This
compact nucleus formed the original town, and must be considered
first when looking at London's customs. It is the province of the Lord
Mayor who heads the oldest municipal body in the country, older
than Parliament itself, for which it served as a prototype. During his
year of office, the Lord Mayor holds powers that exceed those of any
similar office in Europe. He becomes Chief Magistrate of the City, as

well as Admiral of the Port of London, and as Viceroy of the City is the first to be informed of the death of the sovereign. The Lord Mayor shares with the Queen the right of being informed of the daily passwords to the Tower of London. In the past when a reigning monarch visited the City they might have the City gates deliberately closed as their carriage approached and be obliged to state their purpose before being allowed to proceed. Today on official visits the

[Figure 22: The Lord Mayor's Procession, from
Hogarth's *Industrious Apprentice*.]

158

Lord Mayor will greet the sovereign at Temple Bar in great style and surrender his Pearl Sword as a token of his fealty, but immediately have this returned.

The Lord Mayor's Show in November, on the day of his, or her, accession, is a major pageant of international acclaim. The Lord Mayor rides from Guildhall to Mansion House (the official mayoral residence dating to 1752) to take the traditional salute of the great procession. Thereafter the Lord Mayor will follow at the rear in a gilded coach, with the City sword and mace, as the procession makes its way to the Royal Courts of Justice in the Strand. There the newly elected incumbent signs a declaration in front of Her Majesty's judges promising to respect the Crown while carrying out the duties of this 800-year-old office.

There are other impressive ceremonies like this, such as the Coronation and Trooping the Colour, which have ancient pedigrees and contain much interesting detail, but like the fascinating medieval proceedings of the City livery companies, these are impossible to cover here. What follows can be no more than a sample selection from the great number of customs that take place in London throughout the year.

The mute swan, our largest and most elegant bird, has always been considered royal property. It has been one of the royal badges since the fourteenth century, and as late as the mid-nineteenth century the penalty for the unlawful killing of a swan was transportation for seven years. A Royal Licence was necessary before a 'game' or 'royalty' of swans could be owned, and only a few favoured individuals or bodies were ever granted this privilege. Two of the City's livery companies, the Vintners and Dyers, still hold swan rights on the Thames, which were granted in the 1470s.

The *Ceremony of Swan Upping* dates from this period, when it was necessary to establish the ownership of all new cygnets and mark them accordingly. It must be remembered that at one time swans were kept to be eaten, and the Swan Voyage began simply as an annual check on the swan population from London Bridge to Henley-on-Thames. By the eighteenth century it had developed into a grand celebration and was accompanied by the livery companies' state barges, with music playing, guns firing, and much eating and drinking. Nowadays it starts at Sunbury in Surrey on the last Monday in July and finishes a few days later at Pangbourne in Berkshire. Six skiffs form the colourful convoy, which is commanded by the Queen's swan warden or master, who wears a scarlet livery. His two skiffs each fly the Royal Standard and a flag with a swan on it, and the Queen's oarsmen wear scarlet jerseys and white trousers.

Behind them come the Vintners' two boats flying their company flag, with their swan warden and men dressed in green. The Dyers follow in similar fashion except their colour is blue. When a family of swans is spotted a shout of 'All up' is given, and they are surrounded and gently taken up into the boats while the identity of the parents is ascertained. Formerly the birds were marked by nicking the beak, with the Vintners having two and the Dyers one and any unmarked ones being considered the property of the sovereign. Nowadays they are distinguished using rings around the legs. Swans mate for life and the cygnets are ringed according to their parents. In cases of mixed parentage the cygnets are shared, and any odd birds are given to the cob or male bird. A time-honoured salute is observed when they pass Windsor Castle, the men standing to attention in the boats with upraised oars and crying, 'Her Majesty the Queen, Seigneur of the Swans.'

Doggett's Coat and Badge Race is the oldest continually contested sculling race in the world. It was founded in 1715 by Thomas Doggett, a well-known actor and Drury Lane theatre manager, who announced its inauguration with a notice fixed to London Bridge. He offered prizes of a handsome orange coat (now red) and a large silver badge that were to be rowed for by six first-year watermen every year 'on the same day forever'. At this period theatre-goers relied heavily on the watermen for river transport, and this announcement no doubt further improved relationships.

Doggett was a strong supporter of the Hanoverian dynasty, and wished to commemorate the accession of George I on 1 August in some way. The idea for a race came to him after being rowed home to Chelsea late one stormy night by an obliging young waterman, whose skill, rowing against the tide, had impressed him. The race is now from London Bridge to Cadogan Pier at Battersea Park, a little over four miles. It is no longer against the tide and sculls are used instead of the heavy passenger wherries; however, there are now eleven new bridges to negotiate. The race is administered by the Fishmongers' Company, and the winner is presented with his splendid coat and badge at their annual dinner in November. As always there will be a Guard of Honour of former winners in their livery, who are also invited to wear their uniforms at other royal and civic functions.

The *Butterworth Charity* takes place every Good Friday morning at the priory church of St Bartholomew-the-Great at Smithfield. This graveside dole has existed for the benefit of twenty-one poor widows of the parish since at least as far back as 1686, when it was first mentioned in the church warden's account. Twenty-one sixpences would be laid on a tomb in the churchyard, and each widow would kneel to pick one up before crossing the tomb to receive a bun. The twenty-two pounds and ten shillings confidently left in 1887 for its 'perpetual endowment', by a Joshua Butterworth (from whom it takes its name) to save it from extinction, in no way covers even this much.

A procession from the church, headed by clergy and choir, makes its way to a convenient flat-topped tomb in the graveyard which, in this case, has no connection with any donor. In the past, the instigation of such a charity was seen as an ideal way to ensure one's grave was well kept and one's name remembered. No poor widows have claimed the dole since the 1970s, nevertheless a short service, with Easter hymn singing, still takes place among the graves and is punctuated by the distribution of buttered half-buns to the assembled crowd and a collection taken for the homeless.

The well-known incident following the Royalist defeat at the Battle of Worcester in 1651 when King Charles II evaded the Roundheads by hiding in the branches of an oak tree near Boscobel House so caught the nation's imagination that oak leaves became forever associated with his memory. Because of this, the day chosen for the annual celebration of the Restoration of the Monarchy became known as *Oakapple* or *Royal Oak Day*. The date is 29 May, which is both the King's birthday and the anniversary of his triumphant entrance into London after the Restoration in 1660.

For a while it even exceeded May Day in popularity and everyone would wear oak leaves, and any without would be beaten with nettles by the children. One place where this day has been faithfully kept up, even through the wars, is at the Royal Hospital in Chelsea, which was founded by King Charles in 1682 for the benefit of veteran soldiers without a livelihood. He never lived to see the completion of this fine Wren building in 1692, but on every Founder's Day since, his equestrian statue in Figure Court has been decked with oak boughs.

In the morning the Chelsea Pensioners, resplendent in their famous scarlet frock-coats, each sporting a sprig of oak, parade for inspection by a member of the royal family or high-ranking army officer. At the end of this parade they give three cheers for 'Our Pious Founder, King Charles', and three more for 'Her Majesty the Queen'. The rest of the Hospital is now inspected, while a military band plays in the Figure Court, and the Pensioners go for a well-deserved meal.

The *Stow Commemoration Service* is held every three years in April in the Church of St Andrew Undershaft in St Mary Axe. John Stow (1525–1605) is famous for his *Survey of London* of 1598, a comprehensive historical work that is still invaluable to present-day historians. Stow's alabaster tomb effigy in this church (where he once worshipped), depicts the beruffed historian studiously working at his desk, quill pen in hand. It is unusual in that the quill pen is a real one, and at each commemoration, to honour his memory, it is ceremonially replaced by a fresh quill pen.

During the commemoration service, a procession is formed, and makes its way to the Stow Memorial in the north-east corner of the church. Included in the procession will be the Lord Mayor and the Master and Clerk of the Merchant Taylors' Company. Stow started out as a tailor and was a Freeman of the Company, and it was only in later life that he devoted himself to the study of his native city that brought him such renown. An invited historian, who will later give the customary historian's address from the pulpit, removes the old quill and presents the new one, on a cushion, for the Master to insert.

The Church of St Andrew Undershaft obtained its curious name from the large maypole that once stood before its south door. In 1517, after the May Day celebrations got out of hand and the apprentices ran riot, the pole (which was taller than the church tower) was taken down and hung along the house fronts of nearby Shaft Alley, never to be re-erected. There it hung for over thirty years, until a zealous churchman persuaded the inhabitants that it was a pagan idol, when it was sawn up for firewood. Maypole dancing may still be seen at several London venues. It is a traditional part of the spring celebrations that hail in the summer, and survives from the old festival of Beltane, which was associated with the promotion of fertility for crops and livestock.

The *Trial of the Pyx* is the ritualized counting and testing of a representative sample of the coins minted during the previous year. It takes place at Goldsmiths' Hall, Foster Lane, in February or March. The maintenance of accurate standards for coin of the realm has been of paramount importance for centuries, and some form of monitoring has existed since at least Saxon times, with the first regular testing beginning in Henry II's reign. However, the procedure we can recognize in today's independent check was instigated by an ordinance in Edward I's reign, which laid down that 'a standard should be made . . . And the money shall be made according to the form of the standard and of the same fineness.' The vital trial plates were kept secure for centuries in the Pyx Chamber at Westminster Abbey, right up until 1843, but nowadays the Standards Department of the Board of Trade produces the necessary plates. The Royal Mint also originated at Westminster, but its home from 1300 to 1811 was the Tower of London, after which it moved to the Royal Mint Building on Tower Hill, and since 1971 it has been in South Wales.

The ceremony is presided over by the Queen's Remembrancer, who swears in the jury of eminent City businesspeople. Each jury member, seated round the long table, has two bowls, one of copper and one of wood. They are handed a series of sealed bags taken from the mint boxes or *pyx* (from which it takes its name) placed in readiness. They open the bags, retaining the seal, and count the contents to ensure that each has the correct number of fifty coins (one having been taken from each batch minted). A coin is selected at random for testing, and is put in the copper bowl while the remainder are placed in the wooden bowl, which is cleared by the staff, who bring another bag. The selected coins go to the Goldsmiths' Hall Assay Office for testing, which takes about eight weeks. When the jury is reconvened, the Queen's Remembrancer will ask for their verdict, and if it is satisfactory, as it usually is, the Pyx Luncheon may go ahead that evening, when the Chancellor of the Exchequer, as Master of the Mint, will be principal speaker.

Certain observances that were laid down by the Vintners' Court 700 years ago are still faithfully followed during the Worshipful Company of *Vintners' Annual Installation Procession.* On the day that their new Master is installed in July the officers and members of this Company process from their Hall in Upper Thames Street to their home church of St James Garlickhythe for divine worship. The ancient ruling still ensures that before setting out the Master, Wardens and Brethren of the Assistants are 'provided with nosegays of sweet and fine herbs that their noses be not offended by any noxious flavours or other ill-vapours'. It further stipulates that a party of tackle porters (the now redundant occupation of wine porter) should lead the procession and sweep the way clear, so that they should 'step not in any foulness or litter'. Today a single porter wearing the traditional white smock and a silk top hat walks in front symbolically performing this task with a birch besom that never touches the ground. He is closely followed by the anciently attired Beadle, Stavesmen, Swan-Markers, Barge Master and their new Master, each carrying their brightly coloured nosegays, while other members of the Company follow at the rear.

During the era of the stage coach, the main route into London from the north was through Highgate, and several inns flourished here on this trade. At most of the inns, the strange and amusing custom of *Swearing on the Horns* was practised, and over half the travellers were said to have taken part:

It's a custom at Highgate that all who go through,
Must swear on the Horns sir, and sir, so must you.

The horns referred to were a pair of ram's or stag's horns attached to a pole, which were in the care of a man dressed in black called the 'Clerk'. As many travellers as possible would be persuaded to swear the oath, under the direction of a suitably robed and bewigged 'Judge'. A small fee was required at the end of this light-hearted ceremony, when the person swearing the oath would be declared a Freeman of Highgate and informed of its peculiar privilege: 'If at any time you are going through Highgate and you want to rest yourself, and you see a pig lying in a ditch, you have the liberty to kick her out and take her place, but if you see three lying together you must only kick out the middle one and lie between the other two.'

If this custom derived from an earlier more serious ritual is now impossible to say. It declined in the nineteenth century with the coming of the railways, but was revived in the twentieth century and today various inns at Highgate perform the ceremony. Often this is on a twice-yearly basis in the evenings when the bar staff usually don appropriate period costume. The black-clad 'Clerk' holds the horns, as of old, but can now issue fines for the slightest misdemeanour (such as smiling during the ceremony), and the 'Judge' in a red robe, administers a version of the oath published in 1796. Up to half-a-dozen people may participate at a time, holding on to the horns with their left hand while repeating the oath:

I swear by the Rules of Sound Judgment that I will not eat Brown Bread when I can have White, except I like the Brown better; that I will not drink Small Beer when I can get Strong, except I like the Small Beer better; but I will kiss the Maid in preference to the Mistress, if I like the Maid better; but sooner than lose a good chance I will kiss them both. So help me, Billy Bodkin.

They must then turn completely around to fulfil the oath and become a Freeman or Freewoman of Highgate, when its dubious privilege will be made known to them. A certificate is now issued,

[Figure 23: *The Swearing on the Horns, Highgate,* from a print of 1796.]

and a donation expected, which, together with the fines, goes to help some local charity.

The City of London Corporation has exerted control over carriers plying for hire within the City for hundreds of years. The Corporation not only limited numbers but also obliged each carter to display a numbered brass plate and have the shafts of their vehicle branded with the City coat of arms. After 1838 all Freemen of the Fellowship of Carmen were required to appear annually at Guildhall to have their carts branded with a different letter of the alphabet.

The necessity to license and mark all vehicles privileged to work within the Square Mile has, of course, long since passed, yet the kudos attached to this mark of distinction has not diminished and today there are no shortage of drivers applying to attend the annual *Cart Marking Ceremony.* Proud owners bring their meticulously kept period vehicles from all over the country to acquire this badge of honour and some return annually.

All carts once had ample surfaces for branding, but that is not the case with modern vehicles, so the brandings are now done on temporarily attached hardwood panels, which afterwards are displayed as trophies. Each panel bears two enamel badges – the City arms and the Carmen arms – plus three large brass digits, which make up the designated number of the vehicle. The panel of first-time attendees is branded with the City coat of arms in addition to that year's letter.

This colourful and historic custom is organized by the Worshipful Company of Carmen and the branding is done by the Master Carman and the Master Glover, whose Company provides the necessary fire-resistant gloves. Also wearing heatproof gloves are a team of young men who relentlessly re-heat the irons between each application. The third member of the branding party is the Lord Mayor who customarily arrives some way through the proceedings, which take about two hours.

Up to fifty vehicles may be marked each year and the audience benefits from a running commentary identifying each vehicle. The majority of the vehicles date from a bygone era and the range is truly startling. There are nineteenth-century horse-drawn vehicles, steam-powered road locomotives and vintage Rolls-Royces side by side with the very latest vehicles, and also part of the mix might be Smithfield meat carts, police motorcycles and forklift trucks!

After a vehicle has received its mark it resumes its place among the heterodox collection lining Gresham Street to await a drive past through Guildhall Yard so that even latecomers can admire the splendidly turned-out procession. The event is concluded by a reception for participants in Guildhall.

The *Ancient Druid Order* holds three public ceremonies each year, the most famous being their midsummer ceremony at Stonehenge. Both of their lesser-known ceremonies are held in London. Primrose Hill has been used for the Autumn Equinox ceremony since the formation of the modern order in 1717, and Tower Hill for the Spring

Equinox since 1956. There is a Druid Temple marked on the map of Roman London near to Tower Hill and the Druid Ceremony held here overlooking the Bryn Gwyn, or sacred mount, within the Tower might be considered a renewal of a very ancient rite.

At the Spring Equinox the white-robed and banner-carrying procession forms a circle at noon in the garden adjoining the church of All-Hallows-by-the-Tower, with the Chief Druid standing in the east. The Herald announces the imminent commencement of the ceremony with four blasts on his massive horn to the north, south, west and east. This is followed by the Chief Druid holding a partially drawn sword, once again to the four quarters, and asking in turn 'Is it Peace?' When this is affirmed each time by the rest of the company the ceremony can proceed in earnest.

The Presider begins by reminding his companions (consisting of equal numbers of men and women) that they are there at the command of the Lord of the Radiant Light to acknowledge their indebtedness for the promise of the Great Fulfilment that is to come. This is followed by the formal barring and then admittance of a young woman and two flower-bedecked girls, representing Ceridwen as Earth Mother and her maidens. They scatter seeds as tokens of recurrent growth and the Chief Druid and others drink from a horn before its contents are poured on the ground. Throughout the rest of the ceremony stress is placed on selfless personal development and the acquisition of wisdom. Before the procession exits past the bemused office workers and the clicking cameras they send peace to the four quarters of the world. The ceremony held at the Autumn Equinox is similar, but fruits are scattered on the earth, rather than seeds.

The practice of *Beating the Bounds* each year, when a party of people perambulated a parish's or other property's boundary to ensure that everyone knew its course and no encroachments had been made, is very ancient indeed (see Chapter 11). Its origins go back at least to two Roman festivals: the Terminalia, when the god of fields and landmarks was celebrated, and the Ambarvalia, when animals were sacrificed for the benefit of the crops and processions made around the fields. In this country it was commonly practised from the fifth century right up until recent times, and at one period boys would be taken round and be either bumped, beaten or thrown in ditches at mark points to make sure they would never forget these positions.

The Tower of London beats its bounds every three years on Ascension Day. After a short service at the Chapel of St Peter ad Vincula, a party of children, armed with hazel withies and accompanied by Tower officials, perambulate the twenty-nine accessible mark points on the Tower Liberty boundary. At each stop the Chief Yeoman Warder commands, 'Whack it, whack it,' and so each mark point in turn is thrashed with withies.

The adjacent property of All Hallows-by-the-Tower beat their bounds earlier the same day and as their parish boundary runs along the centre of the Thames they board a boat so that one of the children can beat the water through a window. Their beating party reassembles in the evening to 'greet' the Tower beating party as it passes their church. What then occurs is known as the 'Confrontation', when both parties line up and humorously insult each other in remembrance of a bloody dispute over their shared boundary line that happened in 1698. However, after a few minutes of exchanging verbal abuse the Resident Governor of the Tower will cordially raise his feathered hat to salute the rector of All Hallows and the two groups will part amicably.

The Tower of London is officially locked up each night using a 700-year-old ritual called the *Ceremony of the Keys*. This short ceremony begins a little before 10 p.m. each night, when the Chief Yeoman Warder leaves the Byward Tower with the Keys, carrying a lantern, and joins his escort of four Guardsmen at the Bloody Tower. He hands the lantern to the only Guardsman without a rifle, and they proceed in formation to the West Gate. There the Sergeant of the Guard halts the escort, and they present arms while the gate is locked.

The same procedure is repeated at the Middle Tower and the Byward Tower, and as they approach the Bloody Tower the sentry challenges them: 'Halt, who comes there?' The Chief Warder replies, 'The Keys' and the sentry asks, 'Whose Keys?' and the reply is, 'Queen

Elizabeth's Keys' whereupon they are allowed to proceed to the main body of Guardsmen waiting at the steps beside the Jewel Tower (the depository of the Crown Jewels).

The Officer in Charge commands all Guards to present arms, and the Chief Warder steps forward and raises his Tudor bonnet and cries, 'God preserve Queen Elizabeth', and the soldiers respond with 'Amen'. All this has been precisely timed so that the clock now strikes ten o'clock and the bugler sounds the Last Post. The Chief Warder takes back the lantern, and proceeds to the Queen's House to hand over the Keys to the Resident Governor for safe-keeping overnight.

Quit Rents are symbolic or nominal rents, paid for land or property, and would be granted by a sovereign, or other landowner, to a special favourite, or as a reward for services well done. It meant that after the performance of some simple duty the tenant would be considered quit or free of any other obligation. These rents, which originated in medieval times, mostly took colourful or amusing forms, so that they acted as public reminders that the original owner still retained the right to the property.

An example is the Knollys Rose, which is presented to the Lord Mayor every Midsummer's Eve. The story goes that while the renowned military leader Sir Robert Knollys was away fighting in France in the fourteenth century, his wife, Lady Constance, had a footbridge built between their house and a garden across Seething Lane. Just as today, official permission should have been obtained first, and the City Fathers were displeased to learn of its omission. However, all they requested from so eminent a soldier was a single red rose from his garden, to be paid each year by Sir Robert, 'his heirs and assigns forever'! This debt he honoured until old age, and so it has been paid – apart from a long break prior to its revival in 1924 – from 1381 to the present day.

The ceremony, which takes place at Mansion House, is now arranged by the Company of Watermen and Lightermen. The verger of All Hallows-by-the-Tower, carrying the rose (still obtained from a garden in Seething Lane) on a blue altar cushion, heads a procession which includes the Master and Clerk of the Watermen, and the Chief

Escort to the Rose – someone of note invited from the City. It passes down the Saloon between a guard of honour formed by Doggett Coat and Badge winners, and when it reaches the Lord Mayor and Lady Mayoress, the Chief Escort will present the rose.

Two other quit rents are rendered together at the Royal Courts of Justice in the Strand in late October. Both have been paid (except for the interruption of Cromwell's Commonwealth) for over seven and a half centuries, a staggering persistence that can only be marvelled at. The first was granted by King John in 1211 for a piece of land at Eardington in Shropshire. Two knives, one 'good enough to cut hazel', and one 'so bad that it will bend in green cheese', have to be rendered each year – but from what private joke this derived is now a complete mystery. About 300 years later the ownership was transferred to the City of London, and at some point the knives became a billhook and a hatchet.

The ceremony is officiated by the Queen's Remembrancer, who commands that the 'tenants and occupiers of a piece of waste ground called "The Moors" in the County of Salop come forth and do your service.' Whereupon the City Solicitor steps forward and attempts to cut a small faggot of hazel on a wooden block with a billhook, but with no success. He then produces a hatchet, with which he has no difficulty whatever in chopping the faggot in half. Satisfied with the outcome, the Remembrancer pronounces 'Good Service'.

The second rent was first mentioned in 1235, and concerns a piece of land in the parish of St Clement Danes called 'The Forge', which was granted to one Walter Le Brun Mareshal for use as a smithy. It was on Fickerts Meadow, which stretched from Lincoln's Inn Fields to the Strand, and though its precise site is uncertain, it is now thought to be occupied by Australia House. The smithy adjoined the jousting ground of the Knights Templars, who owned all this area, and the rent was six horseshoes and sixty-one nails. The shoes are massive and would project beyond the hoof, because they are all for the forefeet of the great Flemish horses used in the joust. The Remembrancer once more commands the respective tenants to 'Come forth and do your service.' The City Solicitor then counts out the six horseshoes and the sixty-one nails – ten per shoe 'and one more'. Once again the conditions of rent have been fulfilled for another year, and the Queen's Remembrancer pronounces 'Good Number'. In this case the horseshoes and nails are retained for use the following year.

It is curious that these customs have endured for so long. Some obscure process seems to have checked the passage of time and presented us with a living piece of history. Most of them could not be described as tourist attractions because they are so little known, and even if a particular custom's history is fully understood, the reasons why it has persisted are still difficult to fathom. It may be they are continued because a superstitious apprehension has become attached to the idea of their non-performance. But it is more than that – these customs have their roots in our everyday lives and encapsulate certain moments that were once important in themselves (although now only important in the form of the repetition). We are familiar with reassurance gained by our own personal little rituals, and in a similar way the public performance of these ceremonies seems to satisfy an undefined communal need.

Perhaps it is nostalgic longing for the past, but nonetheless there is an essential rightness and almost familiarity experienced when witnessing one of these old ceremonies, even for the first time. A feeling of kinship can be sensed, not only between the participants and spectators of our day, but also, one feels, with all those other participators who have preceded us; a palpable link between the living and the dead is created, and if these old customs were to disappear, something precious would be lost forever. Thankfully the Londoner is essentially conservative and naturally inherits a respect for these ancient observances, realizing they are under siege from our modern way of life and instinctively maintains them.

As will be seen from the following select calendar, Londoners possess a wonderful opportunity to witness many fascinating ceremonies throughout the year. It is an intriguing part of our heritage that can be experienced at no cost, and ought to be taken more advantage of.

Select Calendar of London Customs

January
King Charles I Procession — Horse Guard's Parade

February
Blessing the Throats — St Etheldreda's Church, Ely Place
Cakes and Ale Ceremony — St Paul's Cathedral
Sir John Cass – Red Feather Day — St Botolph's Church, Aldgate
Trial of the Pyx — Goldsmiths' Hall, Foster Lane

March
Bridewell Service — St Bride's Church, Fleet Street
Clown's Service — Holy Trinity Church, Dalston
Oranges and Lemons Service — St Clement Danes Church, the Strand

March/April
Butterworth Charity — St Bartholomew-the-Great
Widow's Buns — Widow's Son Tavern, Bromley-by-Bow
Druid's Vernal Equinox Ceremony — Tower Hill

April
Stow Commemoration Service — St Andrew Undershaft (three-yearly)

May
Swearing on the Horns — Highgate
Florence Nightingale Service — Westminster Abbey
Beating the Bounds — All Hallows-by-the-Tower annually & the Tower of London (three-yearly)
Spital Sermon — St Lawrence Jewry, Gresham Street

May/June
Pepys Commemoration Service — St Olave Church, Hart Street
Beating Retreat – Household Division — Horse Guards Parade
Skinners' Election Day Procession — Skinners' Hall to St James Garlickhythe

June

Bubble Sermon (Stationers')	St Martin-within-Ludgate
Trooping the Colour	Horse Guards Parade
Beating Retreat – Royal Marines	Horse Guards Parade
Election of Sheriffs	Guildhall

July

Vintners' Installation Procession	Vintners' Hall to St James Garlickhythe
Swan Upping	Thames
Cart Marking Ceremony	Guildhall Yard

July/August

Doggett's Coat and Badge Race	Thames, London Bridge to Chelsea

September

Battle of Britain Sunday	Westminster Abbey & St Clement Danes
St Matthew's Day Procession	St Sepulchre-Without-Newgate (start)
Druid's Autumn Equinox Ceremony	Primrose Hill
Admission of Sheriffs	Guildhall
Election of Lord Mayor	Guildhall
Swearing on the Horns	Highgate

October

Procession of Judges	Westminster & Law Courts, the Strand
Pearlies' Harvest Festival	St Mary-le-Bow, Cheapside
Quit Rent Ceremonies	Royal Courts of Justice, the Strand
Lion Sermon	St Katherine Cree, Leadenhall Street
Trafalgar Sunday	Trafalgar Square & Old Royal Naval College
Basketmakers' Service	St Margaret Pattens, Eastcheap

November

State Opening of Parliament Procession	Palace of Westminster
Cenotaph Ceremony	Whitehall
Lord Mayor's Show	Mansion House to Law Courts & back

December
Pensioners' Cheese Ceremony   Royal Hospital, Chelsea

Other Regulars
Changing the Guard   Daily   Buckingham Palace
Ceremony of the Keys   Nightly   Tower of London
Gun Salutes   About six times a year   Hyde & Green Parks
                                                 & Tower of London

II

London's Boundaries

Geraldine Beskin

In London once I lost my way,
In faring too and fro,
And asked a ragged boy
The way that I should go.

He gave a nod and then a wink,
And told me to get here,
Straight down Crooked Lane
And all around The Square.

Thomas Hood, the man that wrote these lines, was the son of a
Scottish bookseller, who was in turn the son of the man who opened
up the book trade between Britain and America. Born in 1799 in
Cheapside, he spent his forty-six years writing poetry, humorous
fiction and knowing everyone who was anyone at the time. He was a
true Londoner, who relied upon the hidden shape of the city to find
his way.

This mysterious landscape was marked out by the boundaries of
each parish; invisible lines marked at significant nodes that everyone
local to each area would have known.

According to *Vogue* magazine for August 2015, Peckham is currently
the artistic epicentre of London, while its next-door neighbour,
Nunhead, is hot on its heels for a cutting-edge urbanista lifestyle,
having revived the ancient rite of 'Beating the Bounds' in its parish.

Traditionally this ancient ceremony was as much about the way
people come together for a good day out as anything. As they went
in procession through the streets, they would beat walls and hedges
between markers with stripped willow wands. Small boys and girls

were turned upside down and their heads gently knocked, or 'dunted', at each stopping point so they would not forget the place or the experience. Hot pennies used to be thrown, too, as part of the fun, but always following the strict rule that no blood should ever be spilt at a boundary site. Minor burns, bruises and jostling were all fair in the cause of defence.

Nowadays when the boundaries are beaten, significant points and changes are noted along the way, as skylines change from one year to the next and building sites become buildings. Important places are suddenly not important any longer and lovely views of them may be eclipsed forever. Comparison with a Victorian map will show how market gardens, woodland or light industry was lost in the urban sprawl.

The walking of the boundaries is one way that local history is remembered – recalling informally and immediately where a street fair was held some years ago, or where a famous person lived, or a garden that used to have gaudy gnomes, or a house with bright paint-work or lots of bird feeders, or a scary old couple who terrorized children, or whatever the distinguishing feature was.

Various traditional fixed points are used to trace the boundaries. Stones, rivers, and trees are the most obvious ones, while in the marvellously named area of Elephant and Castle lies St George's Circus, there is an obelisk dedicated to His Majesty 'Mad' King George III, who sits atop a milestone. Some closely guarded boundary points are etched or painted and often marked high up on the sides of buildings. In one case a plaque marks the point of the parish boundary in the middle of the floor of a Marks and Spencer store in Oxford.

The names of streets tell their own stories, as do the names of pubs. Knowing from the name who built a particular street and where they got their money from is all part of the pattern. Maps showing how the area looked in Victorian times can help us to make comparisons with the present, and earlier maps may amaze us all with how little was there even two hundred years ago.

Stones that mark the boundaries are sometimes given names – as on Dartmoor where they have Little Anthony, Old Jack, Grey Mare and Woodley's Post as well as the Sitting Down Stone and Trolls

Table. In towns many of these markers are in inaccessible places, in basements or high up on walls, so that agile children are necessary for physical contact to be made. Touching the marker lays claim to it for another year and there are witnesses to prove that it belongs to the parish.

Water is vital to life and commerce and many parish lines go down the middle of a river or stream. A boundary line adjacent to the Tower of London is no exception to this and its splendid ceremony involves a police launch and a teenager from one of the local schools being lowered over the side of the boat until their hair touches the Thames. The boundary of the parish of St Clement Danes Church in the Strand leads into the river, too, and has twenty-five markers with anchors on them, not all easily visible. There is one in the vaults of a sometime bank in Fleet Street, another in the Outer Temple; and Essex Court, New Court and Middle Temple lawn all have them too, among other places. An unprepossessing cobbled triangle lies at the front of St Clement Danes. It is centuries old and marks where City and State meet. This is why Margaret Thatcher's funeral stopped there to allow her coffin to be transferred from a hearse to a gun carriage.

Markers evolve over the centuries often with conflicting dates attached to them. These may well refer to the creation or expansion of civic wards, as well as religious boundaries. If you want to discover the old boundaries for yourself, you may need to spend a little time at the local church finding the plan of religious boundary markers, while the council will have the civic ones. The local history library will have copies of memoirs, maps, photographs of streets, newspapers and the staff usually have answers to everything.

The *Church Times* in 2007 carried a story illustrating why the beating of the bounds should not be thought of as anachronistic. A vicar in Fulham received a leaflet about 'a new church for Fulham', which showed only half his parish. The Area Dean knew nothing about it and neither did the Central Fulham Churches Forum. The vicar was understandably agitated.

The new church proved to be under the auspices of the nominally Anglican Co-Mission Initiative, apparently known for being largely indifferent to parish and diocesan boundaries. The new bishop responsible for this Initiative was not even in communion with the Church of England and refused to submit to normal selection procedures. Churches such as this have proliferated in the last few years.

Older reasons why the beating of the bounds should be carried out include the promise it conveys with it of a blessing for the fruits of the field. It brings justice in its preservation of the bounds; offers charity, in living, walking and accompanying one another in neighbourly fashion; and it helps reconcile the differences of that time, if there be any. It also offers mercy, because the parish should relieve the poor by a liberal distribution of largesse wherever this is needed.

Traditionally, the beating of the bounds is scheduled for the end of April. They are walked, or ridden on horseback (as in Cumbria where the geographical area is vast) or even driven or sailed around. Increasingly the tradition is revived as a jolly day out and ends up in the village hall for tea and cake or drinks at the local pub.

According to the vagaries of the shifting church calendar, Ascension Day, or Holy Thursday, is the 'proper' day to walk the boundaries of the parish. This is forty days after Easter and critically, the Rogation days fall on the four days from the fifth Sunday after Easter, determined by the Sunday following the full moon of the Vernal (Spring) Equinox. The Latin verb *rogare* means to ask or beseech and the hymn written by John Keble, 'Lord in thy name, thy servants plead', is still favoured by some Church of England vicars as it requests the blessing of the newly sown crops. The even more familiar 'We plough the fields and scatter' is actually another Rogation hymn, rather than a harvest festival one as is often assumed. Harvest Home is a long way off at this stage in the year and all the uncertainty of how the seeds have survived the early sowing remains in country people's minds.

Within the church calendar this is also a time of death and resurrection, just as it is in the pagan year. The Anglo-Saxon *gangen* meant 'to go' or 'to walk'. And although there was a cessation of the tradition of walking the bounds due to nineteenth-century Enclosure Acts, where it survived, so did the offering of 'ganging beer' and 'Rammelation biscuits' on 'gang days'.

Long before these enclosures, the Anglo-Saxon charters that set out the division of lands were re-enforced once a year. They would subsequently be associated with the royal and baronial charters of the late medieval period, demonstrating the power the charter holder, often the lord of the manor, had over his serfs and tenants, and asserting the primacy of law. They defined the rights of tenants to sow and harvest, the extent of their holdings, and how much tithe, if any, was to be paid to the landowner and his agents.

Burnham Deepdale church in Norfolk has a very splendid piece of Norman carving on its font that shows the activities of the village nine hundred years ago and underlines the structure of their year. What it shows is typical of most of the country at this time. January shows someone drinking from a horn and February people warming their feet by the fire, so that they were rested enough to dig the earth during March. April was for pruning and May shows a Rogationtide banner with the beating of the bounds. Weeding and scything kept them busy in June and July, while the binding of a sheaf of corn depicts August. Grain was threshed in September and ground in October. In November they turned their attention to slaughtering the animals for the winter meat and finished the year by feasting throughout December. The Bounds were important enough events in the calendar to be set in stone.

In secular terms a parish was a taxation unit, and an annual record of businesses and the numbers of the employed and the poor was helped by this kind of boundary tradition. It was a sensible thing to do in a manageable area and an undemanding timeframe. Fishing and grazing rights were jealously guarded and infringements were noted and corrected when the people from one village met at the boundary with another one.

Traditionally, wherever the beating the bounds procession stops, chaos ensues as the musicians play, dogs bark, drinks are drunk, stones are whacked as the cry, 'Whack it boys, whack it!' is taken up by the crowd. People clamber over walls, children are manhandled and, if the timing is right, the people from the area next door are there to greet and do the same to their children. Friendly jeering at neighbouring parishes' poorer soil, uglier men and worse beer has gone on since time immemorial.

To beat the bounds, to walk the boundaries, is still a constructive thing to do. Fences may need repairing, and if people know the homeowners are too old or hard up, the problem can sometimes be

The London Stone, Cannon Street.

William Blake's gravestone,
Bunhill Fields, City Road.

Cleopatra's Sphinx, Embankment,
Westminster.

Cleopatra's Needle, Embankment, Westminster.

The Wyvern guardian, Tower Hill

The Wyvern guardian, Holborn.

Roman pavement at All-Hallows-by-the-Wall, Southwark.

The Crossbones Cemetery, Southwark.

Medieval roof boss from Southwark Cathedral.

Statue of Elizabeth I at
St Dunstan's Church, Fleet Street.

Magog and Gog, guardians of the Guildhall.

King Lud and his Sons at St Dunstan's Church, Fleet Street.

Memorials of Templar knights,
The Temple Church.

The Temple Church.

The grave of Mary Wollstonecraft
Godwin, St Pancras.

Part of the Medieval London Wall

The Hardy Tree,
St Pancras Old Church.

Magical Guardians of the
City's coat of arms

Lud's Gate, entrance to the City.

St Helen's Church, Bishopsgate.

The Shrine of our Lady of Willsden,
St Mary's Church, Southwark.

The Black Madonna of Willsden.

Epping well-water in the Church of St Mary, Southwark.

Epping Well, Epping Forest.

sorted out. In the country a boundary walking team can also unblock a stream, right a gatepost, and decide when to do the bigger community jobs. In London and other cities, a small number of streets will produce a collection of people with surprisingly varied skills, who might defend a local landmark, paint some scruffy railings or do some guerilla gardening or other repairs as they choose.

★ ★ ★

The beating of the bounds takes place at a time of year when there are spring flowers, fresh shoots, lambs, piglets and, theoretically at least, more sunshine. In Roman times the ancient celebration of Floralia started on 28 April and went on for three days. Janus, the double-headed watcher of the ways, acted as a boundary marker, while the Roman God Terminus, to whom boundaries were sacred, officiated at the April festival of Robigalia.

Here in London, this takes place close to May Day, the possibly more ancient festival when the hawthorn, one of the first trees to blossom, was cut down and used as the maypole, then resurrected by being raised and danced around. The sun is in the zodiac sign of Taurus the Bull at this time, when mad, Tom Jones- or Russell Brand-style male energy runs wild. Cattle would be passed through the Bel fires at this time, to cleanse them and purify them after calving.

The children conceived after the August Lammas celebrations would have been born at this most feminine time, when the ducks and chickens would be laying well and the weather should be good enough to venture outside again. The farmers would be back in contact with their land, having dug it over and pruned it. This was also a time to have a proper spring-clean and get rid of the accumulated rubbish of winter. Teenage boys could go off and seek their fortunes like Jack the Giant Killer with a couple of goslings, their spare shirt and some bread and cheese wrapped in a kerchief and slung over their shoulder on a 'stang' or stout stick. Dick Whittington, so famously four-times Mayor of London, was one such independent youth.

The bounds processions survived the Reformation – albeit with some interruptions. In 1548 Protestant reformers prohibited the carrying of banners in procession by the clergy, although Queen Mary subsequently rescinded that law. In the reign of Elizabeth I the unification of the Church and state led to the annual Rogation service being allowed again, but in a slightly subdued way as small boys were not allowed to be whipped! Cromwell banned all such celebrations as part of the Puritan prohibition of most religious ceremonies. The restoration of the monarchy and the re-establishment of the Church festivals led to the revival of Rogationtide as an important feast day and processions perambulated around parish boundaries again.

In 1604, the Enclosure Acts split up parish and manorial lands among several landowners, and the ceding of Church parish jurisdiction to control by local government followed in the nineteenth century. Manorial and parish maps were incredibly useful at this time, and groups of parishioners, along with the vicar, would take over the duties of maintaining the old boundaries and check that marker stones were still intact. Many clergymen took the opportunity to preach to the accompanying masses, and stopping points under oak trees became known as 'Gospel oaks'. This is how the North London district of Gospel Oak got its name.

In some vestry accounts from 1678, there are entries for the payment of ten pounds for 'the perambulation of the Out Bounds'. This refers in particular to a detached part of Chelsea located at Kensal Green and known as Chelsea-in-the-Wilderness, and shows how specific the boundaries were.

The Bounds procession could cause problems for householders and citizens alike. On one occasion in London a driver refused to move his stagecoach off the boundary line, so those taking part promptly climbed in one side of the coach and out the other. In High Wycombe there was a well-recorded account of the whole procession marching termite-like in the front door of a house built on the boundary and climbing out of one of its windows.

The millennium saw a revival in awareness of boundaries as local councils were awash with money that had to be spent on something significant to mark the great occasion. Seeking to forge a sense of community, so that defining 'Your' space from 'Their' space would become almost obligatory, they explored the restoration of ancient bounds. Unfortunately they did not always respect the age-old marker points and put up beautifully designed ones close to the current footpaths, ignoring the original boundaries, which subsequently became almost forgotten. The new ones were designed to withstand high impacts and gale-force winds and should last another millennium, but why not put them where they should be? Land has never been more valuable and councils know how costly boundary disputes can be.

★ ★ ★

It was no accident that willow was the most often used wood to create the boundary-beating switches, employed to whack the stones and other useful activities. The switches are usually about 8 feet long and not prone to breaking. Willow itself had its own mythology, of course, often associated with death. In mythology Jason, in his search for the Golden Fleece, passed a strange grove dedicated to the Goddess Circe, planted with funeral willows, in the tops of which corpses hung. The classical Greek travel writer Pausanias speaks of a grove consecrated to Proserpine, planted with black poplars and willows, and Orpheus, while in the infernal regions, carried a willow branch in his hand. When Aeneas forsook Dido, Shakespeare says:

> In such a night stood Dido, with a willow in her hand,
> Upon the wild sea-banks, and vowed her love
> To come again to Carthage.
> The Merchant of Venice, Act 5, Scene 1

Willow has long been associated with the planet Saturn and astrologers say the moon rules it. Traditionally it is sacred to Ceres, Goddess of the Corn, and in the medical Doctrine of Signatures it is considered to be a sterile plant, like lettuce or fern. It remains a favourite instrument for divination and dowsing. Some magicians favour it for their wands, as it has a pliability it never loses.

Richard Folkard Jr in his 1884 book, *Plant Lore and Legends and Lyrics*, concurred that since remotest time willow has been considered a funeral tree and an emblem of grief. So universal is the association of sadness and grief that 'under willows the captive children of Israel wept and mourned in Babylon' and the ancients hung their harps on 'such doleful supports'. Shakespeare says of Ophelia's death:

There is a willow grows aslant the brook,
That shows his hoar leaves in the grassy stream.
Hamlet, Act 4, Scene 7

In *The Faerie Queene* Spenser writes of 'the willow worn of forlorn paramours'. The poet Herrick says that garlands of willow are worn by neglected or bereaved lovers, and lovesick youths and maids came to weep out the night beneath the willow's cold shade. Happy lovers enjoyed kissing under weeping willow trees at the Pleasure Gardens in Lambeth, as passers-by could not see who was romantically engaged because of the low-hanging branches. Napoleon took a tree to St Helena with him, as he enjoyed resting in its shade.

★ ★ ★

The history of the changing boundaries within London alone could fill a book. At the moment, there is some debate in North London as to where Crouch End begins and Stroud Green ends. This concerns about a dozen streets – or is it fifteen? How far along any of them does the boundary go? Beating the bounds could unravel many such problems.

The rich area of Fitzrovia recently succeeded in a massive land grab into Bloomsbury by referring to itself suddenly as part of Fitzrovia. Bloomsbury is already under threat of becoming known as Mid-Town as landowners and property developers seem not to be interested in preserving history, or reasons why places are named as they are. Bloomsbury, of course, houses the British Museum, and in the 1770s the land there was owned, farmed and closely guarded by two unmarried sisters called Capper. They delighted in stealing the clothes of young men who bathed in their stream, and they also rode up on their old grey mares and cut the strings of kites being flown by young children.

At this time the land was open as far as St Pancras except for a few buildings, partly because it was owned by landed gentry who eventually built a small town on it, along with the magnificent Montagu House, which eventually became the British Museum. There is a legend concerning the rough, open land that lay just behind where the grand house was built. Known as the Brothers Steps, or the Field

184

of the Forty Footsteps, because their footsteps were supposed to be preserved on the ground, it commemorated a love story gone wrong as two brothers fought for the woman of their dreams while she sat and watched quietly from a grassy knoll.

Neither brother survived, and their footsteps marked out a barren land ever after. Where the young men fell, nothing grew again, despite being ploughed up each year. People tried to count the deep outlines of the footsteps, which survived for a long time, and were celebrated in a melodrama that told the whole sorry tale.

John Aubrey, the discoverer of the Avebury stone circle and noted man of letters, said that at midnight on Midsummer Day 1794, he saw twenty-three young women in 'the parterre behind Montague [*sic*] House, looking for a coal, under the root of a plantain, to put under their heads that night, and they should dream who should be their future husbands.'

The land behind Montagu House stretched to Lisson Grove and Paddington, north to Primrose Hill, Chalk Farm, Highgate and Hampstead and east to Islington and St Pancras and beyond. The vista to the north was left open to be enjoyed. The perfume of the gardens, a fine grove of lime trees and the open space created a 'wholesome and pleasant air' and it became a fashionable place to stroll and be seen. But it was no more than a few hundred yards from the infamous St Giles Rookery, a centre of pestilence, horrible social habits and living conditions. This area was also known as a vast Thieves' Kitchen. The Whig MP Horace Walpole recorded in January 1750 that Lady Albemarle was robbed there by nine men, but we can only presume that she felt a little better about it when the King himself presented her with a new watch and chain the very next day.

As the museum grew, so the area became a home for the intelligentsia and academics of London. Lawyers spread over from the Inns of Court to live around Southampton Row, and London University grew around the museum. It is hard to believe that Senate House was Britain's first skyscraper – all 210 feet or 64 metres of it.

Gower Street runs alongside it and has seven blue plaques along its walls, commemorating medical pioneers, as well as Charles Darwin and the Pre-Raphaelite Brotherhood.

On the other side of the street is Bedford Square where one of its residents, Duchess Anna Bedford, invented afternoon tea as we know it. She would have an energy dip in the afternoon so had a snack and a pot of tea sent up to her rooms. Her friends thought it was a great idea and then, as now, where the fashionistas led, others followed. Lady Albemarle was a lifelong friend of Queen Victoria, and we know that Her Majesty liked the idea. Her great, great granddaughter, our current Queen, famously holds tea parties every summer at Buckingham Palace.

★ ★ ★

These details from history are remembered in the boundaries that once divided London into convenient wards, though many think that postcodes are the only important boundaries today. First introduced in Croydon in 1966, the whole country had them eight years later once the system became automated.

These new divisions were actually the outcome of a problem that started in the 1840s, with the growth of London leading to several streets having the same name and the landowners being reluctant to change them, as many were named after their ancestors. Postmaster General Sir Rowland Hill's response to this was to divide London into ten districts and the still-familiar EC (East Central), WC (West Central), and so on, radiated out for twelve miles from the centre of the city.

During the First World War, when women worked for the Post Office and had neither the familiarity nor speed of men who had worked there for many years, a number was added according to the area's position in the alphabet to make identification easier. Bethnal Green became E2, Bow E3, Eastern Central EC1, and so on. A big boundary was established in 1889 when the London County Council (LCC) was created and the boroughs as we more or less know them today were formed.

It seems strange now that the great Victorian sprawl of London had no central, unifying governance for the basics such as schools, roads and transport until a little over a century ago. The LCC existed until 1965 when it became the Greater London Council. The

Conservative government upset a lot of Londoners by abolishing it in 1986, believing it to be both inefficient and unnecessary.

★ ★ ★

The City of London is still ruled by the world's oldest continually elected governmental body, having its first Lord Mayor elected in 1189. Even when Magna Carta was signed in 1215, the men of the City claimed ancient liberties. They kept the area separate from what was happening elsewhere, though neither the King nor the barons adhered to the agreement in the end.

The barons' plan was to limit the monarch's power and to protect their own privileges and this has held true within the City, which can still do more or less what it likes. The Court of Common Council, the hundred Livery companies, the twenty-five wards and the old Guilds are all laws unto themselves. Even when the Queen visits, she meets a red cord raised by the City police at Temple Bar, and engages in a colourful ceremony involving the Lord Mayor, his sword, assorted aldermen and sheriffs, and a character called the Queen's Remembrancer. During the ceremony the Lord Mayor politely recognizes the Queen's authority, but it is a complex relationship, with the Mayor reminding Her Majesty of the right of the City to run its own affairs. Meaning: we will buy you lunch, Your Majesty, and then tell you what we are going to do, whether you like it or not!

The City is the centre of banking and finance for Britain. It has huge wealth, massive landowning, and holds the fiscal fate of many a nation in its grasp. Those who operate from within its bounds are very secretive about themselves and after many years of ill grace and delay, recently disclosed the contents of just one of their many bank accounts. It had £1.8 billion in it and had been open for eight hundred years.

★ ★ ★

The reorganization of the City into areas, with the establishment of new boundaries, has often been forced upon it by circumstances beyond its control. When the Great Fire of London started in 1666, about 70,000 people had to try and escape through the seven gates in the old Roman wall. Ludgate, Newgate, Cripplegate, Bishopsgate, Aldersgate, Moorgate and Aldgate were simply not enough and many thousands were trampled and burnt. When the fire started, the Lord Mayor, Mr Bloodworth, did not think it was all that serious and famously said, 'Phish, a woman could piss it out.'

Samuel Pepys and John Evelyn, the diarists, both have streets named in their honour, partly because of their diligence in recording the decimation of everything they knew. Evelyn's boots became so hot, his feet got burnt. The fire that had begun in the baker's shop in Pudding Lane destroyed the medieval city and the Monument was erected to commemorate the tragedy.

If the Monument, which stands on Fish Street Hill, to the north-eastern side of London Bridge, was laid down due east, the top would reputedly rest at the site of the Pudding Lane bakery. The fire forced the redesign of the City and Sir Christopher Wren, who designed the elegant Doric column, topped the Monument with a drum to sound the alarm and a flaming urn representing the fire.

★ ★ ★

A June day in 1780 started off like any other in the City until Lord George Gordon headed a riot to repeal the Catholic Relief Act. They burnt houses belonging to Catholics. They also ransacked breweries and eventually burnt down Newgate Debtors Prison. The two thousand debtors got drunk with the rioters and decided to attack the Bank of England, as money is the root of all evil, or some such.

Soldiers were sent for, a few people were killed, and Lord George Gordon was imprisoned in the Tower of London, where he reputedly converted to Judaism and having learnt how to play the bagpipes, died insane. That day of rioting meant that the Bank of England had its own armed guard, the Bank Piquet, which survived until 1973.

When the Reform Riots happened in 1830 and 1848, the bank was sandbagged, loopholed and fortified. The sandbags stayed in position until 1924 when the bank was rebuilt with the windowless walls at ground level that we see today. The gilded bronze figure on the top of the building is named Ariel, after the Spirit of the Air from Shakespeare's *The Tempest*. It symbolizes the dynamic spirit of the bank, carrying credit and trust all over the world.

★ ★ ★

London was successful as a development because it commanded a piece of high ground next to the River Thames, back when it was the *Tamesis*. In pre-Roman times the legendary King Lud was said to have founded London on the high ground closest to the river. It was all of 58 feet above sea level at Ludgate Circus, the name of which commemorates its supposed 'founder'. St Paul's Cathedral is said to have a temple to the Goddess Diana underneath it and the urban myth is still prevalent that this is why Prince Charles and Diana Spencer were married there. Royal ceremonies are so full of esoteric and arcane symbolism that it will be forever a source of speculation, but the story of Diana having to kill a stag when she was engaged lends some strength to the idea.

Westminster Abbey was chosen for the wedding of Prince William and Catherine Middleton, making it the seventeenth such royal event in its thousand years of history. In the sixth century it was a low-lying island of boggy ground, where the Tyburn River met with the Thames. The Anglo-Saxon King Sebert was a Christian convert and built a church he wanted dedicated to St Peter. The night before the first Bishop of London, Mellitus, was due to consecrate it, St Peter himself appeared in a blaze of glory with a heavenly choir of angels and did it for him – or so legend says. The current building dates from the thirteenth century and even now they are still adding to it.

The House of Commons in the Palace of Westminster lies north across another boundary and across the road from Westminster Abbey. To this day the Government and Opposition parties are still kept eight feet, two inches apart within the chamber where they meet. This measurement is said to be two sword lengths, and prevents them from inflicting physical harm on each other. There are still loops of pink ribbon in the cloakrooms for them to hang up their swords, should they so desire. The Lord Speaker oversees the House of Lords and the benches to his (or her) right are the Lords Spiritual and those to the left the Lords Temporal, showing that even here boundaries are observed.

The Houses of Parliament were bombed not once but fourteen times in the Second World War and by the time it was rebuilt, the Chamber was not large enough, as the four hundred and fifty MPs had become six hundred and fifty – due to boundary changes.

The Queen has a very splendid Robing Room in the House that she uses when she attends the State Opening of Parliament each year. As she puts on her ermine robes and the State Imperial Crown in the Robing Room, she is surrounded by King Arthur and his Knights, represented in paintings executed by William Dyce. Many Victorians, including Victoria and Prince Albert, saw Arthur as the source of our nationhood.

★ ★ ★

We complain about the weather and our public transport in equal measure, although we have a rail system with seventeen termini, an enormous number of taxis, and an extensive and improving Tube system. The familiar 'taxi' sign is to show the passenger a fixed price will be charged for a distance travelled and that it is taxed at a standard rate. A *cabriolet* was a smart little carriage from France and 'cab' is in use all the world over.

We have 7,000 buses on 700 routes serving about 1,800 bus stops. George Shillibeer started a big business in 1850 supplying horse-drawn carriages to the gentry. A few years later Thomas Tilling set up in opposition to him, but soon Shillibeer's fight was with the London General Omnibus Company, whose buses were painted the uniform red we know today. Eventually they reached a truce and amalgamated. Other entrepreneurs did the same thing and chaos reigned as they took each other's routes and stole each other's numbers, and the remnants of those crazy routes lasted a hundred years before everything was tidied up. Echoes of those days can be seen in the eighty different pay grades in use among the various transport companies whose staff drive the same routes.

★ ★ ★

This brief trip around London's boundaries brings us back to Peckham where we started. Thomas Tilling had his bus station there and the tree-lined streets were very convenient to live in, as a single bus would take people to Kent in one direction and Hampstead in another. Just as today, they passed through parishes and districts seeing all manner of sights and buildings great and small, new and old, known and unknown to them. London has been such an important city since it began on the shore of the mighty Thames thousands of years ago that we can only hope visitors and residents respect the past, enjoy the present, and have a safe future within its great, sprawling boundaries.

PART II

A Guide to the Sites

12

The Hidden Landscapes of London

Chesca Potter

L ONDON IS ESSENTIALLY a city built upon hills that rise between networks of rivers. Along their banks were numerous sacred springs, while the natural hills would originally have been wooded. The most important London rivers are the Thames, the Fleet, the Walbrook and the Tyburn. The River Fleet flows from Parliament Hill on Hampstead Heath, through St Pancras and Holborn, to its meeting place with the Thames at Blackfriars. The Walbrook runs through the City from Shoreditch to the Thames. The Tyburn flows from Belsize Park to Haverstock Hill, past Primrose Hill to Regent's Park, and then beneath Buckingham Palace before it divides into two tributaries into the Thames, forming the Island of Thorney upon which Westminster stands (see map overleaf). All these rivers are now lost in that they have been culverted and cannot be seen. However, one can see that most of London's sacred sites once stood on or near their banks.

The first settlements seem to have been built here as a protection against flooding, since the Thames is tidal. Each tribal settlement would have had its own hill, with its associated sacred sites. If there was no natural hill one would be built, therefore on Thorney Island, Westminster, there was a large artificial mound, the Tothill. From this foundation, order could be established, as the four quarters (north, east, south and west) could be measured and the settler's place in the world assessed. The main sacred hills of London are Ludgate Hill, Parliament Hill, Primrose Hill, Greenwich (Maze) Hill, Penton Hill and the White Mound at the Tower of London. Each of these hills may once have had a central shrine or axis point, which originally may have been either a tree or a stone, replaced in time by a more fully constructed shrine, and finally a church.

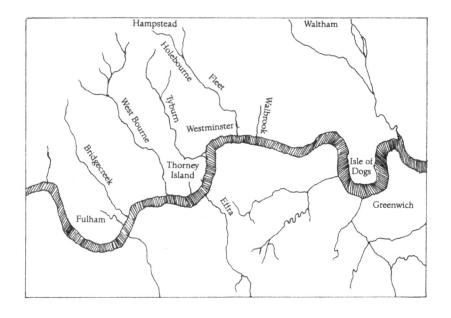

[Figure 24: The lost rivers of London.]

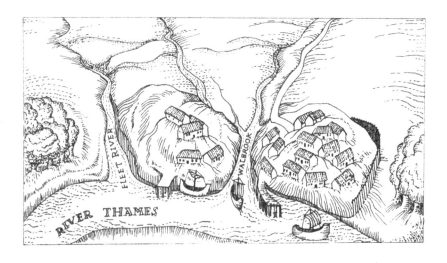

[Figure 25: Reconstruction of pre-Roman London.]

Symbolically both tree and church mark out the three worlds; a tree has its roots in the underworld, the base of its trunk is on this earthly plane and its branches amidst the stars, while the church has a crypt in the underworld, its nave in this world and its spire in the stars. Each hill would be in some way related to the underworld, for example Merlin's Cave at Penton Hill, or a barrow such as Boudicca's Mound on Parliament Hill.

The priest or priestess, king or queen, who were the worldly representatives, or mediators, of the tribal deities, and who were meant to hold the land in balance, were enshrined or enthroned at the central axis. This sacred place was intended to be seen as the hub of the wheel, the central point of creation from which all else radiated.

The Wheel of the Year

Each sacred hill or primal mound represented the womb of the earth from which the sun rose at the dawn of creation; every dawn, every midwinter, when the sun was reborn out of darkness, depicted the primal creation, and because the position of the rising sun in relation to the land changes throughout the year, every mythology had to take into account its various aspects. This was done by dividing the year into eight, a pattern that formed the basis of most Western mythologies.

First, the year can be divided into four, giving us the solstices and equinoxes. Then it is divided again to give the cross-quarter days. These are the pre-Christian festival days of Brigantia, or Imbolc (1 February), Beltane, or May Day (1 May), Lammas or Lughnasad (1 August), and Samhain (1 November). The four directions are also placed on this wheel.

The eight-spoked wheel can also be divided into two crosses. One is the 'solar' or equal-armed cross, where each aspect of the sun's journey through the year is personified by a male archetype.

At midwinter the sun is born out of darkness, growing in strength throughout the spring, and becoming the Solar King at midsummer, the height of the sun's power. As the sun's strength wanes, the king is sacrificed and descends into the underworld. There he is initiated into the knowledge of his ancestors – those who have been buried before him. He then becomes Lord of the Underworld and a protector and guardian of his people and the kingdom above.

The second cross relates to the feminine cycle, and is based on the so-called 'saltire' or St Andrew's cross. Here the pattern is connected to the way the land itself changes throughout the year.

At the beginning of spring the Maiden rises out of the dark winter earth. She is not born as a child like the male, but emerges refreshed like annual plants after winter. As spring advances, she blossoms into the Flower Bride. Then, when the land is at its most fertile, she becomes the nurturing mother, the Empress giving birth to the harvest. When that has been reaped, she descends into the underworld, becoming the Dark Maiden. In some mythologies, she becomes a female warrior defending her land, while in others she becomes the initiator, the wise enchantress, directing the land's destiny. She next becomes the Dark Mother, the Goddess of Death, but also Guardian of the Dead, the holder of the knowledge of all the ancestors.

The interaction between the two crosses forms the basis of all Western mythology. Every aspect of the year was equally valid and sacred, dark not being a qualitative term. Certain tribes, however emphasized particular aspects of the wheel. For instance, a culture that was basically matriarchal (i.e. Neolithic) concentrated more on the importance of the Goddess. Later tribes increasingly emphasized the aspects of the solar male. Thus references to the Goddess in London are rare and fragmentary, though we can be sure that behind every Sun King was a great Goddess!

The hub of the wheel symbolically would have been represented by the central shrine, and it was here that the representative of the sovereignty of the land would be enthroned. He or she then represented all aspects of the wheel in harmony. The person of the priestess or queen would thus form a complete archetype, symbolically crowned with the stars, emblazoned with the sun, rising from the moon, standing upon the earth.

Male Archetypes Associated with Sacred Sites in London

Deity	Archetypes	Date	Associated Place
St Pancras	Sacrificial Youth	12 May	St Pancras Old Church
Apollo	Solar Youth	24 May	Ludgate Hill
Lugh or Lud	Sacrificial Youth	1 Aug	Ludgate Hill
Mithras	Sacrificial Youth	b. 25 Dec	Temple of Mithras Walbrook
Balin	Solar King	21 June	Billingsgate
Magog	Solar Oak King	24 June	Ludgate
St Martin	Lord of Underworld	11 Nov	St Martin-within-Ludgate
Bran	Lord of Underworld	21 Dec	Tower of London
Cadwallo	Lord of Underworld	7 Nov	St Martin-within-Ludgate
Merlin	Lord of Underworld	21 Dec	Merlin's Cave
St Peter	Solar Hero	29 June, 1 Aug	Westminster Abbey
John the Baptist	Sun throughout the year	24 June	Temple Church
Gog	Holly King	21 Dec	Ludgate Hill

Feminine Archetypes Associated with Sacred Sites in London

Deity	Archetype	Date	Associated Place
Brighde (St Bride)	Reborn Maiden	1 Feb	St Bride's Well
Elen (St Helena)	Flower Maiden Empress Fertile Mother	23 June	St Pancras
Hecate	Dark Maiden Initiatrix	Dark moon	Elephant and Castle; Tyburn
Brigantia	Dark Maiden	1 Aug	Boudicca's
Boudicca	Female Warrior Initiatrix	21 Sept	Mound
Black Mary	Dark Maiden Black Madonna	1 Nov	Black Mary's Hole, St Mary's Willesden

Matronae (Four Mothers)	Fertile Mothers	1 May	Blackfriars
Isis	Mother	23 July	Blackfriars
St Mary Overie	Mother	21 March	Southwark Cathedral
St Mary	Mother	13 Aug	Southwark Cathedral
Artemis	All aspects of the Goddess	–	St Mary-le-Bow
Fflur Estrildis/Yseult	Sovereignty of London	–	London

13

The Mythology of London:
Gazetteer of Sacred Sites in London

Compiled by John Matthews,
Chesca Potter and Caroline Wise

T HE ORIGINAL GAZETTEER of sacred sites was compiled by
Chesca Potter, with additions by John and Caitlín Matthews.
Some of the entries required updating; some have changed over the
past ten years and have been deleted. The present gazetteer therefore
consists of an updated and re-edited version of the original, with
additional sites and information collected by John Matthews and
Caroline Wise, with help from the contributors to this new edition.
This is by no means a comprehensive list of all the sacred sites in
London, but consists of places to which access is possible, and that
maintain a special or sacred atmosphere.

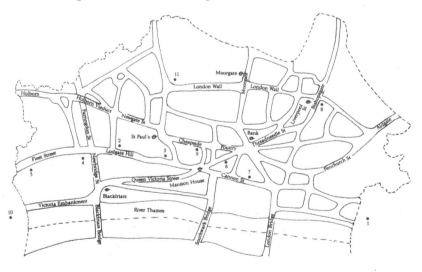

[Figure 26: Map of Central London sites.]

The mythology of London may seem confusing and disparate, not only because many of the ancient places have been destroyed, but also because of the advent of numerous incoming peoples of different cultural backgrounds, who rededicated these sites to deities of their own pantheia. However, beneath the many variants in name and place one can still glimpse remnants of a cohesive mythology, and though most of the sites included here are mentioned individually at greater length elsewhere in this anthology, our purpose is to link them together by pointing to some underlying patterns.

Table of contents

CENTRAL LONDON AND CITY

1. The Tower of London, EC3

The Tower, which lies hard against Tower Bridge, is one of the most impressive monuments within London. It has been a royal fortress, an armoury, a menagerie and a prison over the nine hundred or so years of its existence. Although the site was fortified on the orders of William I, and the subsequent structure built in the reign of successive Norman and Plantagenet kings, the site of the Tower was of strategic military importance to both the Romans and Saxons. The mythic underlay of the British legend of Bran the Blessed, whose head was buried at the Bryn Gwyn (The White Mount) in order to repel foreign invasion (see Chapter 4), probably antedates the building of the Tower of London, seen by the British as the epicentre of the Norman control over England and Wales.

The White Tower

The White Tower, or central keep of the Tower of London, is the oldest surviving edifice. It originally accommodated the Sovereign and his Constable. The Chapel of St John the Evangelist, once gorgeously adorned with wall paintings and stained glass, holy images and a painted rood screen, now appears plain and functional, due to the excesses of the Reformation. However, its stark beauty is still impressive, giving a focused stillness to the hurried comings and goings of tourists who come to see the arms and armour currently displayed in the White Tower. The White Tower was the prison of the Welsh prince, Gryffydd ap Llewylyn, who fell to his death in 1244 in an attempt to escape. In 1358 King John the Good of France and his son the Dauphin and in 1415 Charles, Duke of Burgundy were all interned in the Tower as a result of capture during the Hundred Years War.

The Crown Jewels

The Crown Jewels are presently housed in the massively secure treasury of the Jewel House, where visitors may see the coronation regalia, which though most of it dates from after the Restoration of Charles II, does include some jewels said to have been part of the original pre-Norman regalia of the Saxon kings. Some pieces have interesting stories.

The mysterious Koh-I-Noor diamond, the 'Mountain of Light', currently sits in the crown of the late Queen Mother. It has a sinister reputation, and legends tell of it being cursed. It was mined in India around 1100 and was once set as an eye in a statue of a Hindu Goddess by the Kakatiya dynasty of Southern India. Maharajah Ranjit Singh requested on his deathbed that the diamond be offered to the Hindu god Lord Jaggannath in his temple in Odisha. The British administrators did not honour this, and in 1850, a child, Ranjit's son Duleep Singh, was brought to Britain to surrender the diamond to Queen Victoria and the British Crown.

A Hindu text from 1306 states that 'He who owns this diamond will own the world but will also know all its misfortunes. Only God or a Woman can wear it with impunity'. Many male owners and rulers did indeed have bad luck and come to blood-soaked ends, and the crew of the ship bringing it to England was struck down with cholera. The diamond is sensibly placed in the crowns of female consorts, and this seems to have worked in keeping the curse at bay. Debate continues concerning its rightful home.

The Royal Sceptre symbolizes the temporal authority of the monarch under the Cross. It was redesigned in 1905 to contain the diamond known as the Great Star of Africa; one of nine gems cut from the largest diamond then discovered, the Cullinan. This jewel was given as a gift to King Edward VII. The Sceptre of the Dove, or the 'Rod of Equity and Mercy', represents the spiritual authority of the monarch. The monarch holds both sceptres when the Archbishop places the crown on his or her head during the Coronation ceremony. The Sovereign's Orb, a golden sphere topped with a cross, represents Christendom, the world governed by Christianity. It is no longer used in the coronation ritual.

The Ravens

The Ravens at the Tower are the last remnants of the tradition that the head of Bran the Blessed guards Britain from foreign invasion. Bran's name means 'raven' and the legend runs that if they fly the Tower, the Crown will fall and Britain with it. The Tower ravens' wings are kept clipped to avert this occurrence. As these birds mate on the wing, replacements would be sought when one died, for there must always be at least six ravens at the Tower, according to a tradition started by Charles II. There is a story that during the Second World War only one raven survived the stress caused by the bombardment of London during the Blitz. The ravens couldn't respond naturally and fly away due to their clipped wings. Winston Churchill understood the effect that losing the ravens could have on the morale of the country, and ordered more ravens to be brought in.

The Tower ravens are enlisted as soldiers of the kingdom and they can be sacked for 'unsatisfactory conduct'. Birds of the corvid family have been known to hold 'funeral gatherings' and according to the Raven Master, in 1990, when a chaplain of the Tower died in his room, the ravens gathered on the Tower Green near the chapel, cawed, and then became quiet, as though to pay their respects. There is currently a successful breeding programme for the Tower ravens, and if needed, replacements are brought in from bird sanctuaries, too. The birds are often given names of mythical characters, such as Odin and Merlin.

Prisoners

The Tower is redolent of history and legend, but is perhaps most famous for its prisoners and as a place of execution. Such notable political prisoners as Sir Thomas More and Rudolf Hess have been housed in its precincts. The Wars of the Roses saw the expedient political assassinations of Henry VI, the Princes in the Tower, and George, Duke of Clarence, here, while the Tudor period saw the executions of Henry VIII's two wives, Ann Boleyn and Catherine Howard. Their remains, together with those of the nine-days queen, Jane Grey, rest in the Chapel of St Peter ad Vincula, freed at last of the chains of mortality. Elizabeth I was more fortunate than her sister prisoner, Jane Grey, for though she was committed to the Tower by her sister, Mary Tudor, Elizabeth lived to incarcerate both political and religious prisoners such as the Earl of Essex and Philip Howard during her reign.

All Hallows-by-the-Tower

This beautiful church is the oldest dedication in the City, founded in 675, some 300 years before the Tower was built. Much of it was damaged in the Second World War and rebuilt and rededicated in 1957. The crypt is a treasure trove of London history, and includes a Saxon arch and a well-preserved second-century Roman pavement. The crypt also houses a chapel, known as the Vicar's Vault. The chapel's altar, according to church history, was brought back from Palestine by the Knights Templars from Château Pèlerin (Castle Pilgrim). A Templar Cross is carved on to the front of it.

There are other links with these warrior Knights. The later British Templar trials were held in All Hallows, some in the church, and some in the medieval Royal Lady Chapel in the grounds. The Templars got off lightly here, but on a more gruesome note, later in the sixteenth and seventeenth centuries, the bodies of those beheaded at the Tower were laid out here before burial, including Archbishop Laud and Thomas More. The church was saved from the Great Fire by the efforts of William Penn's father.

In June each year, the Knollys Rose Ceremony takes place, celebrating a fourteenth-century judgement. The wife of Sir Robert Knollys bought a threshing field opposite her house in Seething Lane. She turned it into a rose garden as the chaff dust bothered her, and built a bridge to it over the mud, without permission. Her fine was to provide, as rent, one red rose, placed on the altar cushion of All Hallows, presented to the Lord Mayor at the Mansion House each June. This ceremony continues. All Hallows also observes the Beating of the Bounds of its parish on Ascension Day.

2. Temple Bar, WC2

The Temple Bar is the gateway from Westminster to the City, at the point where the Strand joins Fleet Street, and it is named for the nearby Temple Church. The earliest mention of the bar comes from 1293. Its original function was to control trade, and traditionally the monarch's carriage stops here on state occasions so that the Lord Major can offer his sword, and in the popular imagination this is seen as a gesture of loyalty to the Crown. In the 1690s, Sir Christopher Wren was commissioned to build an arched gateway of Portland stone at the spot. This was moved to Paternoster Square, beside St Paul's Cathedral, in the nineteenth century. A Victorian monument marks the bar today, incorporating a statue of Queen Victoria. It is topped by the statue of a silver dragon, a symbol of the City of London.

3. Ludgate, EC4

King Lud, whom we met earlier in this book, is remembered in the names Ludgate Circus and Ludgate Hill. Lud's Gate, one of the six original gates of the City, stood at the crossroads at the base of the hill where it joins Fleet Street. The gate arched over the road and contained the statues of Kind Lud and his two sons. It also held the only statue of Queen Elizabeth I that was made in her lifetime. The statues of Lud and his sons may be over 700 years old.

4. St Dunstans'-in-the-West, Fleet Street, EC4

The ancient and crumbling statues of King Lud and his sons can now be seen in a porch on the right of St Dunstan's Church. They were moved here when the old Lud's Gate was demolished. There is currently access to view these important statues on weekdays during office hours, when the small churchyard is open to a coffee stall. The best time to see them is on a Sunday, between 11 a.m. and 3 p.m. when the church is open to the worshippers of the Romanian community who use the church. The statue of Queen Elizabeth is incorporated into the outer wall of St Dunstan's, as is the Gog and Magog Clock. This splendid clock was made in 1671, the first in London to have a second hand. Gog and Magog turn their heads outwards and strike the bell with their clubs at the quarter hour, half hour, and on the hour. Gog and Magog appear in the Old Testament as two giants who are descendants of Noah. They have become unofficial tutelary guardians of London. Effigies of Gog and Magog as the 'Giants of Albion' feature in the Lord Mayor of London's annual show, and have been paraded in it since the time of Henry V.

The clock is mentioned in this 1782 poem by William Cowper:

> *When labour and when dullness, club in hand,*
> *Like the two figures at St Dunstan's stand,*
> *Beating alternately in measured time*
> *The clockwork tintinnabulum of rhyme,*
> *Exact and regular the sounds will be,*
> *But such mere quarter-strokes are not for me.*

St Dunstan was one of the foremost British saints. Born in the early part of the tenth century, he was taught by Irish monks in Glastonbury and rose to hold the important offices of Abbot of Glastonbury, Bishop of London, and Archbishop of Canterbury. Legends attached to him include the tale that when his mother Cynethryth was in church, all the candles went out. However, Cynethryth's reignited, and all present lit theirs from this flame. This indicated that she would give birth to a special and saintly child.

5. St Martin-within-Ludgate, EC4

St Martin's is not a very spectacular church to visit; however, it is included because of its mythological importance. Initially, St Martin's was a gate church attached to Ludgate, one of the main gates to the city. The name Lud could also be another form of the Celtic sun god Lugh, whose festival Lughnasad fell on 1 August.

The Feast Day of St Martin (of Tours) fell on 11 November, or

Martinmas, a day also known as Old Winter's Eve. Traditionally Martinmas was a day of sacrifice, when agricultural communities, even as late as the eighteenth century, slaughtered their fattened oxen. 'Mart' means ox in Gaelic/Irish and it is interesting to note that numerous oxen bones were dug up in St Paul's churchyard next to St Martin's.[1]

The church itself has a curious foundation legend. The first building was supposedly built about AD 600 by Cadwallo, King of the Britons. When he died in AD 677, his ashes were allegedly placed in an image of himself mounted upon a brazen horse, which was then buried in a secret crypt. This legend is almost identical to that of Silbury Hill, Wiltshire, in which a king named Zel is supposed to be buried on a brazen horse. The fact that this artefact was not found during archaeological digs indicates that it may be a symbolic image. King Lud was also said to be buried in an underground chamber beneath Ludgate. The tower of St Martin's was struck by lightning in 1561.

St Martin's is now used by some of the City's wealthy guilds and masonic lodges, and is also the chapel of the Honourable Society of the Knights of the Round Table.

6. St Paul's Cathedral, EC4

There is a legend which relates that St Paul's was originally the site of a temple of the Goddess Diana, and was erected by Brutus, London's mythical Trojan founder. It thus became the main temple of the city of Troynovante (New Troy) the original London. There are also traditions referring to a Roman temple of Apollo on the site, while the twelfth-century historian Geoffrey of Monmouth states that Bladdud, the semi-mythical founder of Bath, crashlanded a magical flying stone on the spot.

Here also, according to Arthurian tradition, stood the stone and anvil containing a sword, placed in the churchyard by the enchanter Merlin as a symbolic reference, so that when the future King Arthur withdrew it, he was proclaimed sovereign. It is often wrongly assumed that this sword was the famous Excalibur, but in fact it later broke during combat and was replaced by the magical weapon given to Arthur by the Lady of the Lake, whose name is also sometimes given as Diana.

The Hellenic equivalent of Diana was Artemis, the sister of Apollo. Although originally an ancient solar woodland goddess, Artemis ceded her solar aspect to Apollo, becoming a lunar Goddess of the Hunt. This may perhaps account for the rededication of the site to St Paul, renowned for his suppression of the cult of Artemis at Ephesus. The survival of a curious pagan ceremony called the 'Blowing of the Stag', which was still enacted until recent times, suggests that the earlier associations with Artemis had not been forgotten. The ceremony consisted of a stag's head being brought into the church by clergymen and laid on the altar, at which point huntsmen from the forests surrounding London blew their horns at the four quarters. Great feasting and celebrations followed this. St Paul's is built at the summit of Ludgate Hill and this previous shrine to Artemis may have been the geomantic centre of the original city.

At one time a famous stone called St Paul's Cross, or 'Pol's Stump' stood in St Paul's churchyard. It was a site for the local folkmoot, and a place of religious and secular freedom of speech. Rebuilt after an earth tremor in 1382, 'Pol's Stump' was finally destroyed by Cromwell and his followers and is now replaced by a tall pillar with a gilded statue of St Paul, overlooking the City and the river.

7. St Bride's Church, Fleet Street, EC4

This church was built upon one of the earliest known places of pre-Christian worship in London. It was sited beside the Thames at the mouth of the Fleet River, and beside a natural spring, St Bride's Well. On this site are the remains of the only known Roman building between the heart of the City and present-day Westminster. Historians are puzzled as to why the Romans built outside the city walls, but this may have been because they understood the sacredness of the site, or because it was a significant source of fresh water.

The first stone church of which we have knowledge (it may have had wattle and daub predecessors) was built here in the sixth century and dedicated to St Bridget of Kildare, Ireland. It is possible that the spring was once sacred to the Gaelic Goddess Brigid, who was Christianized as St Bride. In the west of Scotland and Ireland, she was known as 'Mary of the Gaels' and was a major goddess of the Celts in Scotland and Ireland. The Gaelic Brigid was a goddess of sun, and fire, and wells, and of the spring when the lambs were born. In both her Christian and pagan guises she was associated with healing, poetry and the smithcraft of the forge.[2]

It is possible that here, as at Kildare, the nuns had taken over the role of an earlier enclosed order of priestesses, continuing some aspects of the earlier worship of St Bride. St Bride's Well, which is a natural spring, can still be heard running beneath the church, though there is no longer access to it. During the fifteenth century it is recorded that processions to the well took place on the Feast to St Bride (1 February). Inside the crypt is a small medieval chapel with an exhibit showing the history of the church, its Roman pavement, archaeological finds and an exhibition of the history of Fleet Street (see also pages 56–8).

8. Postman's Park, St Martin's Le Grand, EC1

Lying just north of St Paul's Cathedral and bordered by Aldersgate Street, St Martin's Le Grand, and King Edward Street, Postman's Park is one of the largest parks within the ancient walls of the City. Built on the site of the former burial ground of St Botolph's, Aldersgate, it was the site of the General Post Office headquarters, until it became a park in 1880, following the demolition of the building. In 1900 it was selected as the site of the Memorial to Heroic Self Sacrifice, established by the artist George Frederic Watts. Until recently this was also the site of a magnificent bronze statue of the Minotaur by Michael Ayrton, but the sculpture was moved in 1997 to St Alphage Highwalk, and moved again to its present resting place beside the Barbican Lake. Eventually it will be installed as part of a new development at London Wall Place.

9. The Temple Church, EC4

Consecrated in 1185, the Temple Church is, like most Knights Templar churches, round. Based on the circular design of the church of the Holy Sepulchre in Jerusalem, this is one of the finest surviving examples of the design. The rectangular chapel was added in 1240. The architecture of the whole is magnificent, especially the six hollow porphyry columns in the centre of the round church. Around the walls are stone seats where the knights sat in chapter. Above are grotesque heads and on the floor are effigies of knights, though not all are Templars. These suffered badly during the last war from bomb damage, but perfect pre-war copies can be seen in the Victoria and Albert Museum.

Following the publication of Dan Brown's novel *The Da Vinci Code*, it became the centre of pilgrims seeking the Grail. The long story of the Templar association with the sacred vessel is told elsewhere, and though no proof exists of the links between the Order and the Grail, people still go there to seek harmony and enlightenment. (For more details on the history and rituals of the Knights Templars, see Chapter 5.)

10. The Mithraeum – A Roman Temple to Mithras, EC4

In the nineteenth century a marble relief of the Roman god Mithras slaying a bull was uncovered beside the Walbrook stream in the centre of the City. It was thought to have been associated with the Roman temple to Mithras, the site of which lay undiscovered. In 1954 during the construction of Bucklersbury House, Queen Victoria Street, workmen found the perfectly preserved foundations of the temple along with a remarkable collection of Roman cult objects, including heads of Minerva, Serapis, and Mithras. These can now be seen in the Museum of London.

It is thought that the temple was dedicated to the Persian god Mithras, who was adopted by the Romans and became the central cult of the legions. The London site was probably in use between AD 240–350.

When work on the office block, Bucklersbury House, began in 2004 it was decided to move the Mithraic temple stone by stone to a site in nearby Temple Court. There it remained until 2009, when it was stated that the entire temple would be relocated once again to its original location, in a specially created vault beneath the rebuilt Bucklersbury House on Queen Victoria Street. However, the project was put on hold while archaeologists continued to explore the huge site along the banks of the Walbrook River. So far more than 10,000 objects have been discovered there and the dig is set to continue until at least 2016. In the meantime the stones of the Mithraeum remain in boxes catered by the Museum of London.

It is likely to be several years before the temple is once again open to the public, but some artefacts belonging to the temple can be seen in the Museum of London.

11. *The London Stone, EC4*

The London Stone can be found on the north side of Cannon Street, next to St Swithin's Lane, opposite Cannon Street Station. It is shrouded in mystery and tradition, yet is sadly neglected today, set as it is within a grilled cavity in the wall of a building currently occupied by WH Smith. Plans to move the stone to the nearby Walbrook Building caused an outcry in 2012. Currently any decision remains unknown.

What is left of this once great pillar of oolite limestone is just a fragment, some three feet across and wide. Yet in the past, according to John Stow in his *Survey of London* (1598), it was 'pitched upright' on the south side of Candlewick Street (Cannon Street). It was 'very tall' and was sunk deep into the ground. Apparently, if carts ran into it, it might break their wheels but the stone itself would remain undamaged.

The London Stone is traditionally connected with the preservation, safety and wellbeing of the capital. Legend says it was originally placed there by Brutus, London's founder, and there is an old saying which states that 'so long as the stone of Brutus is safe, so long shall London flourish'. If genuine, then this legend suggests that the monolith was considered to be a stone of destiny, similar to the Stone of Scone, the coronation stone that was in Westminster Abbey and was returned to Scotland in 1996, or the King Stone on which the Saxon kings were crowned at Kingston-on-Thames.

It would also suggest that the London Stone was present before the Roman Conquest, a view not shared by many historians, like Camden who, in his *Britannia* of 1586, considered the stone to be a 'milestone' like that in the forum of Rome 'from which the dimensions of all roads or journeys were begun since it stood in the middle of the city as it runs out in length'.

Camden said that the first documentary evidence of the monolith comes from the Saxon chronicles of Athelstan, King of the West Saxons. There the London Stone was mentioned as being next to lands owned by the King. Camden says that in the year 1135 it was again mentioned, this time as being near the house of one Ailward, which was burnt down in a fire, which consumed 'all east to Aldgate'.

The importance of the London Stone to the wellbeing of the city is first hinted at in references to the earliest Lord Mayor of London, the chief magistrate of the city, Henry Fitzailwin. He had a stone house by the London Stone in 1188 and both he and future mayors were given the title 'de London Stone', showing their link with the monolith.

H.C. Coote, FSA, in his *Transactions of the London and Middlesex Archaeological Society*, first series, Vol. V, 1881, suggested that the Lord Mayor lived in a stone house of which the stone was the last remaining part.

The London Stone, regardless of its actual origin, has always been a remarkable centre of rites, ceremonies and traditions. The most quoted example of its importance as a stone of destiny comes from an incident that, according to tradition, took place when Jack Cade, a leader of the Peasants Revolt, entered the city. He apparently struck his staff (or sword in some accounts) upon the stone and proclaimed, 'Now is Mortimer Lord of this City.' This again shows the close link between the position of Lord Mayor and the stone, and also strengthens the view that it was very possibly an inauguration stone. There are also traditions that say it was used to proclaim bills, an act that was accompanied by 'drums and trumpet'.

After the Great Fire of 1666 the remains of a Roman building complete with pavement were discovered adjacent to the London Stone, and this prompted Sir Christopher Wren to put forward the theory that the stone was a surviving part of a Roman dwelling place. It would appear, however, that Wren's idea was not taken too seriously.

By 1720 the London Stone had been encased within a stone cavity to protect it, presumably because it was beginning to get damaged. In 1742 what remained of the stone was transferred to the north side of Cannon Street, and in 1798 it was built into the south wall of St Swithin's Church. It stayed there until the church was demolished in 1962. Somewhere in its past it has diminished in size from a tall, erect pillar to a small, insignificant-looking fragment.[3]

12. St Ethelburga-the-Virgin, Bishopsgate, EC2

As one of only seven medieval churches to survive from the medieval period, it is small, but full of atmosphere. It is dedicated to an obscure saint, the daughter of the Saxon King Offa, who reigned from 757 to 796. Ethelburga became abbess of Barking and the church was part of her foundation. Its dates are uncertain, but it was first recorded in 1250 as the church of St Adelburga-the-Virgin. The church was rebuilt around 1411 and some of this fabric, notably the south arcade, still remains.

From 1366 to the Dissolution of the Monasteries, the patronage of the church was in the hands of the prioress and convent of St Helen's, Bishopsgate. In 1954, St Ethelburga's became a guild church particularly concerned with healing and some of the atmosphere of the nunnery (long since gone) still lingers there. The church was one of the few to survive bomb damage in the Second World War, but in 1993 an IRA bomb detonated just outside the church, demolishing much of it. A fund was set up to restore the building, which continues to this day, and a Bedouin tent now occupies the area behind the building dedicated to peace and reconciliation between religious groups. An extraordinary stained-glass window, created by Helen Whittaker and using some pieces of the original glass damaged by the bomb blast, dominates the church today. The artist describes the glass as follows:

> St. Ethelburga is shown as an abbess . . . striding across the composition as if seen through the cloister openings – her upward gaze held by the radiant vision of the Heavenly Jerusalem . . . From a crack in the tiled floor of the first light grows a Hazel bush (*Corylus avellana*) shedding leaves and fruit – a symbol of Peace and Reconciliation . . . The composition of St. Ethelburga is carried through the five existing window lights and reflects the moving forward of Faith. The fragments of the previous window remind us of the tribulations of the past – but give us Hope for the future.

13. St Mary-le-Bow, Cheapside, EC2

The site of St Mary-le-Bow is one of ancient sanctity. There were Celtic, Roman and Saxon buildings preceding the famous Norman church and the crypt in particular, now a chapel, is full of atmosphere. St Mary was, of course, the mother of Christ, and St Mary-le-Bow is, in some sense, a mother church with many smaller parishes annexed to it. St Mary's as mother church is depicted in the window designed by John Hayward in 1964. It shows St Mary carrying and protecting Bow church in her arms with representations of the bombed London churches and their saints around her. (St Bride's church can be seen in the top right-hand corner.)

St Mary-le-Bow houses the famous Bow Bells and it is said one can only be a true Londoner if born within the sound of these. Before London was built up, the Bow Bells could be heard over a much greater distance, and Dick Whittington is said to have heard them at Highgate on his way into London.

In the eleventh and twelfth centuries the church was reported to have held a number of black masses. These were rituals where the officiator would hold requiem masses for the living rather than the dead. In 1196 an illicit congregation was caught holding such a mass, led by a murderer named William Fitzosbert. The perpetrators barricaded themselves in the tower, and had to be smoked out. They were hung at Smithfield gallows. Since this time the church has supposedly been cursed.

14. The Walbrook, EC4

This small lane off Queen Victoria Street follows part of the route of the Walbrook stream, which flowed into the Thames. It was culverted in the fifteenth and sixteenth centuries. It had once been important as both a source of fresh water and a conduit for waste, as well as useful for transport into the city and beyond. In the 1860s, the archaeologist Augustus Pitt Rivers found a large quantity of human skulls in the riverbed during excavation work. They may have been the soldiers referred to in Geoffrey of Monmouth's *History of the Kings of Britain*. These soldiers were apparently slaughtered on the command of the Praetorian Prefect Julius Asclepiodotus, following their surrender when he was asserting the re-establishment of Roman rule in Britain. Geoffrey tells of their heads being cast into a stream called the Gallobroc.

Some historians think that the skulls could be from victims of Boudicca's destruction of London during her brutal rebellion of AD 61. Others suggest that the skulls were offered to the river as a ritual practice. Over a hundred skulls have been found in the course of various archaeological digs. The stream does possess some ritual significance, with many votive offerings being placed there, including statues of deities, and precious metal items that were deliberately crushed or bent. More sinister offerings included curses, written on lead tablets.

15. *The Guildhall, Gresham Street, EC2*

Open Monday–Saturday, 10 a.m.–5 p.m.; Sunday, 12 noon–4 p.m.
This magnificent building was built in the fifteenth century and
reflects the pomp and wealth of the City guilds. In legend, Brutus is
believed to have built his palace on this site, and statues of his associ-
ates, the giants Gog and Magog, can be seen inside. These statues
were commissioned by popular demand in the 1950s to replace the
earlier ones lost in the bombing during the Second World War. Those
had replaced even earlier images.

In 1988, a spectacular Roman amphitheatre was discovered under
the Guildhall's art gallery, with a capacity for 6,000 people to watch
the gory gladiatorial games and entertainments.

16. *Alsatia, Magpie Lane, off Bouverie Street, EC4*

Alsatia was the name given to an area lying north of the Thames on
a site once occupied by a Carmelite monastery. Between the
fifteenth and seventeenth centuries it was one of the few places
within the city granted the privilege of sanctuary, and it thus became
the refuge of criminals, prostitutes and wrongdoers of every kind,
forming what was virtually a tiny kingdom outside the walls of
London. Within it lay a number of boozing kens, brothels and even
a theatre in which the poet Michael Drayton (1563–1631) had a
stake. Drayton was the author of the epic poem *Poly-Obion,*
published in 1612 and 1622, which contained a summary of the
myths and legends of Britain.

The original building occupied by the Whitefriars Theatre had
been the refectory of the monastery known as Whitefriars, remembered still in street names around the area. According to Walter
Thornbury in his 1878 book *Old and New London*, Alsatia was named
after Alsace, an area of France fought over by the French and Germans
during the Thirty Years War, which was considered to be outside the
law. The name is thought to be a slang term for the area, first
mentioned in *The Squire of Alsatia*, a play by Thomas Shadwell dating
from 1688.

Almost nothing of the original site remains, though there is still an ancient doorway, hidden away in Tudor Street and now bricked up, that led into Alsatia at one time, and the remains of a crypt were discovered in the basement of a house in Whitefriars Street in 1895 and again in 1927. Part of this still exists and can be reached via Magpie Alley, off Bouverie Street. There is something quite strange and mysterious about the area. See Michael Moorcock's amazing story in *The Whispering Swarm* (2015).

17. St Helen's Bishopsgate, Great St Helen's, EC3

There is a tradition that pre-Conquest churches existed on this site, including a fourth-century one that St Helena's son Constantine had built and dedicated to his mother after her death. If this is true, this site links London closely with the time of St Helena, the empress who became confused over time with the Celtic Elen of the Hosts, and whom Harold Bayley suggests was based on an earlier guardian spirit of London called Elen (see page 61).

18. The London Wall

The London Wall, built around AD 200, gave its name to the dispiriting modern road that follows its route from Wormwood Street to the Museum of London. It originally enclosed the City in a four-kilometre area, and housed the gates that led to the Roman roads out of the City. These included Ludgate, Bishopsgate, Aldgate and Cripplegate. The wall was maintained, rebuilt and patched up well into the eighteenth century, but then much of it was demolished and its foundations lay beneath city roads and buildings. Substantial remains of the old London Wall can be seen just north of the Tower, and in a small garden area beside the Barbican, which is worth seeking out as an interesting historical oasis of quiet in the City. In legend, the wall was built on the command of the empress and saint, Helena, as noted by John

Stow in his 1603 *Survey of London*: 'howsoeuer those walles of stone might bee builded by Hellen . . .'

19. Smithfield, EC1

Smithfield originally came from the name Smooth Field, an area of land outside the walls of the City of London. The Romans used the area as a cemetery and a rubbish dump. A Roman stone altar dedicated to Mercury was found at Farringdon Road beside the banks of the River Fleet. It is thought to have been part of a Mithraic shrine to the dead. The altar is now in the Museum of London. The area continued its associations with death, being renowned for its gallows.

In 1381 Wat Tyler and his followers confronted Richard II and the Mayor of London at Smithfield. Wat Tyler, wounded by the Mayor, sought refuge in St Bartholomew's Church but was brought out and beheaded. Smithfield has been a livestock market for over 800 years and still runs with blood today.

20. St Bartholomew-the-Great, Smithfield, EC1

St Bartholomew's is Central London's oldest parish church. Only a part of the church survives today: the chancel, crossing transepts and Lady Chapel. These date mainly from the thirteenth century. Despite the loss of much of the original building, St Bartholomew's is still spacious and atmospheric. After the Reformation, parts of the church were rented out for extra income. By the seventeenth century the Lady Chapel was a printing workshop and the north transept a blacksmith's. The Victorians carefully restored the church. Every Good Friday, sixpences are placed on a tomb in the churchyard and are collected by the poor widows of the parish. These women then step across the tomb and each is presented with a bun. The origin of the custom is obscure, but it is probably connected with 'sin-eating', in which the living ritually assumed the sins of the dead by eating a piece of bread over the corpse (see the Butterworth Charity, page 161.)

St Bartholomew's is a dark and compelling place. It is also haunted by the ghost of its founder, the monk Rahere, who was reputed to be able to fly through the air on artificial wings.

NORTH LONDON

21. *The Clerk's Well, 14–16 Farringdon Lane, EC1*

Visits can be arranged by appointment free of charge. To book a visit, please contact the Local History Society, Finsbury Library, 245 St John Street, London, EC1V 4NB.

The Clerk's Well is the only one remaining of the many that once existed along the River Fleet. It is now part of a modern building that has been built around what is left of the original structure. There is a good exhibition describing its history, and one can lift off the well cover and see the now almost-dry spring. It is hard to imagine that in the Middle Ages it gushed with sweet, clear water amidst the fields outside the city. It is shown on a map of 1542 flowing through a retaining wall of the large Nunnery of St Mary, where it ran into an enclosure for public use. The Clerk's Well takes its name from the parish clerks of London, who performed miracle plays nearby.

It is known that the Skinner's Well was close to the Clerk's Well and in Stow's *Survey of London* we are informed that on St Bartholomew's Day, 1390, the parish clerks of London played a series of miracle plays at Skinner's Well in the presence of King Richard II and his queen. The performance lasted three days. After the Dissolution of the Monasteries, the well continued in public use until the nineteenth century, when the water became polluted and was built over. In 1924, during building work, the well was rediscovered and a lease secured by the council to ensure public access. The Clerk's Well is an important relic of the once numerous healing springs in London.

22. *St Pancras Old Church, Pancras Road, NW1*

Open all day from approx. 9 a.m. until dusk.

A notice board outside this small and beautiful church declares that here 'stands one of Europe's most ancient sites of Christian worship, possibly dating back to the early fourth century'. There is a tradition that St Pancras was the first church to be built in London. The

Maximillien Mision is quoted in Richard Duppa's *Travels on the Continent* (1799) as saying of St John Lateran, in Rome: 'This is the head and mother of all Christian churches, if you except that of St Pancras-under-Highgate, near London.' St John Lateran was founded by the Emperor Constantine in AD 324. St Pancras was martyred in Rome at the age of fourteen in AD 304, during the persecution of the Christians under Diocletian.

In legend, the church's early foundation dates from AD 313. Constantine may have had some contact with a Roman shrine on the site during the period he stayed in London between AD 306 and 311. It may have been used as a place of encampment for Constantine's legions. In 1845 a hoard of Constantinian coins was found in an urn on nearby Maiden Lane (now York Way). The church is more likely to have been founded in the late sixth century.

Sir Montagu Sharpe in his book *Middlesex in British, Roman and Saxon Times* (1932) includes St Pancras Church among forty-eight Middlesex churches to be built on the site of pagan shrines. Remains of a Roman building have been found beneath the church, and it is possible that this small hill, rising beside the Fleet River, has been a sacred place for thousands of years. There was at one time a raised, ditched and moated enclosure opposite the church called the Brill (see Chapter 14). According to the entry for 24 October 1826 in Hone's *Everyday Book*, a labourer dug up a series of red figure tiles from the Brill in 1825, as well as many arrowheads. If this is true, it suggests Roman as well as pre-Roman occupation.

The church had a special status during Elizabethan times, since it was the last church where mass was officially said by a priest kept on by the Queen.

The grave of Mary Wollstonecraft, the English writer, philosopher, and advocate of women's rights (and mother of Mary Shelley, who wrote the gothic horror story *Frankenstein*), can be seen in the churchyard.

The Mythology of St Pancras

According to the poet Aidan Andrew Dun in the notes of his epic poem *Vale Royal*, St Pancras himself is the perfect example of the young and pure sacrificed solar youth. The association of the site with

Constantine and Helena gives us clues as to its pagan past. The legends of the life of St Helena are almost interchangeable with those of Elen, an earlier pagan goddess (see page 61). Constantine himself, prior to his Christian conversion, saw himself as an incarnation of the sun god Apollo, while Apollo's sister Artemis was the Hellenistic equivalent of Elen, and possibly had a temple on the site of St Paul's (see pages 210-11). In Greece the Festival of Constantine and Helena (21 May) falls only a few days from the pagan festival of Artemis and Apollo (24/25 May). Perhaps Helena and Constantine could have founded St Pancras Church on a site which had previously been sacred to Apollo and/or Artemis and before that had been a woodland shrine to Elen. (It was part of the great forest of Middlesex even in the late Middle Ages.)

Until the Hanoverians, the church and area maintained a connection with royalty. The king and queen were regarded as physical incarnations, like the emperor and empress, of the sovereignty of the land, and there are shreds of evidence to show that royalty were aware of the importance of the site. The manor of Tothele (later Tottenham Court) once stood at the top of what is now Tottenham Court Road. It was one of the royal residences of King John (1199–1216), who used the nearby forest for hunting. Its use by royalty continued and King Edward IV (1462–83), resided there with his mistress Jane Shore. It was still owned by the Crown under Elizabeth I and Charles II, whose mistress Nell Gwynn held Tottenham Court as one of her residences. There is persistent legend that a tunnel ran from Tothele Manor to St Pancras Church, mentioned in Samuel Palmer's book *St Pancras* (1870):

> From it (the manor) ran a subterranean passage to the Old Church, which some enterprising antiquarians explored with lighted torches in about the middle of the last century.[4]

23. Primrose Hill, NW1

Despite the lack of legends associated with Primrose Hill it is clear that it was once a sacred place. Iron Age barrows were excavated at the bottom of the hill and the area is still called Barrow Hill. Primrose Hill rises over North London and from its top there is a 360-degree view. This panoramic vista would not only have been protection from hostile invaders, but would have been the natural focal point of the area, giving a sense of being centred within the landscape. In May 1829 a Mr Willson proposed to turn Primrose Hill into a necropolis, forming a pyramid of bodies laid on different levels within the hill. There would have been a lift running down the centre of the hill to deliver the bodies to the various levels. Fortunately this plan was rejected.

The Druid Ross Nichols (1902–1975) in his *Book of Druidry* tells how, at the Autumn Equinox of 1917, John Toland and John Aubrey inaugurated a neo-Druidic grove on Primrose Hill, and it has continued to be used by subsequent groups for yearly Equinox and Solstice celebrations until the present time.

There are two apt prophecies, written by the famous nineteenth-century seer Mother Shipton, that concern Primrose Hill:

> *When London surrounds Primrose Hill,*
> *The streets of the Metropolis will run with blood.*[5]

and

> *Carriages without horses shall go*
> *And accidents fill the world with woe*
> *Primrose Hill in London shall be*
> *And in its centre a Bishop's see.*[6]

It is clear that when these lines were written, Primrose Hill stood some way from Central London, which does indeed now stretch for miles around it.

24. Hampstead Heath, NW3

Hampstead Heath is probably the most richly varied and unspoilt of the sacred places of London. In the Middle Ages it was still part of the great forest of Middlesex, inhabited by red deer, wild boar and even wild cattle. Now, only the small Kenwood and Queen's Wood, Highgate, survive.

In this great forest our ancestors lived a nomadic life, moving from one campsite to another as they hunted animals and gathered plants for food. There was a Mesolithic campsite near Leg-Of-Mutton Pond where hundreds of flint implements were found, together with an axe and the postholes of primitive shelters from 8000–6000 BC.[7]

Key:

A   Parliament Hill
B   Boudicca's Mound
C   Kenwood
D   Kenwood Springhead
E   Vale of Health

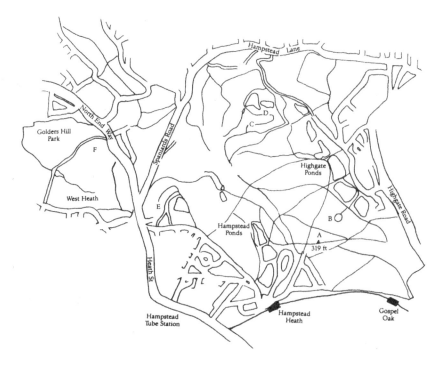

[Figure 27: Map of sites around Hampstead Heath.]

There was also a Neolithic settlement for thousands of years on the west heath from 4000–2000 BC. The sandy soil proved ideal for both crops and for grazing cattle. It is certain that the presence of a settlement would have meant that there were sacred sites close at hand.

Boudicca's Mound

This is a small tree-covered tumulus now surrounded by an iron railing. It is popularly called Boudicca's Mound and is said to be her burial place. This is because of the tradition that Boudicca and 10,000 Iceni warriors were defeated by the Romans at Battle Bridge a couple of miles to the south (Battle Bridge was the earliest name for King's Cross).

This is, however, historically unlikely. According to the Inner London Archaeological Unit, 'The tumulus of Parliament Hill may be a grave mound dating from the Bronze Age. Though a small excavation in 1894 found no evidence of burial, this may be because the body had decomposed without recognizable trace.'[8]

William Stukeley drew the mound, writing below it, 'This is a tumulus on an eminence by Caenwood, which I drew on Mayday 1725. It was the tumulus of some British King before Christianity, probably enough, of Immanuence monarch, here just before Caesar's invasion.'

There is a local tradition that the mound was added to and planted with Scots pine in the late eighteenth century to form a picturesque view.

Parliament Hill

This is one of the highest hills in London (319 feet), and would have given an important view out from the forest, across the northern heights and south towards the City. Elizabeth Gordon in *Prehistoric London* writes:

> The structure of the hill is London clay at its base, gradually changing to a sandy loam. The central boss would appear to have been sculpted from the highest level, since there is a circular terrace still distinct. Half a century ago the sighting lines (somewhat similar to those at Silbury

Hill) and graded slopes were to be traced, but a pathway over the summit and trees planted on the sides have destroyed the original contour. A vestige of the trench remains which once enriched the base, but the spring has been diverted and now forms a series of ponds.[9]

The hill, in fact, sits between the source tributaries of the River Fleet, and thus rises as a primal mound out of the waters below it.

The hill was called Millfields Hill until 1800; however, since sacred hills were the traditional meeting places of tribal leaders, and later of local government, perhaps the name 'Parliament' harked back to this. On the north-east slope there is a stone with an inscription stating that public speaking is allowed. This is popularly called the Stone of Free Speech. Unfortunately the inscription has now been white-washed over.

St Paul, the patron saint of London, is said to have preached from the summit of Parliament Hill. Such a blatant Christianization shows the original importance of the hill, since this legend obviously sanctions a long-held pagan assembly.

The Gospel Oak, which stood nearby, has a similar legend that St Augustine preached beneath it. However, it probably stood on the site of one of the ancient pagan oaks that were common all over Britain:

One of the first acts of Edward the Confessor after his coronation at Winchester was to renew the charter of rights to the citizens of London, seated under the Gospel Oak.[10]

It is notable that these two sacred centres are used to emphasize the civil rights of the 'ordinary' people. This is a memory of a time when such places were for the benefit of all the tribe and that when such harmony existed, the fertility of the land was assured.

Kenwood

This small wood is all that remains of the once great forest of Middlesex. It suffered badly in the hurricane of 1988. There is a natural chalybeate (iron bearing) spring, rising at the edge of Kenwood Lake. At the bottom of Kenwood Farm there is a sculptured wellhead.

The Vale of Health

The name given to an area of the heath supposedly because those who came there were protected from contracting the plague. This cannot have been true, because the area at that time was a malarial swamp. The Vale of Health was probably a gentrifying name given to the area previously known as Hatches Bottom.

25. Highgate, N6

Highgate is one of the most interesting and unspoilt areas of London.

Whittington Stone

On Highgate Hill, a milestone topped by a bronze cat marks the spot where Dick Whittington supposedly heard the bells of St Mary-le-Bow. These summoned him to return to the city that was to make him Lord Mayor.

Lauderdale House

Lauderdale House was built in the 1660s, and Nell Gwynn and Charles II were said to have had one of their many residences there. In 1960 a bricked-up sacrifice was discovered near a first-floor fireplace. This consisted of four mummified chickens, two strangled and two buried alive, and also a strip of plaited rush and a candlestick. These items can now be seen in the Museum of London, and Lauderdale House is open to the public with an exhibition space and regular craft and antique fairs.

The custom of sacrificing animals under or within buildings was once almost universal. Cats, dogs, horses and oxen were all used as foundation sacrifices. They are often found near fireplaces and were perhaps believed to act as guardians of the house. As late as 1913, a cart-horse was buried beneath the terrace foundations of Arsenal football stadium at Highbury in North London.[11]

Queen's Wood

Queen's Wood is one of London's ancient habitats. It is probable that there has been some kind of woodland there since prehistoric times.

Even in the Middle Ages, red deer, wild cattle and wild boar were found in London's forests. Modern pagan revivalists, including the witch Doreen Valiente, held ritual meetings in these woods in the late 1960s and the 1970s.

The Swearing on the Horns Ceremony

Although once a very small village, Highgate has always had many pubs. This is because it was on a cattle drovers' route to Smithfield market, and many would stop here for refreshment. These pubs upheld a custom called 'The Swearing on the Horns', which has existed since at least 1638.

The ceremony seems to be a memory of an ancient fertility rite. Originally each inn in the locality would keep a pair of horns, either those of stags or bulls, and new travellers to the inn would be asked to swear on them and 'kiss a maid', thereafter succumbing to riotous drunkenness (see pages 164–6). Hone's *Everyday Book* states that in 1826 nineteen inns still continued to practise it. By the late nineteenth century, it had fallen out of fashion but was revived in 1898 at The Gatehouse public house and in recent years at The Red Lion and The Sun.

Highgate Cemetery

Highgate Cemetery was opened in 1839. It was built to replace Old St Pancras Churchyard, which had acquired a sinister reputation due to body snatchers and the chronic overcrowding of corpses. The cemetery itself now has the reputation of being one of the most eerie and haunted places in London. Managed by 'The Friends of Highgate Cemetery', an organization formed to help restore it, the feeling of neglect and decay add to its atmosphere.

In the 1970s, Highgate Cemetery became associated with strange incidents. In August 1970 the *North London Press* reported the first of many disturbances there:

Police are investigating the possibility that the headless body found at Highgate Cemetery last week may have been used in black magic rites. Two young girls made the important discovery of a charred woman's body – minus head. The body, which had been buried in

1926, came from a family vault in the catacombs of the old cemetery. Although charred, 'It was very well preserved, like a fossil', a police spokesman said. Two weeks later a man, Allen Farrant, was arrested, carrying a stake and crucifix, with which to destroy the Highgate Vampire. He and other colleagues from the British Occult Society claimed to be keeping watch over the cemetery as they were convinced of a vampire's presence there. Many graves had been smashed and corpses dispersed. In 1974 Allan Farrant was jailed for four years after being found guilty of damaging a memorial to the dead, interfering with a body and sending two 'Poppets', or death spell dolls to two detectives. He was also alleged to have conducted black magic ceremonies in a vault in which a French woman danced naked over desecrated coffins.

26. Willesden – The Black Virgin Shrine and Holy Well
St Mary's Church, Neasden Lane, NW10

There has been a church on this site since AD 938. The original Black Virgin statue was burned during the Reformation, and a modern replacement sits in the Lady Chapel. The well is in the crypt but there is currently no public access to it. Water is available in a glass container adjacent to the statue.

EAST AND SOUTH-EAST LONDON

27. William Blake's Grave, EC1

A stone stands at Bunhill Fields, outside 38 City Road, EC1. It is a memorial to the last resting place of William and Catherine Blake.

The exact location of the grave was recently rediscovered by Luis and Carol Garrido. Since 1965, the exact location had been lost and Blake's grave is still commemorated by a stone that reads 'Nearby lie the remains of William Blake and his wife Catherine Sophia'. This memorial stone is situated approximately twenty metres away from the actual grave site, on the edge of a lawn within the burial ground. It is still unmarked, though plans are afoot to place a marker there.

William Blake, poet and visionary, left his mark on London, which he saw as the place of 'Dark Satanic Mills', grinding the poor into the ground. His vision of the fourfold city (see Chapter 8) transformed London into a myth-haunted place.

28. The Isle of Dogs, E14

The Legend of the Wild Hunt

The name of the Isle of Dogs possibly derives from a fascinating legend. For hundreds of years the site is said to have been haunted by a ghostly huntsman riding through the sky with a pack of phantom hounds. There is a legend attached to this apparition. A nobleman celebrated his wedding by going hunting in the forest at Hainault, which used to cover the island. His bride got lost, and became trapped in a marshy swamp near the river. Both she and her horse suffocated in the quagmire. Her husband also drowned in the bog while trying to find her. Although nothing now remains of the forest, the huntsman and the noise of barking hounds continue to haunt the area.

The legend of the tragic bride and bridegroom was probably an attempt to explain the apparition. The sightings of the huntsman are more likely to be connected with the ancient god of the forest, Herne the Hunter who, along with Arthur and the Norse god Odin, led the

Wild Hunt, (a pack of white hounds with red eyes and ears) across the skies and through the forests. The Wild Hunt also haunts Windsor Great Park. From Island Gardens one can walk through the foot tunnel under the Thames to Greenwich.

29. Greenwich, SE10

Greenwich was an area of great maritime importance, long before its current associations with the British Navy. This must originally have been partly strategic as Greenwich Hill rises out of the Thames at a point where the river narrows. In Roman times the Thames was narrower at this point, and it is thought that there may have been a ford connecting Greenwich to the Isle of Dogs, where the foot tunnel now runs.

There are Bronze Age tumuli in Greenwich Park, which were reused by the Saxons. There are also traces of a large Roman settlement at Greenwich, and the remains of a villa lie among the mounds. It is thought that Watling Street ran diagonally across the park.

In the centre of the park there is an old hollow oak tree, now dead and ivy-covered, surrounded by railings. There is a notice stating that Henry VIII and Anne Boleyn danced around the tree, and that Queen Elizabeth I had tea inside it. Perhaps this was once the location of a sacred oak. In 1902–3, an excavation of Roman remains suggested that there had been a temple to the Roman goddess Diana Venatrix in the park.

There are still a number of interconnecting tunnels beneath Greenwich Hill. These form a drainage system, without which the hill would be marshy. They were used and repaired throughout the Middle Ages, but are originally pre-medieval, probably Roman.

30. Blackheath, SE3

There is evidence of prehistoric occupation on Blackheath (the top of Greenwich Hill). There used to be numerous round barrows there, and also some dene holes. Dene holes were small holes made in the chalk – mysterious, as their function remains unknown. Most collapsed in the 1880s. Nearby at Charlton House, there was at one time a seventeen-acre Iron Age hill fort, though nothing of this remains.

Whitfield's Mount

There is only one round barrow left on Blackheath, between Goffers Road and Mounts Pond Road. It is tree-covered and clearly visible beside a pond. It is named Whitfield's Mount after the famous preacher, who used to gather audiences of up to 20,000 people there. It was a place of free speech, and this usually means it was previously a place of ancient sanctity, like other places of free speech in London such as St Paul's, Tower Hill, Parliament Hill and Tyburn.

Maze Hill, SE10

A straight processional path once led from the top of Maze Hill to a large turf maze that was situated between what is now Wemyss Road and the front of Morden College at Blackheath. According to Elizabeth Gordon in *Prehistoric London*, ridges and depressions could still be discerned here in 1925. It is well known that turf mazes, also known as labyrinths, were built at important sacred centres, and were the focus of local folklore and ritual.

Jack Cade's Cavern, SE10

There is a subterranean cavern hewn out of chalk underneath the bank of Maidenstone Hill, stretching for a considerable distance under the steeply rising ground known as The Point. This cavern is popularly called Jack Cade's Cavern after the famous rebel. The cavern consisted of four irregular chambers, in the furthest of which was a well of pure water, twenty-seven feet deep. The caves are cut out of stratum chalk and flint, and communicate by small avenues. The plan is similar to the so-called Hell Fire Caves at West Wycombe, Buckinghamshire. The main chamber was large: $58 \times 30 \times 12$ feet.

It was rumoured to have a 'Celtic' carving of a horned god within, but this may have been no older than the eighteenth century. A builder accidentally discovered an entrance to the cave in 1780, and the cave was opened up for drinking parties. Unfortunately it has now been sealed off from the public. Its age and original function are unknown. Perhaps like the nearby Chislehurst Caves in Kent, which both possess a well and a pre-Roman altar, Jack Cade's Cavern was used as a place of worship and as a chalk mine.

31. Charlton, SE7

Horn Fair

Charlton in South-east London once celebrated an annual Horn Fair, and to this day is home to a deer park. The legend of the origins of the fair tells of a miller, cuckolded by King John. When caught in the act, the King offered the miller land as far as he could see, which stretched from Charlton to Rotherhithe. There was a condition attached, that once a year, on the anniversary of the event, the miller must walk the length of the land with buck antlers on his head, to the place now known as Cuckold's Point. The story may reflect an act enshrined in the *Carta de Foresta* that saw more land, once held as royal deer-hunting parks, being released to the common people. The Horn Fair may have been a celebration of that. The fair was stopped in 1874 due to complaints about drunkenness and revelry. Daniel Defoe said of it:

> . . . a village famous, or rather infamous for the yearly collected rabble of mad-people, at Horn-Fair; the rudeness of which I cannot but think, is such as ought to be suppressed, and indeed in a civiliz'd well govern''d nation, it may well be said to be unsufferable. The mob indeed at that time take all kinds of liberties, and the women are especially impudent for that day; as if it was a day that justify''d the giving themselves a loose to all manner of indecency and immodesty, without any reproach, or without suffering the censure which such behaviour would deserve at another time.

Charlton House, which stands at the top of a steep hill, was built between 1607 and 1612. It is the finest Jacobean mansion in the London area. Horns in the form of cornucopia, the horns of plenty, adorn a decorative arch at the front of the building.

32. Waltham Abbey and the Eleanor Cross, Essex, EN9

Waltham Abbey, near Epping Forest, is a magnificent Norman church with a rich historical and legendary background.

Legend of the Holy Cross

A carpenter living in the village of Lutegaresbush (now Montacute), Somerset, was told in a dream to go to the hill above the village and dig there. This he did, and found a cracked marble slab. Beneath it a magnificent black stone crucifix was discovered, with an exquisitely carved figure of Christ. The lord of the village, Tovi the Proud, was a high official under King Canute. He owned many estates, one of which was at Waltham.

Loading the cross on to an ox-wagon, drawn by twelve white cows and twelve red oxen, Tovi decided to take it to one of the great religious centres of England. The oxen refused to budge until Waltham was mentioned, so the cross was taken there, and a small church was built to house it. In 1057, the abbey was built on the site of this church, and it was consecrated on 3 May, the day that St Helena was said to have discovered the True Cross. The abbey subsequently housed the relic of the Holy Black Cross, which was said to have worked powerful miracles. The abbey is correctly called Waltham Holy Cross.

King Harold was brought to Waltham after his death at the Battle of Hastings in 1066, and was buried behind the high altar. The abbey was enlarged in the fourteenth and fifteenth centuries, but after the Dissolution of the Monasteries by Henry VIII, much fell to ruin, and what can now be seen is mostly the original Norman building.

The architecture is magnificent and the church atmospheric. The fifteenth-century Lady Chapel survives with one of the original statues of Our Lady, although she is now headless. On the wall is a rare, late-medieval painting of The Last Judgment.

The nave ceiling, executed by Sir Edward Poynter in 1860, depicts the signs of the zodiac, the four elements, the Labours of the Months and Past and Future. The east windows are by the Pre-Raphaelite artist Sir Edward Burne Jones. It is tragic that Waltham's Holy Black Cross has disappeared without trace.

Waltham Eleanor Cross

When Edward III's wife, Queen Eleanor, died at Lincoln in 1290, her body was brought back to Westminster, resting at several sacred places along the way. A special cross, called an Eleanor Cross, was erected at these places. Twelve crosses were made, three of which survive, including the Victorian copy at Charing Cross; the one at Waltham being the only original one left. Eleanor's body actually rested in Waltham Abbey, but the cross stands about two miles away, presumably built on the site of an earlier wayside cross.

33. Epping Forest, Essex

This was once part of the huge Forest of Essex, stretching from Bow in London to Cambridge and Colchester. It is still quite substantial.

After the Norman Conquest the forest became a royal hunting preserve, where poachers were punished with branding, mutilation and sometimes death. Certain parts of the forest were reserved as common land where local people would graze cattle and gather wood. To maintain the right of tree lopping, it was customary for the villagers to enter the forest on Old Winter's Eve, 11 November. The oldest inhabitant of the village would then embed his axe in a branch of one of the trees.

The forest has always been a refuge for vagrants and outlaws, and still maintains a sinister reputation. In the eighteenth century, the feared gangs of 'Waltham Blacks' roamed the Epping neighbourhood, plundering and robbing, their faces blackened with charcoal. At the beginning of the eighteenth century, a hermit, Old Dido, who was renowned for his knowledge of healing herbs, lived in a tent near Hainault. A contemporary of Old Dido was a white witch known as Old Mother Jenkins, the Goose Charmer. Farmers paid her to bless flocks of geese, so that they would fatten and thrive.

There are two first- or second-century hill forts in this area: Ambresbury Banks and Loughton Camp. Ambresbury Banks is said to be haunted by Boudicca and her daughters, and is another of the many places where it is claimed Boudicca was killed.

34. The Birch Well, Epping Forest, E11

A small, muddy path from the birch wood near the Eagle Pond by
Snaresbrook Road leads to this chalybeate spring at Leyton Flats in
Epping Forest. It is known as the Birch Well, set in an egg-shaped
surround among silver birch trees, holly bushes and the sound of
blackbird song. It is now the home to frogs and toads. It was an
important public source of fresh drinking water for local people.
Those outside the parish had to pay a penny for three bucketfuls. It
lies next to an old boundary marker, which indicates it was once a
place of some significance.

35. Camlet Moat
Trent Country Park, Cockfosters Road, Enfield, EN4

An intriguing site first noted by Christopher Street, who declared it
to be King Arthur's Camelot, the site has yet to be fully explored.
Excavations in 1888 and again in 1920 uncovered the foundations of
ruins that appear to be medieval. There is also the possibility that the
site dates back to a much earlier time, though precise evidence for this
remains uncertain. Maps dating from the fifteenth century make no
bones about calling it Camelot, and there was a North, South, East
and West Camelot ranged around the central site, which can still be
walked under the shade of trees.

36. Cross Bones Cemetery, 18–22 Redcross Way, SE1

This curious and almost forgotten place is believed to be the original
site where prostitutes were buried in unconsecrated graves. Its origins
lie in the mists of the past, but it is first mentioned by the historian
John Stow in his *Survey of London* (1598), who wrote:

> I have heard of ancient men, of good credit, report that these single
> women were forbidden the rites of the church, so long as they contin-
> ued that sinful life, and were excluded from Christian burial, if they

were not reconciled before their death. And therefore there was a plot of ground called the Single Woman's churchyard, appointed for them far from the parish church.

By 1769, it had become a pauper's cemetery servicing the poor of St Saviour's parish and it was said that as many as 15,000 people were buried there. Perhaps not surprisingly the graveyard was closed in 1853 because it was too full. It was subsequently sold as a building site, but nothing seems to have ever been built upon it – due in part to the opposition of local people. Excavations between 1991 and 1998 confirmed that a large number of bodies were buried there, many of children or prenatal foetuses. Since 1998 at Halloween (All Souls Night) an annual ritual, started by the contemporary poet John Constable, has taken place at the site, remembering the forgotten people buried there. At the heart of the ceremony, coloured ribbons are tied on to the iron gates to the site and memorials to the dead read aloud. This is one of the most recent traditions in the long history of London.

WEST AND SOUTH-WEST LONDON

37. Cleopatra's Needle, WC2

Cleopatra's Needle was one of two obelisks originally set up in 1450 BC by Pharaoh Thothmes III at the entrance to the Temple of the Sun at Heliopolis in Ancient Egypt. The obelisks were eventually moved to Caesareum at Alexandria, hence their supposed link with Cleopatra. In the nineteenth century one of the obelisks was offered to successive British monarchs. In 1877 'Cleopatra's Needle' was put on a tug bound for England. En route, a terrible storm blew up, during which six sailors drowned, and the obelisk was abandoned. In 1878, the obelisk finally reached London and was erected at its present site on the Embankment, flanked by two Victorian bronze sphinxes. Its companion obelisk was set up in New York. Cleopatra's Needle is considered by many to be cursed. And curiously it has become a focus for more suicides and attempted suicides than at any other stretch of the Thames. The sound of eerie, mocking laughter has been heard echoing across the Thames at this point.

38. Westminster Abbey, SW1

Westminster Abbey stands on what was once an eyot on the Thames, Thorney, or 'Thorn Ey', formed by the forking of the River Tyburn as it flows into the Thames. Like all London rivers apart from the Thames, the Tyburn has now been culverted and can no longer be seen. Offa designated Thorney 'a terrible place'. The legend of King Canute famously attempting to hold back the tides became associated with Thorney Island. Its name is remembered in Thorney Street behind the MI5 building on the Embankment.

Westminster is some way from the centre of the city, and the Abbey was referred to as the 'West' minster as opposed to the 'East' minster of St Paul's. The Abbey has a curious foundation legend. Segbert, King of the East Saxons, built the first church on the site of a pagan shrine. Mellitus, the first Bishop of London who died in AD 624, had converted him to Christianity. Segbert died *c.* AD 610 and was buried in his new church of St Peter's. The foundation legend states that the night before the dedication, St Peter, in disguise, appeared to a fisherman. He requested that this man ferry him across the Thames, which was done. When St Peter entered Segbert's new church, the fisherman saw it seemingly aflame with supernatural lights. Heavenly beings were said to scatter the host, and rich fragrances filled the air. The saint sprinkled holy water and oil, lit candles and consecrated the church. He then revealed himself as St Peter.

Segbert's church and monastery badly needed repairing by the eleventh century, and King Edward the Confessor, one of the last Anglo-Saxon kings, rebuilt it, consecrating it on 28 December 1065. It is a magnificent piece of Early English architecture. When Edward

Key:
A   The Crossing
B   The Cosmati Pavement
C   Our Lady of the Pew
D   Edward the Confessor's Shrine
E   The Stone of Scone
F   St Faith's Chapel

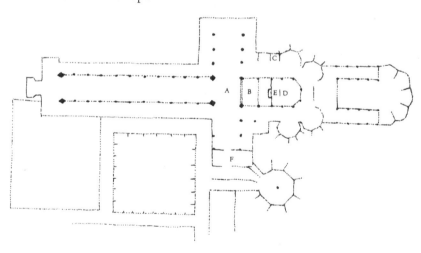

[Figure 29: Plan of Westminster Abbey.]

died on 5 January 1066, he was buried within the church and his shrine is still the central focus of the Abbey. Edward was the only monarch to be canonized.

The first king to be crowned in the Abbey was Harold, on Christmas Day 1066. Previous to this most of the Saxon kings had been crowned at the King Stone at Kingston-upon-Thames. In 1268 King Henry III had the famous Cosmati pavement laid. From that time, all coronations have taken place upon it, which makes its design of the greatest significance. It is a large mosaic square (28.3 feet) made mostly of porphyry and glass tesserae, set into Purbeck marble. The predominant colours are green and pink. The bronze inscriptions, now damaged, read when translated: 'If the reader considers prudently all that is set down, here he will find the end of the *Primum Mobile*.'

The *Primum Mobile* represented a primal act of creation, energy that sent the world into manifestation. The Cosmati pavement is therefore a sacred design representing the created world, holding in the pattern all known history, and also the potential for continual creation.

The Boundary was threefold, each circle signifying three periods of the changing earth. The spherical globe represents the microcosm. This was a way of assessing the time span of the temporal world following traditions in both Classical and Celtic worlds that reckon the ages of created beings in threes. The one referred to here probably went:

> Three times the life of a dog is the life of a horse;
> three times the life of a horse is the life of a man;
> three times the life of a man is the life of a stag, etc.

The Cosmati pavement was covered in carpet for a long time, even during the coronation of Elizabeth II, but it has recently been restored and is now on display to the public most of the time. However, it is still worth checking the website if you are making a special trip to see it.

The Stone of Scone

The monarch is traditionally crowned upon an ancient 'King Stone', the Stone of Scone of Destiny, brought from Scotland to Westminster

243

by Edward I and known as the Coronation Stone. This sandstone block previously rested at Scone, Perthshire, where it had been used in the coronation of thirty-four Scottish kings:

> In the monastery of Scone, in the church of God, near to the high altar, is kept a large stone, hollowed out as a round chair, on which their kings were placed for their ordination, according to custom.
> Fourteenth-century cleric Walter Hemingford

In legend, it is said to be the pillow at Bethel on which Jacob dreamt of the angels. The prophet Jeremiah took it with him on his travels, and a Jewish princess who married an Irish king supposedly brought it to Ireland to serve as their coronation stone. It was taken to Scotland in AD 850 by Fergus, King of the Scots.

On Christmas Day 1950, the Stone of Scone was seized by Scottish Nationalists and returned to Scotland. It was retrieved in time for the coronation of Elizabeth II in 1953 but in 1996 it was returned to Scotland and can be seen among the state regalia in Edinburgh Castle. Rumours still circulate that, in fact, the original is still hidden and the one that was used in the coronation of the present Queen was a copy.

The Throne

The throne is called King Edward's Chair and is named for St Edward the Confessor. The chair was commissioned in 1296 and is the earliest known piece of furniture especially made to house a sacred ceremonial object, the Coronation Stone. All British monarchs since 1308 have been anointed and crowned on this chair, apart from Queen Mary who was jointly crowned with her husband.

The most sacred place in the Abbey is Edward the Confessor's shrine (D). There the throne with the Stone of Scone (E) stood, behind the high altar. At the end of the south transept is St Faith's Chapel (F). This is reserved for private prayer, and has a medieval devotional atmosphere, giving some welcome peace from crowds of tourists.

The thousand-year-old garden of the college of Westminster is an oasis of peace in Central London, and worth seeking out for contemplation and meditation.

The Tothill

A large artificial hill, called the Tothill, once stood on Thorney Island. Nothing remains of it now, but its memory lives on in the names Tothill Street and Tothill Fields. Elizabeth Gordon writes in *Prehistoric London*:

> That the mound was standing in Queen Elizabeth's time is certain, from the following mention of it by Norden, the topographer of Westminster who wrote in this reign 'Tootehill Street, lying in the West part of the City, taketh name of a hill near it, which is called Toote-Hill in the great field near the street.' This hill is marked in Rocque's map (1746) on Toothill Fields, just at the bend in that ancient causeway, the Horseferry Road.

There were many Tot or Toot hills all over Britain. These artificial mounds were ancient places of assembly and local government. The name 'Toot' is sometimes said to be a word meaning breast.

39. Battersea Village, SW11

The present-day 'village' of Battersea was once an island bounded on the north side by the river and surrounded by marshlands. Its earliest known name was written as Batrices Ege – Badric's Isle – though by the time of Domesday it was called Patricesey from which, through various changes, it gained its present name.

St Mary's Church

This church was originally a medieval foundation granted to the See of Westminster by the English Pope Nicholas Breakspear (Adrian IV) in 1157. It was rebuilt in its present form in the eighteenth century and contains several interesting memorials, including one to Benedict Arnold, the American Civil War general.

The church has strong associations with the river and its traffic, and sports two ancient cannon that flank the present-day entrance. It is also notable for the fact that the great poet and prophet William Blake was married here in 1782, to the daughter of a Battersea market

245

gardener. It still retains an air of somnolent quietude, which makes it an ideal place for meditation among the hum of local power stations and the busy scene of nearby Chelsea Reach Harbour (see also Chapter 9).

MUSEUMS OF INTEREST

40. Museum of the Order of St John, St John's Gate, Clerkenwell, EC1

Open every day from 10 a.m.–5 p.m. (Occasional closures for special events. Please check ahead of your visit.) Guided tours at 11 a.m. and 2.30 p.m. on Tuesdays, Fridays and Saturdays.

The Order of the Knights Hospitallers, along with the Knights Templar, were the premier defenders of the Christian kingdoms during the Crusades. Although the Knights Templar were dissolved in 1306, the Knights Hospitallers, because of their emphasis on caring for the sick, continued until Henry VIII suppressed their convent. The Priory of Clerkenwell, the headquarters of the Order in England, was founded in 1140 on open ground outside the City. The original Grand Priory crypt survives, as does a magnificent sixteenth-century gateway, a copy of the original. The museum is comprehensive and fascinating for anyone interested in the Orders of Chivalry.

41. Sir John Soane's Museum, 13 Lincoln's Inn Fields, WC2

Open Tuesday–Saturday: 10 a.m.–5 p.m. Closed Sunday, Monday and bank holidays. Admission free.

This building was designed by the architect Sir John Soane as his home in 1792. It is one of Britain's greatest pieces of domestic architecture. There are numerous small rooms and careful attention has been paid to give each a special ambience. Some are domed, many have carefully placed mirrors, and all are unique in design. It is the perfect setting for an amazing collection of antiquities that seem to grow out of every niche and corner. There is a 'Gothik' monks' cloister containing medieval fragments. There are many Greek and Roman plaster casts, including a superb replica of the cult statue of Artemis from her temple at Ephesus. There is also an Egyptian alabaster sarcophagus of Seti I, beautifully carved with an Egyptian goddess.

42. Museum of London, 150 London Wall, EC2

Open Monday–Sunday 10 a.m.–6 p.m. Closed 24–26 Dec. Galleries begin to close at 5.40 p.m. Admission free.

The Museum of London is the main place to visit for any aspect of London lore and history. It covers every aspect of London's history, but especially of interest in relation to this book are the Roman, Celtic and prehistoric exhibits. There is a comprehensive exhibition of the earliest inhabitants of London and their artefacts and there are votive statues of the Romano-Celtic inhabitants of London. The most impressive of these is the large stone sculpture of the *Matronae*, or *Mothers*. They hold various symbols of nurturing and fruitfulness upon their knees. They hold bread, fruit, a baby, and, unusually, a hound, guardian of the Goddess of London.

Nearby is exhibited the magnificent treasure from the Temple of Mithras. The marble head of the God Mithras shows him as a beautiful solar youth; the head of Serapis crowned by a corn measure shows his connection with fertility and is magnificently carved. This is also home to the wine-jug bearing the inscription *Londini ad fanum Isidis*, which the museum translates as 'At London at the Temple of Isis', one of the oldest remaining objects with the name of London upon it (see also Chapter 3). There are many other items of interest within the museum and frequent important exhibitions.

43. The British Museum, Great Russell Street, WC1

Open Monday–Sunday 10 a.m.–5.30 p.m.

It may seem obvious to include the British Museum here, but this is just a reminder that it contains one of the largest collections of sacred and magical items in the world. It is a place of endless interest. Particularly impressive is the Egyptian sculpture gallery. The site of the museum is interesting in itself, as it is built on a spring of a tributary of the River Fleet.

44. *The Horniman Museum, 100 London Road, Forest Hill, SE23*

Open Monday–Saturday 10 a.m.–5.30 p.m. Admission free.
The museum was founded by Frederick John Horniman, a rich tea merchant, and his daughter Annie persuaded him to install Samuel Liddell Mathers as its curator. Both Annie and Mathers were members of the occult group known as the Hermetic Order of the Golden Dawn, whose other members included the poet W.B. Yeats and the notorious magician Aleister Crowley. Mathers' influence still pervades the museum. It contains an exhibition of shamanic masks, including models of Yoruba magicians from Nigeria. Other African exhibits include medicine vessels and votive figurines.

Other displays include a Hindu section, with the Goddess Kali dancing over the corpse of Shiva in a five-foot high tableau, and a rare pack of Devatara cards, a possible Indian ancestor of the Tarot. There is also an Egyptian section, including a mummy that Mathers is reputed to have tried to bring to life, and a unique item, a Navajo sand painting made by a Native American medicine man. He did not finish the design, for otherwise he would have had to destroy it. Instead it is covered with glass and even the rumble of traffic has yet to blur its fine lines.

Upstairs is a section on divination and magic, with implements from Africa, Australia, China and Europe. This is a remarkable collection and it is hard to imagine more items of magical interest in so small a space.

45. *The Cuming Museum, 151 Walworth Road, Southwark, SE17*

The Cuming Museum houses an extraordinary collection, bequeathed to the people of Southwark by Henry Syer Cuming in 1902. The museum opened in 1906. It was described in Cuming's own words as, 'My Museum illustrative of Natural History, Archaeology and Ethnology with my coins and medals and . . . other curios.'

On 25 March 2013 a fire seriously damaged the museum and library and destroyed some artefacts, including relics dating from the Roman period. The museum remains partially closed for restoration, though a programme of events still takes place. The contents of the museum were moved to alternative locations following the fire. For more information and details of their full programme of events visit: http://www.southwark.gov.uk/info/200162/the_cuming_museum.

46. Dennis Severs' House, 18 Folgate Street, Spitalfields, E1

One of the most extraordinary buildings in London, and a closely kept secret, it was described by its creator (and curator) Dennis Severs (1948–99), as a 'still-life drama' created as an 'historical imagination' of what life would have been like for a family of Huguenot silk weavers. Between 1979 and 1999 Severs gradually recreated what can only be described as a time capsule in the style of eighteenth- and nineteenth-century life. Each room is set up as if the occupants had just left, creating a strangely spooky effect, of which Peter Ackroyd, in his *London, the Biography*, wrote: 'The journey through the house becomes a journey through time . . . it resembles a pilgrimage through life itself.'

Severs left the house to the Spitalfields Trust shortly before his death. It is now open to the public, who are encouraged to participate in a living journey to another time. Brian Selznick's extraordinary novel *The Marvels* describes the lives of the imaginary family invented by Severs. For more information, visit: http://www.dennis-severshouse.co.uk/the-tour/.

45. The Atlantis Bookshop, 49a Museum Street, WC1

Very much part of the hidden history of London, the Atlantis Bookshop was set up by magicians for magicians and has a long and proud history of helping shape the occult landscape for the last ninety-odd years. There is still a thrill to shopping where Aleister Crowley,

Austin Spare, Dion Fortune, Gerald Gardner and W.B.Yeats bought their books. All sorts of lectures, workshops and exhibitions are still held in there. If you are PSI-curious, a committed witch, or in town for the day or exploring inner London, it is well worth visiting this curious link to the living history of magic.

PART III

Stories from London's Past

14

The Brill: Caesar's Camp at Pancras

William Stukeley, October 1758

EDITORS' NOTE: MANY of the spellings of personal names and places are written as they were at the time of Stukeley's essay and do not necessarily equate with the spellings used today.

Many and large volumes have been written on the celebrated city of London, which now, beyond doubt, for magnitude, splendour, riches, and traffic, exceeds every city upon the globe: the famous Pekin of China only boasts itself to be larger. London, then called *Trinobantum*, was a considerable trading *emporium* in British times, and before Caesar's arrival here. But the greatest curiosity of London, and what renders it highly illustrious, has never been observed by any writer: to give some account of it, is the purpose of this paper.

When I resided in London in the former part of my life, I proposed to myself, as a subject of inquiry, for my excursions now and then on horseback round the circuit of the metropolis, to trace out the journeyings of Caesar in his British expeditions. This I account the *aera* from whence we derive the certain intelligence of the state and affairs of our native country. I was pretty successful therein, and made many drawings of his camps, and mansions; several of which I then engraved with a design of printing the copious memoirs I had wrote concerning them.

No subject concerning our own country antiquities could be more noble. But what I mean to speak of at this time, is a camp of his, which I have long since observed no farther off than Pancras church.

In all my former travels, I ever proposed an entertainment of the mind, in inquiries into matters of antiquity, a former state of things in my own country: and now it is easy to imagine the pleasure to be found in an agreeable walk from my situation in Queen's Square, through the fields that lead me to the footsteps of Caesar, when, without going to foreign parts, I can tread the ground which he trod. By finding out several of his camps, I was enabled, off-hand, to distinguish them; and they are very different from all others we meet withal.

It was the method of Roman discipline, to make a camp every night, though they marched the next morning; but in an expedition like Caesar's, in a new and unknown country, he was to trust to his own head, and the arms of his troops, more than to banks and ditches: yet, for the sake of discipline, a camp must be made every night; it was their mansion, and as an home; where was the *praetorium*, or general's tent, and the Praetorian cohorts, as his guards; it was the residence of the majesty of the Roman genius, in the person of the commander; it was a fixed point, subservient to order and regular discipline military; where and whence every portion and subdivision of an army knew their regular appointment and action.

This camp was very small; designed but for a night's abode, unless the exigence of affairs required some stay: but the third part of the army lying under arms every night, prevented the danger of a surprise.

Caesar, led on by divine Providence, entered our country in the year before the vulgar *aera* of Christ 54. The second time, about the middle of the month of July, as we now reckon, in his own Julian kalendar. I shall not recapitulate what I have observed of the footsteps of this great man in Kent; I hesitate not in believing that Carvilius, one of the four kings, as called, who attacked his camp while he was on this side the Thames, lived at Guildford; the name of the place shows it; the river was called *Villy*, or Willy, a common British name for rivers; so that Carvilius was a local title of honour, as was the British custom, like that of our present nobility: so Casvelhan, Caesar's oponent, was king of the *Cassii*, Cogidubnus of the *Dobuni*, Togodumnus of the *Dumnonii, Taeog* being *Dux* in British. It was the method of the British princes thus to take the names of towns, and of people, as it was the method of their ancestors the Midianites; of which we find an instance in Josephus, *Antiq.* iv. 7. Rekam, a king there, of the same name as his city, the capital of all Arabia; now Petra.

Caesar passed the Thames at Coway stakes, notwithstanding the stakes: the town of Chertsey preserves a memorial of his name, as

Cherburg in France: he pursued the Britons along the bank of the Thames as far as Sheperton, where the stakes were placed, and there pitched his camp with the back of it upon the Thames. At his camp on Greenfield common, near Staines, a splendid embassy came to him from the Londoners; desiring his alliance and protection, and that he would restore their prince Mandubrace, who was then in his retinue. To his little camp, or *praetorium*, on this account he orders another to be drawn round it, for reception of these ambassadors, and their prince, together with forty hostages which he demanded, and corn for his army.

Upon this, ambassadors came to him from the *Cenimani*, people of Cambridgeshire; the *Segontiaci*, Hampshire; *Ancalites*, Buckinghamshire; *Bibroci*, about Berkshire; and *Cassii*, of Hertfordshire; submitting themselves to him. For them he orders another appendix to his camp, to receive them.

When business was done with them, he moves forward to attack Casvelhan, who was retreated into his fortified town at Watford. One of his camps thitherward, is to be seen very fair on Hounslow heath, in the way to Longford; which I showed to lord Hertford then president, and to lord Winchelsea vice-president, of the Antiquarian Society, in April, 1723; who measured it, and expressed the greatest pleasure at the sight.

His next camp was at Kingsbury: it is now the church-yard, and still visible enough: its situation is high, and near the river Brent: the church stands in the middle of it.

From hence he went, and forced Casvelhan's military *oppidum* at Watford, and Rickmansworth; a gravelly island of high ground, *sylvis paludibusque munitum*, as he expresses it; and by this he brought Casvelhan to submit. It is not my present purpose to speak largely on these particulars; but from hence he advanced towards London, effectually to settle his friend and ally Mandubrace, whose protection he had undertaken, in the kingdom of the *Trinobantes*; and reconcile him to his subjects, and to his uncle Casvelhan.

Mandubrace was the son of Immanuence, commonly called Lud in the British story, which signifies the *brown*; who was killed by his ambitious brother Casvelhan, too near a neighbour to London; his residence being at Harrow on the hill, and Edgeware called *Suellaniacis* from him: he likewise forced Mandubrace to fly to Caesar in Gaul, to implore his aid: the great Roman was not averse to so favourable an opportunity of advancing his glory, by invading Britain, a new world.

It was not suitable to his honour, or his security, to quarter in the city of London; but he pitched his camp, where now is Pancras church: his *praetorium* is still very plain, overagainst the church, in the foot-path, on the west side of the brook; the *vallum* and the ditch visible: its breadth from east to west forty paces; its length from north to south sixty paces.

This was his *praetorium*, where his own tent was pitched in the centre; the praetorian cohorts around it. There was no great magnificence in Caesar's tent, here placed; it was not his manner. L. Aurunculeius Cotta, who was here present, in his commentaries writes, when Caesar was in Britain, although he had acquired the highest fame by his great actions, yet was he so temperate in his manner of life, such a stranger to pomp, that he had only three servants in his tent. Cotta was killed the next year in Gaul. When I came attentively to consider the situation of it, and the circumjacent ground, I easily discerned the traces of his whole camp: a great many ditches, or divisions of the pastures, retain footsteps of the plan of the camp; agreeable to their usual form, as in the plate engraved: and whenever I take a walk thither, I enjoy a visionary scene of the whole camp of Caesar, as described in the Plate before us; a scene as just as if beheld, and Caesar present.

His army consisted of about 40,000 men, four legions with their horse. After long debate of authors concerning the quantity of a Roman legion, I infer, from Josephus so very often using the expression of ten thousand, many ten thousands, and the like, that the usual and general number of soldiers in a legion was ten thousand.

Authors generally state a legion at 6,666 men; but they just mean strictly the soldiery, without officers or horse: so that I conclude a complete legion of foot and horse to be 10,000. Polibius, Vol. 2, Book iii, writes, in the war of Hannibal, each legion consisted of 5,000, besides the auxiliaries, together with 900 horse; and therefore we may well judge, a legion with its officers should be reckoned 10,000.

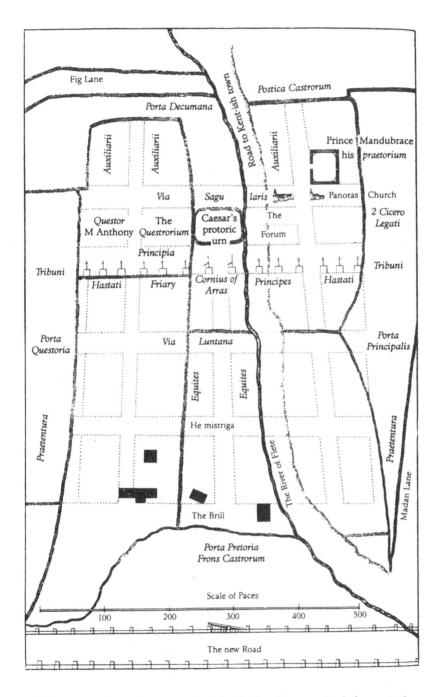

[Figure 30: Caesar's camp called the Brill at Pancras, Stukeley, 1758.]

Romans	5,000
Auxiliaries	4,000
Horse	900
Officers	100
Total:	10,000

Strabo writes the Romans generally had their horses from Gaul.

Caesar had now no apparent enemy; he had leisure to repose his men, after their military toil. He was in the territory of a friend and ally of the Roman state, whom he had highly obliged in restoring him to his paternal kingdom: nor was it his purpose to abide here for any time: he therefore did not fortify his whole camp with a broad ditch and *vallum* for security; but the army was disposed in its ordinary form and manner: it might be bounded by a slight ditch and bank, as that of the whole length of the camp on the west side (the foot-path from the bowling-green accompanying; or it might be staked out with pallisado's called *valli*), which returns again on part of the north side, at the *porta decumana*, till it meets the ditch that passes on the west of Caesar's *praetorium*, and so continued downward, to the houses at the Brill.

This last-mentioned ditch runs on the line that separated the column of the horse from the *Triarii*, on the west side of the camp; the footway from the Brill accompanying it all the way. The *porta decumana* is left open in the back of the camp. The same of the *porta praetoria*; but the bounds of the camp here at the south-west corner are visible in two parallel banks remaining; the upper surface of the earth between them, has been dug away for making bricks.

The oddness of the present division of the north-west pasture, inclosed by that of the *postica castrorum*, preserves evident tokens of the camp: the elbow to the west, concurring with a ditch on the eastern border of the whole camp, preserves the track of the *via sagularis*; here the baggage and carriages were placed: it extended itself behind the *praetorium*. Pancras church stands upon this way.

The north-west field before specified is bounded by a ditch, which marks out the street, that runs along the front of the *praetorium*; along which were set the tents of the officers, the *praefecti* of the horse, and tribunes of the foot; along with the ensigns and standards of the horse and foot, which were pitched in a line in the ground.

On the west side of the *praetorium*, in this pasture, was the open place, a square *area*, comprehended between the *via principalis*, or *principia*, and the *via sagularis*, called the *questorium*: this was the quarters of the quaestor, M. Crassus; a promising young man, who afterwards fell with his father, the triumvir, in Parthia. Pompey married his widow. Hither the soldiers repaired to receive their allowance of pay and provision: on the west side of it was the quaestor's tent, the military chest, the stores: just beyond, northward was the station of Comius of Arras, auxiliary to Caesar, with the Gaulish troops under his command; likewise the tents of the Gaulish princes, which Caesar brought over with him to prevent their revolting in his absence; among whom was the son of Indutiomarus prince of the *Treviri*.

Come we to the *via praetoria*, or principal street of the camp, extending along the middle line from the *praetorium* to the houses at the Brill; where is the *porta praetoria* at the *frons castrorum*. The gate between the two houses at the Brill, leading into the pasture there, which pasture was the station of the horse, is in the very line of the *via praetoria*. The front of the camp is bounded by a spring with a little current of water, running from the west, across the Brill, into the Fleet brook: the lane out of the great road, along this spring, terminates in the *frons castrorum*, as an avenue to it; and may be ancienter than the road along the valley, where the river runs, to Pancras. This Brill was the occasion of the road directly from the city originally going along the side of the brook by Bagnigge; the way to Highgate being at first by Copenhagen house, which is the strait road thither from Gray's-inn lane, and before that of the valley to Pancras, called Longwich in Norden's *Speculum*.

It is not a little remarkable, that the name of *Brill* should through so many ages preserve the sure memorial of this most respectable monument of Julius Caesar's camp. Camden, the Pausanias of Britain, a genius great in his way as Julius Caesar, takes notice, in Buckinghamshire, 'of the ancient Roman burgh, where much Roman money is found, called the *Brill*; which was afterward a royal village of Edward the Confessor's; and, instead of Bury-hill, is by contraction called *Brill*.'

In the additions to Camden's *Britannia*, Sussex, thus we read: 'Hard by Chichester, toward the west, there has been a large Roman camp, called the *Brile*, of an oblong form, four furlongs and two perches in length, two furlongs in breadth: it lies in a flat low ground, with a great ramp and single grass; probably Vespasian's camp, after his landing.' And the like must be said of the Brill in the Netherlands, probably too one of Caesar's camps.

This camp at Pancras has the brook running quite through the middle of it: it arises from seven springs on the south side of the hill between Hampstead and Highgate, by Caen wood: there it forms several large ponds, passes by here, by the name of Fleet, washes the west side of the city of London, and gives name to Fleet-street. This brook was formerly called the River of Wells, from the many springs above, which our ancestors called Wells: and it may be thought to have been more considerable in former times, than at present; for now the major part of its water is carried off in pipes, to furnish Kentish-town, Pancras, and Tottenham court: but even now, in great rains, the valley is covered over with water.

Go a quarter of a mile higher toward Kentish-town, and you may have a just notion of its appearance at that time, only with this difference, that it is there broader and deeper from the current of so many years. It must further be considered, that the channel of this brook, through so many centuries, and by its being made the public north road from London to Highgate, is very much lowered and widened since Caesar's time. It was then no sort of embarrassment to the camp, but an admirable convenience for watering, being contained in narrow banks, not deep: the breadth and depth is made by long tract of time. The ancient road by Copenhagen, wanting repair, induced passengers to take this gravelly valley, become much larger than in Caesar's time. The old division runs along that road between Finsbury and Holborn division, going in a strait line from Gray's-inn lane to Highgate: its antiquity is shown in its name, Madan-lane.

Let us pass the brook, and consider the eastern half of the camp; only remarking, that a ditch at present dividing the two pastures, which was the station of the horse, is continued across the brook and road, to that eastern half of the camp, and marks, when properly continued, the two gates on the west and east side of the camp, called *porta quaeltoria* and *porta principalis sinistra*: below it is the other cross road of the camp, called *via Quintana*.

To the east of the *praetorium* was a square plot, analogous to the *questorium*: this was called the *forum*; this at present includes the church-yard to its eastern fence, with the houses, the grove and kitchen garden precisely. To the east of the *forum* was the quarter of the legates. Sulpitius Rufus, whose coin I have given above, we may justly suppose one of them: he is mentioned by Caesar as his legate in the civil war; all the time with him in Gaul: and we can have no scruple in thinking he was with him in Britain too. The coin is in Goltzius's *Julius Caesar*, but reversed, Tab. ix. I, he gives no explication of it: it is in gold, but imperfect, here supplied. Publius Sulpitius Rufus, mint-master to Caesar, here celebrates a naval expedition of the emperor's; and not unlikely his British. Caesar on a galley with the eagle in his hand: the Genius of Rome follows him. It is said, he was the first of the Romans that leaped on the British shore: finding the soldiers slack in landing, he took a standard in his hand, and went before them. Caesar himself says the standard-bearer of the tenth legion did so.

The coin was struck by him, when governor of some province under Caesar, probably Spain, where at Carthagena, in the Franciscan monastery, remains his monument, thus in Gruter. MCCCCXXIII.

> P. SVLPICIVS Q.F.Q. N.COL.
>
> HIC SITVS EST ILLE PROBATVS
>
> IVDICIEIS MVLTEIS COGNATIS
>
> ATQVE PRIVIGNEIS.

C. Trebonius was another legate, a commander of horse, mentioned B.G.V. 17.

North of the church-yard is a square moted about, in length north and south forty paces, in breadth east and west thirty; the entrance to the west: it was originally the *praetorium* of Mandubrace, king of London, and of the *Trinobantes*. The ditches have been dug deep to make a kitchen-garden for the rector of the church, from whom I suppose in after-times it has been alienated. All the ground of the camp beyond the *via sagularis* was ever allotted to auxiliary troops, and allies.

This honour of a *praetorium* was allotted to Mandubrace, now confirmed in his kingdom, an associate of Caesar's, and friend declared to the Roman commonwealth; and to give him more authority with his own people.

Hither Casvelhan was sent for, and reconciled to his nephew, enjoined not to injure him, as an ally of Rome; assigned what tribute he should annually pay, what number of hostages he should send to him into Gaul: for now he was upon returning, having accomplished all that he proposed, and the time of the autumnal equinox approaching. It was now September, and 54 years before the vulgar Christian *aera*.

To the north of the eastern half of the camp, a bank and ditch marks the outward bound there, in a strait line, and becomes crooked as it goes eastward, just where ends the original northern bound of the camp. To the south, where was the *frons castrorum* at the houses of the Brill, one would reasonably suppose, there might formerly remain much more evident marks of the camp, as it is so far distant from the *praetorium*: there might have been a more considerable *vallum* and ditch quite around the camp, than now anywhere appears; and then it is natural to think, the name of the camp, as called by our Saxon ancestors, the *Brill*, would be fixed to the habitable part, the houses, as now.

In the first field of the duke of Bedford's, by Southampton row, the *vallum* and ditch runs, which was drawn quite round London and Southwark in the civil wars: they afterwards levelled it, and it is now scarce discernible, which is but 100 years ago; Caesar's 1800.

Caesar in his *Commentaries*, B. Gall. iv. 27. writes, the Britons, in asking peace after being vanquished, brought some hostages according to Caesar's command, and promised to bring the rest in a few days, as to be fetched from more distant parts: in the mean time they disbanded their armies; the princes of the country came from all quarters, recommending themselves and their principalities to Caesar. Hence it is obvious, he stayed here many days.

A bank is visible in the pasture between the Brill and end of Copenhagen road, in the south-east pasture, the boundary of the camp: we may discern, it is somewhat oblique, not in a true line with the rest of the *frons castrorum*; but I suppose this owing to the curve of the river eastward to Battle-bridge: they therefore made this bank in a square to the river.

We may observe a portion still visible of the original boundary of the camp eastward, in that part called *latera praetoria*, being at present a watery ditch; and further downward, the foot-path between two banks observes the like direction; and the ground of the *porta principalis*, between them, is open and unfenced.

I judge, I have performed my promise, in giving an account of this greatest curiosity of the renowned city of London; so illustrious a monument of the greatest of the Roman generals, which has withstood the waste of time for more than eighteen centuries, and passed unnoticed, but half a mile off the metropolis. I shall only add this observation, that when I came to survey this plot of ground, to make a map of it, by pacing, I found every where even and great numbers, and what I have often formerly observed in Roman works: whence we may safely affirm, the Roman camp-master laid out his works by pacing. To give some particulars.

The measure is taken from the inside of the ditch, or the line between the *vallum* and the ditch: the space of ground, which the camp-master paces, the workmen throw inward to compose the *vallum*.

The camp on Barham downs contains in breadth thirty paces, length sixty. The camp at Wrotham, in breadth thirty paces, in length forty. At Walton by the Thames, it is a square of fifty paces. The foss here is converted into a mote, as here the *praetorium* of Mandubrace: so the camp at Sheperton is a square of the same dimensions, and the foss turned into a mote, and made an orchard: we observe here at Sheperton the *praetorium* is made on the bank of the river Thames; the *postica castrorum*, beyond the *via sagularis*, neglected. While Caesar was pitched here, the turn of the auxiliaries to be in arms all night, with the other part of the troops, whose duty it was, came on: and the general's intention was but to stay one night in this place; so there was no need to mark out their places in the camp. The stakes placed here in the river, by the Britons against Caesar, were now a sufficient security behind him. Caesar practised the same method when he fought the *Belgae*: passing the river Axona, he placed his camp with the river behind him, that he might not be attacked from that quarter.

Caesar's camp on Greenfield common is forty paces broad, sixty long. Here he received the ambassadors of the *Trinobantes*, desiring their prince Mandubrace to be restored: they bring forty hostages and bread-corn for the army. For their reception another camp is made around this, which is 80 paces broad, 100 long. Another day came in ambassadors from the *Cenimani, Segontiaci, Ancalites, Bibroci*, and *Cassii*. This obliged the camp-master to add the appendix to the camps, which was of the breadth of 100 paces, and equal to the length of the last; 130 in length, stretching out to the east: but in the ground-plot of that camp we see an egregious proof of my position, that they went by paces in marking out their camps; and sometimes by guess-work, in the square; which obliged the camp-master to carry his 130 paces beyond the angle of the former camp. Concerning the method of adding new occasional works to a former camp, we observe a like instance in that camp of Chlorus's between Clarendon palace and Old Sarum; made, we may well presume, on the states of Britain sending their ambassadors hither to him, with submission to his government after the destruction of Allectus.

Caesar's camp on Hounslow heath is very perfect, sixty paces square. His camp at Kingsbury is thirty paces broad, and forty in length.

Come we now to our work at Pancras. The *praetorium* is forty paces broad from east to west, fifty paces long from north to south: the *praetorium* of Mandubrace is thirty paces long from east to west, forty from north to south: thereby it accommodated itself to that part of the camp, that was called *retentura*.

The breadth of the whole camp was 400 paces, not reckoning the valley of the brook: the length of the whole is 500 paces. Examine the intermediate parts, they fall into whole numbers: the breadth of the pasture, comprehending the station of the *Hastati* and *Triarii*, on the west side of the camp, is 150 paces: that of the horse is forty broad: the correspondent, or eastern part of the camp, is likewise 150 paces broad, comprehending the station of the *Triarii* and *Hastati*; so that, subducting the space of the valley where the brook runs, the whole breadth of the camp, where the tents are pitched, contains 340 paces: a space beyond, on each side, of thirty paces wide, is supposed to be left between the tents and the *vallum*, where a camp is fortified: and then the camp contains just 400 paces broad.

The camp is in length 500 paces: the thirty paces beyond, for the way between the tents and *vallum* (where a *vallum* is made), amounts to 560; so that the proportion of length to breadth is as 3 to 2; where strength and convenience is well adjusted, and is often the proportion of Roman cities. This space of ground was sufficient for Caesar's army, according to Roman discipline; for, if he had 40,000 men, a third part of them were upon guard.

The recovery of this most noble antiquity will give pleasure to a British antiquary; especially an inhabitant of London, whereof it is a singular glory: it renders the walk over the beautiful fields to the Brill doubly agreeable, when, at half a mile distance, we can tread in the very steps of the Roman camp-master, and of the greatest of the Roman generals.

We need not wonder that the traces of this camp, so near the metropolis, are so nearly worn out: we may rather wonder, that so much is left, when a proper sagacity in these matters may discern them; and be assured, that somewhat more than three or four sorry houses, is commemorated under the name of the *Brill*: nor is it unworthy of remark, as an evident confirmation of our system, that all the ditches and fences now upon the ground, have a manifest respect to the principal members of the original plan of the camp.

In this camp at Pancras, Caesar made the two British kings friends; Casvelhan, and his nephew Mandubrace: the latter, I suppose, presented him with that corslet of pearls, which he gave to Venus in the temple at Rome, which he built to her, as the foundress of his family. – *Pliny* and *Solinus*.

Mr White of Newgate-street has a gold British coin, found in an urn in Oxfordshire, together with a gold ring set with a pearl.

When Caesar returned, he found letters to him, acquainting him with his daughter Julia's death. – *Plutarch*.

I shall conclude with this observation, that on Caesar's return to the continent, the *Morini*, inhabiting the opposite shore, lay in wait for his men, hoping to obtain great spoils. This was in his first expedition: it shows Britain was not so despicable a country as authors generally make it: much more might they have expected it in return from his second expedition, when the nations of the *Cattichlani, Bibroci, Ancalites, Trinobantes, Cenimani, Segontiaci*, sent ambassadors to him, seeking his favour; all charged with magnificent gifts: and, beyond doubt, the Londoners were not slack, for so great a favour as protecting them from the insults of Casvelhan, and restoring to them their king Mandubrace.

Caesar, having accomplished his purposes here, returned by Smallbury green, in order to pass the Thames again at Chertsey. Smallbury green was then an open place as now, and has its name from his *praetorium*, like this at the Brill: the road lately went round it on the north side; and gravel had long been dug from it, to mend the road; yet I could discern part of it, till, three years ago, they made a new road across the green, and totally ruined the *praetorium*. There is a spring arises at the place.

It is fit we should say somewhat of the city of London, the glory of Britain. Caesar calls the inhabitants of this country *Trinobantes*: it comprehends Middlesex and Essex on this side of the river; Surry on the other. The name of *Trinobantes* is derived from *Trinobantum*, the most ancient name of London: it signifies the city of the *Novii*, or *Novantes*, the original name of the people called *Trinobantes* by Caesar. *Tri*, or *Tre*, in the very old British dialect, imports a fortified city. Many names of this kind still remain, in Cornwall especially.

Noviomagus most certainly is Croydon in Surry. *Magus* in British signifies a city on a down, or heath. Newington on the South of London, and Newington on the north, retain evident remains of the name of the *Novantes*.

In many coins of the great king Cunobeline, nephew of our prince Mandubrace, we have inscribed TASCIO NOVANTVM, meaning the tribute of the Londoners, and of the people *Novantes*, dependent on them, called by Caesar *Trinobantes*.

The *Novii*, or *Novantes*, the original people of this country, knew how to take the proper advantage of the noble river Thames, and built this their fortified city of *Trinobantum* upon a most convenient situation, celebrated by all writers. The inhabitants of this potent city carried on a very considerable trade with the continent, and were rich and flourishing, as those numerous coins of Cunobeline are evidences beyond all exception. *Londinium copia negotiatorum & commeatuum maxime celebre*, says Tacitus. These coins are in gold, silver, copper: I have engraved twenty-three plates of them. Nor, in my opinion, have we reason to doubt of Billings-gate being built by him, as his royal custom-house; and why Ludgate should not take name from Immanuence Lud, father of our prince Mandubrace, I see not.

The business of a society of antiquaries is to separate truth from fable, by evidence, by reason, and judgement. Authors are certainly mistaken in thinking our British ancestors a rude and barbarous people. Need we a further testimony of our continental trade, Caesar speaks of the Gaulish merchants who traded hither: he convened them together to inquire concerning the nature of the country; and I have the strongest reasons in the world to induce me to believe, that Britain was peopled before the opposite continent, by a great and polite nation; and that our British coins are the oldest of any in Europe.

Cunobeline, very young, was carried to Rome by his uncle Mandubrace, four years after Caesar's expedition here, and his restitution to the kingdom of the *Trinobantes*. Cunobeline became well acquainted, and even intimate with Augustus, in the dawning of his power; being about the same age. Augustus entertained a great kindness for him; and he bore a share in his warfare, being praefect of a Roman legion, the XX, VV. called *Cretica*, as Richard of Cirencester informs us; which is the reason that he so often struck the figure of a boar on his British coins, that being the ensign and cognisance of the legion. After he returned, and was king of Britain, he kept up a friendship and correspondence with Augustus, during his whole, and that a very long life. He struck many coins in honour of Augustus, and the plainest imitations of the coins of Augustus. He sent him magnificent presents, paid a tribute to him, built the city of Caesaromagus in compliment to him. He celebrated the Actiac games like those done by Agrippa at Rome, by Herod at Caesarea, and many other states of the Roman empire. By these means he staved off, for his life, an actual subjection of Britain to the Romans.

I cannot agree with my late learned friend Mr Baxter in his derivation of *Trinobantum*, that it is of Belgic original. The word *Tri* or *Tre* of the old Cornish, prefixed, sufficiently confutes the notion: here is none of the Belgic pronunciation, as in the west of England. Caesar's assertion of the supereminent power of the *Trinobantes*, shows they were an aboriginal people: they had indeed been under some sort of subjection to the *callii*, or *Cattichleuni*; but that may have been recent, when Casvelhan invaded them, and slew their king, his brother Immanuence, father to our Mandubrace, as Caesar tells us.

The very name of their neighbours, *Cattichleuni*, confirms our opinion; signifying the clan of the *Cassii*; a most ancient word of the Britons, equivalent to the Latin *civitas*, used by Caesar; still in use in Scotland. Baxter owns the *Cassii* to be of Frisian, or British origin.

This word *Frisian* puts us in mind of the British stories of *Trinobantum* being *Troja nova*, built by the wandering Trojans: so deep rooted among our ancestors is the notion of a Trojan original. I know several foundations that may be assigned for this notion: one seems to come from the utmost source of antiquity, the founder of the British nation, APHER, grandson of ABRAHAM: for which I can bring very large proofs, not so much pertaining to this place. He is the Greek Phryxus, a near relation to Melicerta or Melcartus, the Tyrian Hercules: he founded the Phrygians; he gave name to Africa, and Britain; so that *Phrygii, Frisones*, and *Bryges, Britones, Brigantes*, are all words in different pronunciation meaning the same.

Of it I say no more at present, than that it further illustrates my opinion of the *Trinobantes* being a most ancient, an aboriginal people here; and that their city was fenced about, whether with a wall, or with a *vallum* and ditch, I cannot pretend to say, any more than when it was first called *Londinium*: and it is not my humour to carry conjectures beyond what they will reasonably bear. But I think I am not distant from truth, when I judge the *Novii* to be the same as the *Nubae* of Africa, on the west side the Nile; neighbour to the *Troglodites*, says Strabo: these were neighbours too to the Arabians; the Red Sea between them: natural navigators they must needs be. And Josephus makes the children of ABRAHAM by Keturah to be settled by him in *Trogloditis*, and Arabia the Happy, upon the Red Sea. *Antiq.* i. 15. The colony of these people at Cadiz is always said to come from the Red Sea. Pliny mentions the *Nubaei*, a people of *Arabia Deserta*.

Further, *Novantae* are a people in the west of Scotland, now Galloway. *Novantum promontorium*, the Mull, *Chersonesus*, and *Novaritae*; and the city *Novantia*, north of Severus's wall. The river Nid, in Scotland, is called *Novius*. No reason to think either one or the other of Belgic original, but undoubtedly a colony of our *Trinobantes*.

Josephus, in his xiv. of the *Antiquities of the Jews*, gives us the decree of the senate and people of Pergamus, in favour of the Jews; setting forth, 'Since the Romans, following the conduct of their ancestors, undertake dangers for the common safety of mankind, and are ambitious to settle their confederates and friends in happiness, and in firm peace—'

The decree proceeds as at large set forth by Josephus, and well worthy perusal; concluding, 'That the Jews would remember, their ancestors were friendly to the Jews, even in the days of ABRAHAM, who was the father of the Hebrews; as we have also found it set down in our public records.' Many useful observations may be made from this testimony:

1. We learn hence, mankind at that time, which was but about forty years before the vulgar Christian *aera*, had the same notion of the Romans, as I have enlarged upon in chap. 1. of the *Medallic History of Carausius*. The Romans, for their valour, virtue, fortitude and temperance, were the nation chosen by divine Providence to conquer, polish, and set free, all the world, to prepare for the advent of Messiah.

2. These Phrygians were a colony of the descendants of ABRAHAM by Keturah. At Pergamus the ancient and famous physician Aesculapius had a shop, and practised physic, as Lucian testifies. Midian, the father of Phryxus, APHER, was a great physician, and no other than the Greek Chiron; as I have shown elsewhere: so our Druids, the people of APHER, were famous for medicine. The Genius of physic remained at the place: the famous Galen was born here.

3. These people assert, what they say is written in their public records; so that they had an early use of letters, from the Abrahamic family: our Druids likewise had the use of letters from the same fountain.

4. What they say is confirmed by the Lacedemonians claiming like kindred to the Jews; as we read in Maccabees, xii. 19. 23. and Josephus, xii. 4. 10. Mr Whiston mentions, on this occasion, the testimony of

the Armenian writer, Moses Chorenensis; affirming that Arfaces, founder of the Parthian empire, was of the seed of ABRAHAM, by Kenturah: and thus we find this posterity of the great patriarch, from Britain by sea, to Parthia by land; the extent of the habitable world: and Josephus often mentions his countrymen the Jews exceeding numerous, in after-times, in every country and city throughout the habitable world; which is true to this very day, both in respect to Jews, properly speaking, by Sarah, as well as the Arabians by Hagar, and Keturah: for by these latter all Asia and Africa are at this day peopled: the signal favour of God to the greatest of all men, ABRAHAM.

Return we to the city of *Trinobantum*. I shall mark out the original form, which we may conceive it to have been of, in the time we are writing of. If we look on the plan of London, which I engraved long ago in my *Itiner. Cur.*, we discern the original ground-plot of the oldest part of the city is comprehended, in length, from Ludgate to the present Walbroke; in breadth, from Maiden-lane, Lad-lane, Cateaton-street, to the Thames. This makes an oblong square, in proportion as 2 to 3: I have there made it to be composed of two principal streets, crossing two other principal streets; which makes nine principal quad-rangular spaces, for the habitations, *area's*, and public buildings.

I have reason still to acquiesce in this disposition of the most ancient city of London; as we must suppose it in the time of Immanuence, father to Caesar's ally Mandubrace, whom he now resettled therein. I am very much confirmed in my opinion, by the ground-plot I have lately made of *Caesaromagus*, now Chelmsford, built by Mandubrace's nephew, the great king Cunobeline, to the honour of Augustus, his great friend and ally; for that city was exactly of the same form and disposition.

Hence then we gather, the oldest London was bounded on the west by Ludgate, and the wall there; on the east, by the current or rivulet called Walbroke, coming from the morass of Moorfields; which morassy ground extended to Smithfield, and guarded the whole north side of the city; as the Thames on the south: it is well known, that the Mansion-house stands on a great and deep morassy ditch; that the foundation of it cost a very great sum, in driving piles, and the like, to set the building upon. The city of London is situate much as Alexander projected for Alexandria, between a morass and the sea.

Here was a natural and good boundary on all sides. To the west was a steep cliff hanging over the rivulet of Fleet: its steepness is very considerable now, as may be seen about the Old Bailey, where is at present a flight of steps, through the old wall: in former days it was much more considerable: the other sides had the river and water; so that the spot pitched upon for the city must be reckoned very judicious: the soil a hard and dry gravel.

There is the strongest confirmation for this assignment, deducible from observing three principal roads leading from the gate of Walbroke, at the end of the Poultry, at Stocks market, or the Mansion-house: Cornhill was the great road directly into Essex: Lombard-street conducted to Cunobeline's custom-house, Billingsgate: Threadneedle-street and Broad-street went obliquely toward the north-east, and the present Bishops-gate, and so in later times to the great Roman road called Hermen-street, crossing the Thames where London bridge now is; making a meridian line through the length of the island.

By collating several old plans of London, I discern there were four principal streets running from west to east.

1. The Watling-street, from Ludgate.

2. Thames-street, the boundary toward the river: this on the right hand of Watling-street.

3. On the left hand, Cheapside, Pater-noster row being originally part thereof: at the end of it, beyond the Poultry was the eastern gate of the city.

4. That called Maiden-lane, and Cateaton-street, which was the north-ern boundary of the city, and running along the original wall of it.

This being the first form of the city, its proportion of length to breadth was as 3 to 2. Now, for the cross streets, I conceive one to have been that of St Martin's lane from Aldersgate continued downward to Paul's wharf: the next was from Aldermanbury and Bow-lane, to Queen-hithe: the other, Walbroke to Dowgate, or Watergate, being the outfall of the rivulet; boundary of the eastern wall of the original city, as in the time of Mandubrace. The street which accompanied the western wall, on the inside Ludgate, is quite absorbed by houses at present.

There might then have been many lesser cross streets both ways, of which we cannot now take any account, our purpose being to consider it only in the great; but there are many collateral indications of the justness of our alignment: it would be a trifling minuteness to push conjectures farther, than to observe the gate on the south side was at Queen-hithe.

Thus we see a great conformity between old London and Cunobeline's *Caesaromagus*, especially as to the general distribution and design; the four gates of the sides corresponding to different streets obliquely.

Afterwards, when the Romans became possessed of the island, and made the great roads across the kingdom, three of them had respect to this metropolis, but none went precisely through it; and such was often their method. The Watling-street, from Chester to Dover, came by Tyburn, crossed the Thames at Stanegate, by Lambeth, and so to Shooters' hill: this is crossed at Tyburn by another equally strait, but unnoticed by any writer, reaching across the kingdom from Chichester to Dunwich in Suffolk: I call it *via Iceniana*: it goes by Old-street north of the city, and is the high road of Essex to Colchester; but, when the Romans found it useful to enlarge this city by a new wall, they made a branch to proceed from St Giles's, which we call Holborn, and so built a gate at Newgate, and continued the road to Cheapside.

A third road is the Hermen-street from the sea-side in Sussex to Scotland: it went by Bishops-gate, but on the eastern and outside of the city, till its enlargement; and that enlargement was done by Constantine the Great, or by his mother the empress Helena, our country-woman: and we may well credit the reports of the Britons concerning this matter. Then it acquired the title of *Londinium Augusta*: then it was that the Tower was built; an *armamentarium*, as the castle of Colchester, of the same manner and mode of building, Roman brick and stone; a chapel with a semicircular window, as Colchester, and dedicated to St Helena. This in aftertimes; but in regard to the age we are treating on, that of Caesar and our aboriginal

Britons, it is a just enquiry, after we have given the plan of primitive London of the *Novantes*, where may we suppose their temple to have been? For assuredly we must pronounce, that, whenever the ancients built a city, they certainly took care to erect a temple for divine worship.

In answer to this enquiry, we are to reflect, that the Britons were under the ecclesiastic regimen of the Druids, who were of the patriarchal religion, the religion indeed of ABRAHAM: for they came from him. We find in sacred writ, wherever he removed from one country to another, 'there builded he an altar to Jehovah, and invoked in the name of Jehovah', who sometimes personally appeared to him: consequently we must infer *Jehovah* to be the Messiah, or Son of God, in an angelic form.

Other times ABRAHAM removed into a country abounding with groves of oak; sometimes he planted a grove of oak for religious purposes, as a temple. All these things the Druids did; they built such open temples as the great patriarch; they used oak-groves, or planted oak-groves as temples: we cannot say that Jehovah appeared personally to them; yet we may well think they were sometimes vouchsafed the spirit of prophecy, and particularly in regard to Messiah, who they knew was to be born of a virgin, and likewise was to be born at the winter solstice, whence their famous misleto solemnity.

Moreover, at Chartres in France, which was the place of the principal meeting of the Gaulish Druids, there is now a magnificent church, built upon the spot where then was that most celebrated open temple: for the Druids very easily passed over into christianity; the transition was but natural. This church is dedicated to the Mother of God, as they there style the virgin Mary: there is under it a chapel cut in the rock, with a flight of stairs descending to it: on the door of the frontispiece is this inscription in Latin:

To the Virgin who bears the Child.

I apprehend this to be analogous to the caves of Mithras in Persia; for *Mithras* is Mediator, or Messiah; and they say there, that Mithras was born in such a rocky cave; and they worship him therein. Both the ancient Persians and the Druids, who were of the same patriarchal religion, had the same notion of the Messiah to be born in the rocky stable at Bethlehem.

We have many instances of Druid men and women endowed with the spirit of prophecy. I shall mention but one, out of Josephus, *Antiq.* xviii. The Jewish Agrippa fell into the displeasure of Tiberius, who put him in bonds. As he stood leaning against a tree before the palace, an owl perched upon that tree: a German Druid, one of the emperor's guards, spoke to him to be of good cheer, for he should be released from those bonds, and arrive at great dignity and power; but bid him remember, that when he saw that bird again, he should live but five days. All this came to pass: he was made king by Caligula; St Paul preached before him: Josephus speaks of his death, agreeable to the prediction. But concerning the Druids, I have before now opened my mind largely, in some papers read at the Antiquarian Society; wherein I have sufficiently vindicated them from the imputation of paganism and idolatry.

As to the temple belonging to the city of *Trinobantum*, or London, we may be assured, they erected no temple within the city. When the Romans became masters here, they built a temple of their own form, to Diana, where now St Paul's stands: they placed it in the open space, then the *forum*; but the British temple, appropriate to the city, was upon the open rising ground to the west, where now is Knave's-acre. The name of the place both gives a very good foundation to my opinion, and also at the same time acquaints us with the particular form of the temple: for the Druids, as I have shown, had three kinds of temples, of the patriarchal mode.

1. The round, or circular work of upright stones, innumerable to be seen.

2. The serpentine temple, or a snake transmitted through a circle; as those of Abury and Shap.

3. The alate, or winged temple, composed of a circle and wings: and this was the sort of temple here placed; of which the name of *Knave's-acre* is a sure memorial. This was made only of mounds of earth, in Latin *agger*, thrown out of the ditch camp-fashion: this word is

corrupted into *acre*. The word *knave* is oriental, *canaph*, volavit; the *Kneph* of the Egyptians; by which they meant the Deity, in the most ancient times, before idoltary prevailed.

The form of our alate temple here exactly corresponds with that now to be seen on Navestock common, Epping forest; which name of *Nave-stock* preserves its memorial, meaning the sacred tree by the alate temple: it is composed of mounds of earth and ditch; as ours was at *Knave's-acre*.

Observe, the word *agger* remains at Edgeware, the *Suellanacis* of our king Casvelhan, uncle to Mandubrace: it is the Roman road called Watling-street. Egham by Stanes acknowledges the like derivation, being upon the *via Trinobantica* at Stanes, the *Ad Pontes* of the Romans. Many more like instances I could give.

These sort of temples were properly dedicated to the Divine Spirit, the author of motion, which moved upon the face of the new-created matter, as Moses writes, and were more particularly assigned to the religious festivity celebrated at the summer solstice, when the pigeon was the first and peculiar sacrifice of the season. I shall not speak more about them here: but besides this temple, the Britons had a magnificent *cursus*, or place for sports and races on foot, in chariots, on horseback, when they celebrated their public sacrifices and religious observances on the solstices and equinoxes.

These *cursus*'s were likewise made of mounds of earth thrown up in two parallel lines: such a one is that at Leicester in the meadow near the river; it is called *Rawdikes*, from the ancient name of the city, *Ratae*, capital of the *Coritani*: such another there is, called *Dyke-hills*, in the meadow of Dorchester, Oxfordshire, where the Tame and the Isis unite; *Dobuni*.

Exactly such another, belonging to our *Trinobantum*, is that we call *Long-acre*, or *agger*; which, we may be confident, was originally two parallel banks, the whole length of that street, and breadth: it has the same gentle sweep, or curve, as those other *cursus*'s: It then commanded a beautiful prospect over the present Covent-garden to the Thames, and an extensive view, both upward and downward, of the river, and into Surrey. The banks were designed for the spectators, and admirably well adapted to the purpose.

So that we may justly conclude, Knave's-acre was the proper temple to the city of *Trinobantum*, and Long-acre their solemn place of races, accompanying the religious celebrations of the ancient citizens here, in the time of Caesar. Long-acre is 1,400 English feet in length, which is exactly 800 Druid cubits, two furlongs of the east, two *stadia*.

Give me leave to mention my fancy or conjecture of the founder of this alate temple and *cursus*, viz. ELI, father of Immanuence, and of Casvelhan: there was his *tumulus* on Windmill-street edge, at the end of Piccadilly: a windmill was erected on it in after-times. From it descends the street called Hedge-lane, from *agger*, the *tumulus*. I suppose the name of *Piccadilly* may be from its elevation, a Hybrid word composed from *peak cad Eli*, the *tumulus ducis Eli*. *Cad* is a common name of the Welsh kings.

Westminster, in Druid times, was a great wood, called afterward Thorney-isle, where they celebrated the autumnal Panegyre. Mr Denman, a brass-founder, told me of three brass Celts dug up very low in the foundation of the Sanctuary at Westminster, which he melted; they were of whitish metal: also two more of the like, dug up in the bottom of the Thames, on digging the foundation of Westminster bridge, which he melted.

I shall only add a few observations, more than what is already done, concerning the plan of the oldest city of London. Where now is St Paul's was the *forum*, or market-place, comprehending the square *area* between Cheapside, the Old 'Change, Watling-street, and where now is the west end of St Paul's. The highest end of the city, was the north-west corner, guarded by a steep precipice, where Maidan-lane is, which imports as much. The north side of the city had a deep ditch, always filled with water from the morass of Moorfields and Smeethfield, now Smithfield. From hence the name of Lade-lane; for *lade*, in Saxon, is an artificial ditch, or drain: and this discharges the vulgar opinion of Ludgate taking its name from the river Flete, as if *porta flumentana*. Now we may well assert Dowgate to be truly such, the Water-gate.

Our Saxon ancestors had some remembrance of the enlargement of London walls, by their naming of Aldgate, and Aldergate, as sensible of the priority of one in date. It was AD 450, that they beat the Scots at Stamford, which is but little more than 100 years from the time of Constantine the Great, when these walls were built, and the title of *Londinium Augusta* commenced. That the city-walls were made by the empress Helena, is strongly confirmed by the history of the recovery of Britain to the Roman empire by Constantius Chlorus: for Asclepiodotus his general fought the Britons under the dominion of Allectus, under the old walls of London, at Walbrook, then the eastern boundary of the city, as historians particularly recite; and we may easily believe Cornhill to have been originally without the city, where the waggons stood that brought it.

The historians likewise tell us, that the first palace of the British kings was in the south-west corner of the city, where afterwards Baynard's castle stood, which likewise became a palace of our kings, before Bridewell was built: but when the empress Helena built the walls of the enlarged city, which walls for the most part now remain, the palace was then the present tower. Lastly, I apprehend, the oldest city which we are describing was walled about; for I cannot allow the Britons to be any wise inferior to the Gauls in art, either military or civil. When the city was enlarged and encompassed with new walls, the three roads beyond the east gate were converted into streets, as at present, Threadneedle-street, Cornhill and Lombard-street; as well as the Roman road, Gracechurch-street.

15

London in the Time of Arthur

Lewis Spence

W E NOW REACH what may be described as the Arthurian Age
of legendary London, in which the outstanding figures of
Arthurian romance, the great King himself, Guinevere and the
Knights of the Round Table all make their appearance in the city on
several occasions and in connection with various adventures. As we
shall see, most of these are not always among the most celebrated
episodes in the Arthurian story, Caerleon-upon-Usk sharing with
London the body of tradition which wove itself around the figure of
the great British deliverer, because of its close associations with
Celtic sentiment and its proximity to Celtic centres in the West. But
I feel that the very circumstance that London appears at all in
Arthurian tradition is due not so much to the fact of the later importance of the place, which might be regarded as having attracted that
tradition to itself,, as to the genuine character of the folk-belief which
held that London had at one period in its history maintained a position and reputation as the nucleus of the Romano-British struggle
against the Saxons during the century betwixt the years AD 430 and
530.

If Vortigern, Vortimer, Aurelius Ambrosius, and Uther employed
London as a base of operations against the Saxons, it follows that
Arthur must also have done so; indeed we have seen that Professor
Parsons is of opinion that some of these leaders certainly conducted
operations from London, while other authorities entertain the belief
that the prevalence of piratical conditions on the Thames led the
Romano-Britons to undertake 'police-work' on a large scale under
Ambrosius and Arthur in an endeavour to extirpate those river
banditti. If we are to believe in an Arthur at all – and modern criticism is at least affectionate to the belief in his personal reality as a

Romano-British champion – we cannot dissociate him from London, the head and front of the fifth-century stand against the Saxons.

As regards the personal authenticity of Arthur, it is unnecessary in this place to add much to the growing body of matter associated with this theory, but I may be permitted to point out the probable existence of an Artorian clan or gens in Roman Britain from which the hero-king may possibly have sprung. It will be recalled that both Nennius and Geoffrey of Monmouth allude to a great continental expedition made by Arthur, in which, after vanquishing Gaul, he proceeded to the overthrow of Rome. The account appears to be a legendary one, with some slight basis of actual historic likelihood.

Lucius Artorius Castus, a Roman general stationed in Britain, certainly commanded a special expedition sent across the Channel to suppress an insurrection in Brittany. He took with him a picked force of legionary cohorts and cavalry regiments. The fact of a Romano-British force having been sent for the first time to fight on the Continent, and the resemblance of its Roman commander's name to that of the British hero, may possibly have afforded a foundation for the later tradition that Arthur himself invaded Europe. Moreover, Artorius was appointed by the Emperor Probus to the command of the Sixth Legion at Eboracum, or York.

There is, however, some slight dubiety regarding the date of the Roman Artorius, who, it was formerly believed, flourished about the third quarter of the third century. Professor J.B. Bury has given it as his opinion that the expedition in question took place about the era of Magnus Maximus (AD 380–390). The choice of Artorius was due to his previous naval experience, as he had formerly held the post of Praepositus, or flag officer, of the coast flotilla at Misenum. This would seem to be the origin of the tradition that Arthur held the post of 'Count of the Saxon Shore', that is the coastal district of Britain most commonly attacked by the Saxon pirates.

With the mention of Merlin we encounter one of the most obscure yet most interesting problems in British legend. Certain modern critics have recently put forward the theory that the greatest figure of the Arthurian saga, save Arthur alone, is merely an invention of Geoffrey of Monmouth and nothing more. Here I must deal with him mainly so far as he is associated with the legendary side of London, the question of his origin and status demanding much more than the space which can be afforded it.

On the death of Vortimer, says Geoffrey, Vortigern was restored to his kingdom, and at the entreaty of his Saxon wife Rowena sent messengers to Germany, to which Hengist had betaken himself in flight, begging him earnestly to return. The Saxon chief complied with the request, but brought with him an army of such embarrassing dimensions that the princes of Britain were naturally greatly alarmed and resolved to give him battle. In order to lull them into a sense of security the evil Vortigern and his ally arranged the fatal rendezvous at Stonehenge, which ended in the massacre of so many Britons of eminence.

Vortigern, himself terrified at the result, consulted his magicians as to his personal safety. As he had lost all his strongholds, one by one, by siege or battle, they advised him to build a tower of exceptional strength on Mount Eryri. But as the work proceeded it was nightly interrupted by some supernatural agency, the foundations being engulfed as though by a subterranean upheaval. Vortigern's soothsayers assured him that only by seeking out a fatherless boy, slaying him and sprinkling his blood on the foundation stones could he proceed with the building of the tower. At once he dispatched messengers throughout the kingdom in search of such a lad, and after a toilsome quest they succeeded in finding him through the chance remark of a companion, who taunted him with ignorance of his father. Learning that his mother was a nun and a daughter of the King of Demetia, but that his father was unknown, they brought him to Vortigern.

But the lad, whom Geoffrey now calls Ambrosius Merlin, convicted Vortigern's wizards of ignorance and assured him that the real cause of the nightly disturbance of the foundations was the presence of two dragons beneath the spot, which strove mightily and in their struggles overthrew the structure. Vortigern ordered excavations to be made, discovered the monsters lying couchant beneath the foundations, and all regarded the young Merlin as surpassing in hidden wisdom.

At this juncture Geoffrey halts in his narrative and announces that as many men in authority had entreated him to make public the wonderful prophecies of Merlin he had agreed to do so, and he then provides a long account of the same, which, he tells us, is 'translated out of the British'. Here I must confine myself to those which deal with the city of London, but I think it is evident from the language Geoffrey employs in his 'preface' to these prophecies that he was concerned with actual traditional material and was not inventing a fabulous series of oracular and symbolic statements.

He makes Merlin, in the course of his long prophetic deliverance, voice eight separate predictions regarding London. The first of these is connected with the archbishopric of London, which, he says, will 'adorn Dorobernia', that is Canterbury. This, of course, was a retrospective prophecy, but it seems to reveal that a sense of the inappropriate still lingered in Geoffrey's time concerning the transference of metropolitan power to the Kentish area.

The next prediction is greatly more obscure. It reads:

Then shall the calamity of the White be hastened and that which is builded in his little garden shall be overthrown. Seven sceptre-bearers shall be slain, and one thereof shall be canonised a saint. Children shall perish in the wombs of their mothers, and dread shall be the torments of man that thereby may they that were born in the land be restored unto their own. He that shall do these things shall clothe him in the brazen man, and throughout many ages shall keep guard over the gates of London sitting upon a brazen horse.

I take this to refer to Cadwallo, who, as we shall see, waged terrible war against the Saxons for forty years and whose ashes were placed in an image of him mounted upon a brazen horse at the West Gate of London (Ludgate). The expression 'the White' refers to the white dragon of the Saxons, the red symbolizing the Britons.

The third prophecy states that:

From Conan shall issue forth the warlike Boar that shall try the sharpness of his tushes within the forests of Gaul. For the greater oaks shall he stub short each one, but unto the smaller shall he grant protection. The Arab and the African shall be adread of him, for even into furthest Spain shall sweep the swiftness of his career. The He-goat of the Castle of Venus shall succeed, having horns of gold and a beard of silver, and a cloud shall he breathe forth of his nostrils so dark as that the face of the island shall be wholly overshadowed. There shall be peace in his time, and the harvests shall be multiplied by the bounty of the soil. Women shall become serpents in their gait, and all their steps be full of pride. The castles of Venus shall be builded new, nor shall Cupid's arrows cease to wound. Every fountain shall be turned into blood, and two Kings shall encounter in nigh combat for the Lioness of the ford of the staff. Every soil shall riot in luxury, neither shall mankind cease to follow after lust. All these things shall three ages see, until the buried Kings be brought to light in the city of London.

The Conan here alluded to is, of course, Constantine, the father of Aurelius Ambrosius, who is the 'warlike boar' of the prophecy, and was brought up in Brittany by Budec, its King, on whose behalf he tried 'the sharpness of his tushes within the forests of Gaul' against the enemies of his foster-father. The 'greater oaks', Vortigern and Hengist, he 'stubbed short', while, as we shall see, he spared the lesser Saxons. His fabled conquest of the mythical African King Gormund, who had settled in Ireland, accounts for the allusion to 'the Arab and the African'. I would identify 'the He-goat of the castle of Venus' with the later King Maelywn, an able but vicious monarch. The 'buried Kings of London' were, of course, Belinus, Lud, Vortimer and Cadwallo.

The fourth prophecy reads:

Thereafter shall a tree rise up above the Tower of London, that thrusting forth three branches only shall overshadow all the face of the whole island with the spreading breadth of the leaves thereof. Against it shall come the North wind as an adversary, and an evil blast thereof shall tear away the third branch, but the two that shall remain shall occupy his place until the one shall bring to nought the other by the multitude of his leaves. But when this shall be, then shall he himself hold the places of the twain, and offer sustenance unto birds from the lands that are without. And it shall be accounted hurtful unto native fowl, for they shall lose the freedom of their flight by reason of their dread of the shadow thereof.

284

The 'tree' that is to overshadow the Tower of London is certainly an allusion to the three sons of Constantine, 'the three branches', one of whom, Constans, is destroyed by 'the North wind', that is, the Picts, the other two, Ambrosius and Uther, surviving, Uther in time alone remaining.

Later on we are told that 'London shall mourn the slaughter of twenty thousand', 'that a maiden shall carry the bulwarks of London in one hand and the forest of Caledon in the other', and that in the days of 'a fox from the mountains a serpent shall encompass London with his length'. The 'slaughter of twenty thousand', refers, I think, to the battle of Creganford, in which the Britons lost heavily and fled for protection to London. The maiden who held the bulwarks of London in one hand and the forest of Caledon in the other was presumably that Anna or Margawn, sister of Ambrosius, who married Lot, King of Lothian in Scotland, and became the mother of Modred, while the 'serpent which would encompass London with his length' could scarcely have been other than 'the coiling Saxon serpent' of the Welsh Triads or traditions.

So far as I am able to discover, Merlin has little or no association with London except as regards the prophecies he made referring to it, nor am I here concerned further with him except that it may be said in passing that he appears to have been confused by Geoffrey with the boy Ambrosius alluded to by Nennius as having cleared up the mystery surrounding Vortigern's castle. Indeed, Geoffrey in one passage refers to him as 'Merlin Ambrosius'. He may have received this name as having been, according to some ancient Welsh traditions, the bard of Ambrosius, that is 'Merlin of Ambrosius', or 'Ambrosius' Merlin', while the name Merlin itself may arise from the tradition that his birthplace was Caermarthen, its Welsh pronunciation being 'Myrddin', that is 'Myrthin'. For me Merlin is the traditional magician and not a 'god' as Rhys and others appear to think.

All this time the two sons of Constantine, Aurelius Ambrosius and Uther, afterwards called Pendragon, were in the care of King Budec of Brittany, who brought up both to be valiant knights. On one occasion Merlin, in the presence of Vortigern, prophesied their return to Britain. Shortly afterwards they landed at Totnes and their fellow-countrymen joyfully gathered about them. Their first duty was to avenge the death of their brother Constans upon Vortigern, and, following him to his stronghold in the West country, they beleaguered it and gave it to the flames, so that Vortigern and all his company were consumed within its blazing walls.

Aurelius Ambrosius next turned his arms against Hengist and the Saxons, over whom he triumphed in many battles. After one of these victories, that over Hengist at Aylesbury in the year 455, he appears to have entered London, at that time in the hands of the Saxons, as both Hector Boece and 'Tysilio' relate. With great magnanimity he spared the enemy within its walls, and deported them *en masse* to Germany. Finding the churches in sad disrepair, he restored them, filled them once more with priests, broke the idols which the Saxons had placed on their altars, and commanded a day of rejoicing for the city's restoration to British rule. The churches and houses on this occasion were decorated with flowers and the streets with tapestries, while triumphant music resounded through the city ways. Ambrosius, says Boece, had been aided in his conquest of the Saxons by Lot, King of the Picts, and Conrannus, Governor of the Scots, and these chieftains he feasted right royally, and gave them his two sisters in marriage. One of these, Anna, who married Lot, became the mother of the traitor Modred.

This appears to have been Aurelius' sole appearance in London. According to Geoffrey he built Stonehenge – an ascription only about thirteen hundred years out of date – and in the end was poisoned by a creature of Pascentius, the son of Vortigern, who represented the British party, as opposed to the Roman faction of Aurelius. Aurelius was buried at Winchester. He is known in the Welsh Triads and chronicles as Emrys, a Celtic corruption of his Roman name.

Uther Pendragon, the brother of Aurelius Ambrosius and father of Arthur, assumed the leadership now rendered vacant by the murder of his kinsman. The beginning of his rule was marked by a strange heavenly portent. Says Geoffrey:

> There appeared a star of marvellous bigness and brightness, stretching forth one ray whereon was a ball of fire spreading forth in the likeness of a dragon, and from the mouth of the dragon issued forth two rays, whereof the one was of such length as that it did seem to reach beyond

the regions of Gaul, and the other, verging toward the Irish Sea, did end in seven lesser rays.

At the appearance of this star all that did behold it were stricken with wonder and fear. Uther, also, the King's brother, who was leading a hostile army into Cambria, was smitten with no small dread, insomuch as that he betook him unto sundry wizards to make known unto him what the star might portend. Among the rest, he bade call Merlin, for he also had come along with the army so that the business of the fighting might be dealt with according to his counsel. And when he was brought unto the King and stood before him, he was bidden declare what the star did betoken.

Whereupon, bursting into tears and drawing a long breath, he cried aloud, saying: 'O, loss irreparable! O, orphaned people of Britain! O, departure of a most noble King! Dead is the renowned King of the Britons, Aurelius Ambrosius, in whose death shall we all also be dead, save God deign to be our helper! Wherefore hasten, most noble Duke Uther, hasten and tarry not to do battle upon thine enemies! The victory shall be thine, and King thou shalt be of the whole of Britain! For that is what yon star doth betoken.'

Merlin translated the symbol as having reference to the death of Aurelius and Uther's accession. In memory of the event Uther caused the dragon to be wrought in pure gold, after which he came to be known as 'Uther Pendragon' in the British tongue, that is to say 'Uther of the Dragon's head'.

In this connection I am of opinion that the tradition of the British dragon may possibly be reflected in the supporters of the arms of the city of London, sometimes heraldically styled as 'griffins', at others as 'dragons'. The city coat-armour is, moreover, surmounted by the crest of a dragon's ribbed wing. There is good evidence that the coinage of the early British tribes, particularly that of the Iceni, contained several pieces on which a dragon or griffin was displayed,[1] and it seems to me not at all improbable that this figure may have been employed as a cognisance by the early British rulers who had their seat in London. As we have seen, Professor Parsons is of opinion that Vortigern and Aurelius Ambrosius 'must have used London as a base', and this would naturally also apply to Uther. Beale Poste[2] states that the title 'Pendragon' was 'conferred in its fullest extent on Constantine', the father of Aurelius and Uther, and thinks that it implied the ruler- ship of all Britain, 'latterly being merged in the appellation of King of Wales'. Still there seems to be evidence of a kind that the actual title of the Kings of Britain was 'Brennin Prydain Oll', that is 'King of all Britain'.[3]

Having beaten Octa and Ebissa, the kinsmen of Hengist, Uther hauled them to London and imprisoned them there. 'And when the Easter festival drew nigh, he bade the barons of the realm assemble in that city that he might celebrate so high holiday with honour by assuming the crown thereon. All obeyed accordingly, and repairing thither from the several cities, assembled together on the eve of the festival. The King, accordingly, celebrated the ceremony as he had proposed, and made merry along with his barons, all of whom did make great cheer for that the King had received them in such joyful wise. For all the nobles that were there had come with their wives and daughters as was meet on so glad a festival. Among the rest, Gorlois, Duke of Cornwall, was there, with his wife Igerne, that in beauty did surpass all the other dames of the whole of Britain. And when the King espied her amidst the others, he did suddenly wax so fain of her love that, paying no heed unto none of the others, he turned all his attention only upon her.'

Exasperated by Uther's conduct, Gorlois quitted London without taking leave of the King, whereat Uther commanded him to return so that he might punish him for the affront. But Gorlois treated the command with contempt and shut himself up in his castle of Duniloe in Cornwall, placing his wife in the more secure fortress of Tintagel so that Uther might not be able to carry her off. The story of the manner in which Uther gained access to Igerne and became the father of Arthur in the likeness of Gorlois, through the magical powers of Merlin who transformed him into the semblance of her husband, requires no repetition. Layamon and Matthew of Westminster practically follow Geoffrey in their accounts of this affair. Later Uther fell mortally sick and died at London, says Malory, some two years after the birth of his son Arthur.

After the death of Uther, says Geoffrey, Arthur was crowned King of Britain. Malory, in his *Morte d'Arthur*, makes no doubt that Arthur was crowned in London. 'The Archbishop', he says (and it is remarkable how the tradition that London was anciently a metropolitan see runs through medieval romance):

the Archbishop, by the advice of Merlin, sent for all the lords and gentlemen-of-arms that they should come by Christmas even unto London. And many of them made them clean of their life, that their prayer might be the more acceptable unto God. So in the greatest church of London, whether it were Paul's or not the French book maketh no mention, all the estates were long of day in the church for to pray. And when matins and the first mass was done, there was seen in the churchyard, against the high altar, a great stone four square, like unto a marble stone; and in midst thereof was like an anvil of steel a foot on high, and therein stuck a fair sword naked by the point, and letters there were written in gold about the sword that said thus: Whoso pulleth out this sword of this stone and anvil, is rightwise king born of all England. Then the people marvelled, and told it to the Archbishop. I command, said the Archbishop, that ye keep within your church and pray unto God still, that no man touch the sword till the high mass be all done.

So when all masses were done all the lords went to behold the stone and the sword. And when they saw the scripture some assayed, such as would have been king. But none might stir the sword nor move it. He is not here, said the Archbishop, that shall achieve the sword, but doubt not God will make him known. But this is my counsel, said the Archbishop, that we let purvey ten knights, men of good fame, and they to keep this sword. So it was ordained, and then there was made a cry, that every man should assay that would, for to win the sword. And upon New Year's Day the barons let make a jousts and a tournament, that all knights that would joust or tourney there might play, and all this was ordained for to keep the lords together and the commons, for the Archbishop trusted that God would make him known that should win the sword.

But on New Year's day Sir Kay lost his sword, and Arthur, until then regarded as the son of a certain Sir Ector, to make good the loss of the blade, suggested that he should draw out the falchion embedded in the stone. Kay assayed to do so, but could not, yet Arthur drew it out with ease, whereupon he was proclaimed son of Uther and King of Britain, and 'stablished all the countries about London'.

Geoffrey of Monmouth mentions London only once in connection with Arthur, in the second chapter of his ninth book, when he remarks that he returned into the city of London to take counsel for his first war against the Saxons. So we must look to other sources for such information as exists regarding his associations with London. Malory has naturally much to say of his presence there and of the haps which befell him in the city, in Westminster and the neighbourhood of London generally, and with these passages I shall deal first as providing something in the nature of a connected account with which those of other writers may be compared. Of course we are all aware that Sir Thomas selected his materials arbitrarily, that he did not make 'an intelligent précis' of the whole Arthurian legend, that he notoriously wandered from the beaten track and so forth. But the fact remains that he seized unerringly on the main issues of Arthurian romance, and, as a daily journal of high standing once remarked in its advertisements, gave us 'all the news worth printing' about Arthur.

Bearing this in mind, then, and having regard to the truth that his century, the fifteenth, was by no means an inventive one, I feel constrained to say, even in the face of a disapproving higher criticism of the Arthurian literature, that I would trust his purely aesthetic sense of selection before I would pin my faith to the former's documentary and more pedantic preferences, and that I devoutly believe that there was more respect for the element of tradition in the little finger of Sir Thomas's scribal hand than in the whole rather elephantine, though jaded, body of professional criticism – a sentiment in which the sons of Romance will joyfully agree with me.

In a word, and as we shall find, Malory tells us a great deal more about Arthur in London than any other writer – and the sources of his knowledge will emerge as we compare his account with those of others.

Save one fleeting notice of Arthur's presence in the city, and that concerning his coronation, it is in the third chapter of Malory's eighteenth book that we first find him and his queen, Guinevere, involved in an incident which took place in London and which well-nigh issued in consequences the most dire. The Queen had given a gracious banquet in London to four-and-twenty Knights of the Round Table. Now there was present at this banquet a certain Sir Pinel le Savage, cousin to Sir Lamorak de Galis who had been slain by Sir Gawain and his brethren, and knowing that Gawain had a passion for fruit, and out of his desire for vengeance, he poisoned a dish of apples which was set on the board in the hope that Gawain would eat of the same.

But his cowardly purpose went amiss, for another knight, Sir Patrise, ate first of the apples and expired almost instantly. Suspicion at once fixed itself upon the innocent queen, and Sir Mador de la Porte, cousin to Patrise, loudly appealed to her for vengeance. In sheer dismay at the dreadful turn events had taken, the hapless Guinevere swooned away. The King, apprised of the circumstances, hastened to the banqueting-hall, and to him Sir Mador roundly accused the Queen of treason. Arthur explained that his kingly rank made it impossible for him to defend his wife in combat, but he doubted not that some good knight would embrace her cause, where-upon Mador assured him that every man present was convinced of her guilt. Guinevere, who had somewhat recovered, indignantly denied her complicity in the affair, and the King announced that the cause would be tried by issue of combat in the meadow beside Westminster that day fifteen days hence, and should the Queen's champion fail, she would be burnt at the stake.

When the King and Queen were alone, Arthur asked where Lancelot might be. 'He at least would not grudge to do battle for you,' said he. But Guinevere replied that she did not believe him to be then within the realm of Britain. Arthur thereupon suggested to the Queen that Sir Bors might take up the challenge on her behalf, and she sent for the knight and put the question to him. But he called shame on her for that she who had driven Lancelot out of the country should expect such service from himself, on whom suspicion would assur-edly rest did he come to her aid. Did not the whole Table Round hold her guilty of the death of Sir Patrise? Then came Arthur and pleaded with Sir Bors, who at last grudgingly consented to act as the Queen's champion.

But Bors was aware that Lancelot had gone to dwell with a hermit and to him he betook himself and told him all. And Lancelot was sorely troubled and begged him to take the lists as he had promised, but to wait as long as he dared before beginning the combat.

The day of battle arrived and all drew them unto the meadow beside Westminster, where the lists were set. Sir Bors and Sir Mador faced each other and the combat was about to begin when a Knight mounted on a white horse, and bearing a shield with a cognisance unknown to any, came riding out of a wood hard by and asked Bors to grant him permission to take his place. Bors, after the King had granted the needful grace, gave way to him. The champions ran their course and Lancelot, for the unknown knight was none other, bare Sir Mador's steed to earth. But its rider uprose and called upon Lancelot to do battle with him on foot.

A terrific combat followed for the full space of an hour, at the end of which Lancelot dealt Mador a blow so deliverly that he fell prone to the earth. But he rose almost upon the instant and wounded the other through the thick of the thigh. Sir Lancelot reeled as though mortally hurt, but aimed such a blow at Sir Mador's helm that he fell straight to earth and called for mercy. Then Mador, threatened with instant death, withdrew his charge against the Queen for all time, and the King and Queen bestowed their grateful thanks upon Lancelot and did him much honour.

Later it was revealed by Nimue, the Damosel of the Lake, Sir Lancelot's good genius, that Sir Pinel was guilty of the poisoning of Sir Patrise and when this was known he fled incontinent to his own country. Sir Patrise was buried with much pomp in the church of Westminster, the story of his taking-off being engraved upon his tomb so that all men in the future might hold the Queen guiltless of his death.

The sad story of Elaine, 'the lily maid of Astolat', is associated by Malory with London and the River Thames. Long had she nourished a hopeless passion for Sir Lancelot and when he courteously refused her love she fell into a great heaviness. She refused meat and drink, neither would she sleep, until at length she passed out of life. But before she died, she begged her brother, Sir Tirre to write a letter revealing the cause of her death, to place it in her hand, and then to set her on a fair barge, covered with black samite, so that her body might be rowed down the Thames to Westminster.

And all this was done. And as Arthur and his Queen stood in converse at a window looking across Thames, they espied the black barge and had marvel what it meant. They sent Sir Kay the seneschal to see what it might hold and when they learnt that it contained a fair damosel they entered it and, taking the letter from her cold hand, returned with it to the palace. King Arthur had a mind to read it in presence of his assembled Knights. So they gathered in his chamber and hearkened to what the missive held.

> Most noble knight, Sir Lancelot, now hath death made us two at debate for your love. I was your lover, that men called the Fair Maiden of Astolat; therefore unto all ladies I make my moan, yet pray for my soul and bury me at least, and offer ye my mass-penny: this is my last request. And a clean maiden I died, I take God to witness: pray for my soul, Sir Lancelot, as thou art peerless.

Guinevere was wroth with Lancelot, who denied all blame to himself in the matter. So the King commanded Lancelot to see to the worship-ful burial of the maiden, which accordingly he undertook with a heavy spirit.

Modern scholarship, however, will not grant Elaine of Astolat's association with sweet Thames, but gives her a much more northern setting – at Dumbarton in Scotland. Today it may seem incongruous enough that an environment so workaday should once have been the *cor cordium* of Romance. Not that the Dun of the Britons has, from afar, other than a distinctly Arthurian aspect, for to the visionary eye it instantly commends itself as that veritable Astolat, the spirit of which all the vapours of industrialism cannot quench or distort.

'The original of the name, which variously appears as Shalott, Escalat, Astolat, and other forms,' wrote the late Sir John Rhŷs, 'was probably Alclut, the old Welsh name of the Rock of Dumbarton on the Clyde.' Elaine of Astolat, thought Rhŷs, was, like Undine, Fand or Vivien, 'a woman of the lake-lady type', and her magic mirror, which, we will remember, cracked when the curse came upon her, was a symbol of the water in which her rock was islanded. In short, she may have been the genius or goddess of the Clyde, as Sabrina was of the Severn.

The great adventure of Guinevere's capture by Sir Meliagrance, son of King Bagdemagus, who held at that time a castle within seven miles of Westminster, and had loved the Queen passing well for many years, is the next episode associated by Malory with Arthurian London. Meliagrance had it in mind to carry off the fairest of all queens, but so long as she was in the company of Sir Lancelot he dared not. But on one occasion, when the Queen went a-Maying in the meadows and woods near Westminster, Lancelot being absent and her entourage consisting of ten young knights alone, he resolved to snatch her out of their keeping and bear her to his castle.

So with eight score of his following he rode down upon the party and called upon the Queen to surrender herself. The youthful knights, divested of their mail and armed only with their swords, made great execution among the henchmen of Meliagrance, but at last all were stretched on the sward, severely wounded. Guinevere begged the false Meliagrance that, if follow him she must, he should carry the wounded knights with him, and to this he grudgingly consented. In the midst of the confusion, however, she contrived to send a page to apprise Sir Lancelot of what had happened. Meliagrance perceived his going when too late and, guessing his mission, left a band of archers behind him to ambush Lancelot as he passed that way.

So he rode with Guinevere and the wounded knights and the Queen's ladies to his castle, but the Queen would in no wise let her followers out of her sight and Meliagrance dared not dismiss them because of his dread of Sir Lancelot, whom he greatly feared. Meanwhile Lancelot received the Queen's message, armed himself and set forth to achieve her deliverance.

'He made his horse to swim over Thames to Lambeth,' and further on found the signs of the battle betwixt Meliagrance and the ten knights. Following the track, he came to a wood, and there the archers of Meliagrance, who lay in ambush, bade him turn and go back. He refused and they shot his horse. But for hedges and ditches he might not come at the nimble archers, so he passed on. And on the road he came up with a cart, whose driver churlishly refused him a seat within it, for he was a hind of Sir Meliagrance. So Sir Lancelot slew the man and compelled his fellow to drive him to the recreant's castle. Here, from a window, did Guinevere espy a knight standing in a woodman's cart. And soon Lancelot came to the gates of the castle and called with a loud voice upon Sir Meliagrance: 'Where art thou, false traitor? For here am I, Sir Lancelot du Lake, to do battle with you.'

In great fear, Meliagrance begged grace of the Queen. And Guinevere, out of her good heart, went down to Sir Lancelot, telling him that Meliagrance repented him. And to save scandal, the twain agreed that Lancelot should meet the Queen that night at a window which gave on to the garden. And so he did and remained with the Queen in her chamber until dawn, when he left her.

At dawn Sir Meliagrance went to the Queen's chamber and found blood upon her pillow, the blood of Lancelot, whose hand had been wounded by one of the arrows discharged at his horse. And he called treason upon her to King Arthur. Then Lancelot entered from the garden and asked the cause of the outcry. Meliagrance accused the Queen of treachery to Arthur with one of the ten wounded knights, whereupon Lancelot challenged him to battle in the field beside Westminster, which Meliagrance accepted.

But there was treachery in the heart of Meliagrance, for as they passed to dinner, he suddenly cast Lancelot through a trap-door into a cave full of straw. Believing that he had returned to Westminster, the Queen with her knights and ladies took the road thither.

By the good offices of a lady who fed and tended him, Lancelot was delivered from the cavern upon the very day on which he had to do battle at Westminster with Sir Meliagrance. Meanwhile the traitor had sought out King Arthur and had informed him of the Queen's treason to him, demanding that she should be burnt at the stake in default of Sir Lancelot appearing as her champion. But at the last moment Lancelot rode up and took his place in the lists. Quickly did Sir Lancelot overthrow the recreant. But Meliagrance refused to continue the battle until his opponent in very shame offered to uncover his head and tie one arm behind him. Even so handicapped, Lancelot slew Meliagrance out of hand, to the deliverance of Queen Guinevere from the fire. This tale had an extraordinary vogue throughout the Norman-French world as the romance of *Le Chevalier de la charette*, 'The Knight of the cart'.

The rather consistent manner in which Malory makes Arthur hold his Court at Westminster is not a little puzzling. That Roman buildings and perhaps a Roman settlement existed in the Isle of Thorney in Arthurian times seems very probable from the remains which have been found there at various times, but it is difficult to reconcile the possibility of Arthur's residence at Westminster with the general conditions of life on Thames-side during the early years of the sixth century, when the presence of strong piratical bands who had gained a lodgement farther up the river comes to be considered. London itself, as a walled place, would be sufficiently secure, but any unfortified position, such as Westminster undoubtedly occupied at that period, would have offered too great an inducement to raiding Saxons to admit of its reasonably peaceful habitation, and the probability is that after the Roman evacuation the site of Westminster lay practically desolate until its rehabilitation by the Saxon King Sebert, who seems to have erected a primitive church on the Isle of Thorney about the year AD 616.

Malory tells us in the second chapter of his twenty-first book that Guinevere, in fear of the traitor Modred, who would have taken her to wife, so that he might have been crowned King of Britain, shut herself up in the Tower of London. In the end, however, she was delivered from him, as he was slain in the great battle in which Arthur was wounded so severely that he was forced to betake him to Avalon, there to be healed of his hurts. The Welsh *Brut* makes Modred succeed in his fell purpose of marrying Guinevere and adds that he 'had put on the crown of London' and 'had also taken to himself the whole realm', a passage which appears to hold some memory of a time when London was actually a kingdom in itself. That it was so in early Saxon times is, of course, matter of historic fact, and there is good reason to think, judging by the many references to its 'dukes', that during the British period it may have enjoyed a similar independence, even if under a 'pendragon', or some description of native emperor.

If we turn to the chroniclers, both ancient and medieval, for a consecutive or 'chronological' account of Arthur's several appearances in London we shall see that although he had no very close associations with it, those which make mention of his presence in the city do so in connection with incidents which seem not at all improbable, having reference to the circumstances of his campaigns and to what is known of his history generally.

Matthew of Westminster, in the ninth chapter of his *Flowers of History*, tells us that Dubritius, Archbishop of the city of London, in union with the bishops and nobles of the land, made Arthur, the son of Uther, then a youth of fifteen years of age, King of Britain in the year 516. Although no mention is here made of his coronation in London, it seems to be implied in this account. Geoffrey says that the invasion of Britain, with six hundred ships, by Duke Childeric of Germany, which occurred shortly after Arthur's accession to the throne, caused Arthur's withdrawal to London, 'where he summoned all the clergy and chief men of his allegiance and bade them declare their counsel as to what was best and safest for him to do against this inroad of the Paynim'. Accordingly, messengers asking for succour were sent to King Howel of Armorica, the nephew of Arthur, who fitted out an expedition for the deliverance of Britain from the German host.

Layamon tells much the same story. He says that after Arthur's coronation at Silchester he proceeded to London and swore on the holy relics 'that never should the Saxons become blithe in Britain, but he would drive them out', and that at a later time he again took counsel at London against the coming of Childeric, sending to Howel, his kinsman, for aid, which was duly forthcoming, a statement in which he is joined by Roger of Wendover, and Hector Boece.

Daniel Haigh, who probed the literature of this particular period with quite extraordinary faithfulness, was of the opinion that in the course of this campaign, in which the British-Armorican forces are said to have been victorious, Arthur, on learning of Childeric's arrival, first retired to London to oppose those who re-entered Kent. He left Howel to keep the northern Saxon army in check, but the King of Armorica later followed him to London and crossed the Channel to seek reinforcements. Still later, Arthur took advantage of the combined attack of the Saxon armies in the city of Caer Loitcoit to make himself master of Northumberland and subsequently routed them in the pitched battle of Cat coit Celidon.[4] The Childeric alluded to in their narratives has been indentified by Haigh with the Frankish monarch of that name, the son of Merovée – the founder of the Merovingian dynasty, but in this instance, as in others, Haigh's especial system of chronology is employed to fortify the identification.

Hector Boece, in the ninth chapter of his ninth book of *The Chronicles of Scotland*, gives an account of how a second invasion of the Saxons in the Isle of Wight was frustrated by the appearance of a great host of Scots and Picts, who came to London to support Arthur. These were led by Eugenius, son of Congallus, and Modred, the son of King Lot of Lothian, who is here represented as a man of Pictish race, as indeed he must have been were he the son of Lot. Some chroniclers make him the son of Arthur himself, the fruit of an intrigue with his own sister, the wife of Lot, while unwitting of her relationship to him.

But the amazing thing in our legendary history is the consistent political opposition of the Picts to the Britons and I cannot but believe that it has a stronger claim to the status of authentic history than has yet been disclosed or admitted, though the history of the future may perhaps reveal it as authentic. Modred, indeed, made a definite claim to the throne of Britain at the time of Arthur's coronation, as Fordun and Boece jointly aver. Nevertheless the claim was contemptuously rejected by the Britons, although Modred's mother 'Anna' was the daughter of Aurelius Ambrosius.

'The Scottis and Pichtis,' says Boece referring to those who had marched south to help Arthur, 'abaid certaine dayis in Londoun, and returnit hame, richely rewardit be King Arthure.' A long interval ensues during which we hear nothing of Arthur's presence in the city until we encounter Layamon's statement that after his conquest of France the King sailed up the Thames to London 'to the bliss of the people', who sang his praises and made great joy for his victories in Gaul. With this the legendary references to Arthur in his association with London come to a close.

Before his death or disappearance Arthur had chosen his cousin Constantine, son of Duke Cador of Cornwall, as heir to the throne, but the sons of Modred, who had been slain at the last great battle at Camlan, made a bid for the royal power. Modred's position as regards London is not quite clear, but an old chronicle of Devonshire, cited by Leland, says that although Cerdic the Saxon was crowned King of the Angles, Modred was crowned King of the Britons at London.

This refers to the period of Arthur's wars abroad, when Modred seems to have acted as regent of Britain during his absence, an honour with which he was evidently not contented, and it is to this period that we must refer his illegal union with Guinevere which is said to have taken place in London.

But his two sons after his death raised an insurrection against Constantine, who pursued one of them to Winchester, where he was slain, the other, who was in hiding in the monastery of certain brethren in London, being also butchered there by Constantine before the altar.

Gildas provides a typically dramatic picture of their assassination. He says:

Constantine, the tyrannic whelp of an unclean lioness of Damnonia. In this year, after the fearful sacrament of an oath, by which he bound himself never to practise treachery against his countrymen, who trusted in God first and the oath, in company with the choirs of Saints, and the Mother [of God], he has cruelly torn with his wicked sword and spear, for teeth, the tender sides or hearts of two royal youths, and of their fosterers, in the venerable embrace of their two mothers, the church and their carnal mother, under the holy Abbot Amphibalus, amongst the holy altars themselves, as I have said, so that their cloaks, purple with coagulated gore, touched the seat of the heavenly sacrifice; whose arms stretched forth, not with weapons, which scarce any one in this time handled more bravely than they, but to God and the altar, will hang up the venerable trophies of their patience and faith, in the day of judgment, at the gates of Thy city, O Christ.

So with a barbarous scene of bloodshed ends the traditional history of Arthurian London, a scene which, in all probability, is much more typical of the period than the knightly and courteous environment of the Table Round of Sir Thomas Malory. The glimpses we receive of the presence of the great Britannic hero in London are fugitive indeed and it is unlikely that even the most consistent research will now be able to provide us with anything more specific.

But that Arthur the King did once pass through the streets of a Romano-British London I for one devoutly believe, even though it be only with the eyes of the faithful servant of romance that I seem to behold him stalk through those pillared vestiges of Rome athwart which the shadows of barbarian menace were swiftly gathering. How many leagues from London to Avalon? If a man have romance in his heart and vision in his spirit, no more than may be surpassed in the twinkling of an eye!

16

Great St Helen

Harold Bayley

IN 1647 ON the occasion of an exceptionally low tide a votive
tablet was uncovered on the foreshore of Holland with an inscription translated thus:

> *To the goddess Nehalennia*
> *For his goods well preserved*
> *Secundus Silvanius*
> *A chalk merchant of Britain*
> *Willingly performed his merited vow.*

Nehalennia figures at Newlyn or Newline near Truro as 'Saint'
Niwelinae; she figures again at Noualen in Brittany, founded according to legend by the daughter of a nobleman from Britain; she reap-
pears at Tadcaster in Yorkshire, where a local name Helen's Ford is
supposed to be a 'corruption' of Nehalennia.

From the native forms Newlyn and Noualen it would seem that
Nehalennia or St Niwelinae was a Latinized extension of the Celtic
name; the 'corruption' of Noualen into Helen is no greater than that
of Ellen into Nelly. Nehalennia is usually sculptured with a basket of
fruit in her lap symbolizing, it is said, the fecundating power of the
earth: in this respect she may be equated either with Ceres the Mother
or with Persephone the Daughter. Nehalennia is, however, portrayed
not as a formidable *Magna Mater*, but as a young and simple girl: the
first syllable of Newlyn or Noualen is thus, in all likelihood, the
Celtic *nou* which is the same as present-day *new*, a term according to
Skeat identical with *now*. It may also be connected with the Greek *neo*
as in neophite or new convert. If this suggestion be feasible it would
also account for our use of Nellie as a diminutive of Ellen, a British

variation otherwise difficult to explain: whether or not the diminutive Nellie is a name found elsewhere than in Britain, I do not know.

The connection of Ellen with Nehalennia at Tadcaster may be somewhat paralleled at Newlyn, which is particularly associated with a curious festival of the so-called Allan apple. The name of the Celtic St Allan is defined as meaning cheerful: in Welsh *alain* meant exceeding fair, lovely, bright; in Ireland *allen* was synonymous with beauty.

The most ancient building in the Scilly Islands is a ruined chapel dedicated to St Helen: there was another chapel of St Helen on Cape Cornwall, which was at one time known as Cape Helenus. St Helen figures perplexingly in several aspects: the Saint Helen of Christianity is the historic and material daughter of King Cole of Colchester; behind this Helen is however something – indeed almost everything – fabulous. History records that the British princess Helena, daughter of King Cole, married Constantius, a Roman General; that the son of Helena became Constantine the Great (the visionary of the *Chi rho* cross), and that in the region of Constantine an edict was issued granting freedom of worship and citizenship to all Christians throughout the Roman Empire.

Helena, the British mother of Constantine, was beatified by the Church as being the alleged discoverer at Jerusalem not only of the True Cross but also of the Holy Coat, the Three Nails of the Passion and the bodies of the Three Kings. The bodies of these Magi were deposited it is said at Cologne or Collen as it was usually spelled: the Three Kings – that very customary inn sign – are the Three Kings of Collen. The ancient name of Colchester was Colenceaster; the arms of Colchester commemorate the momentous achievements of 'Saint' Helena; so too do coins struck at Colchester confirm the historic truth of the Constantine story. In the London Museum is a medal minted in Brittany to commemorate the deliverance of London from the filibuster Carausius by Constantius; it bears a legend to the effect 'Restorer of Light that shines for ever'.

Although St Helen was undoubtedly historic there are legends current which are seemingly pagan and prehistoric. Elen the Fair of Britain figures, according to Sir John Rhys, like St Ursula, as the Leader of the Heavenly Virgins: Salisbury Plain was known anciently as Ellendune, and at Dunstable is a Dame Ellen's Wood. St Helen, the lone daughter of Old King Cole the Merry Old Soul of Colchester, appears in Wales and Cumberland as Elen the Leader of Hosts, whose memory was preserved not only in Elaine the Lily Maid, but also in connection with ancient pathways such as Elen's Road and Elen's Causeway. 'These,' suggests Squire, 'seem to show that the paths on which armies marched were dedicated to her.'

Stow alludes to the tradition that Helena was responsible for the encircling of London with its first wall; and I surmise that Great St Helens and Little St Helens, both immediately adjacent to the Church of St Mary Axe or St Ursula and the 11,000 Virgins, are connected with Helen the Magna Mater and Noualen or Nelly the Daughter.

In Cumberland the year's allowance of horsemeat was allotted to servants on St Helen's, Eline's, or Elyn's Day, and as horsemeat was banned by the Church (because, supposedly, of its sacrificial consumption by the heathen) it would almost appear that the custom, like the Saint, was a survival of paganism. In the Mediterranean an inauspicious single fire of St Elmo on the masthead of a ship was known as that of ill-boding Helena; which again brings Helena or Nehalennia *en rapport* with the sea.

The Hellenes claimed for themselves descent from a divine ancestor named Ellan or Hellan, a personage esteemed as the Father of the First-born Woman; according to Pausanias, the first prophet at the Oracle of Delphi was Olen the Hyperborean.

Stow mentions the fact that the author of Holinshed's *Chronicles* was Reyne Wolf, but that the executors of this grave antiquary increased and published his work under the pseudonym 'Ralf Holinshed'. It would be interesting to know the identity of the Holin to whose head the *Chronicles* were thus curiously attributed, and it is not irrelevant to this inquiry that Alleyn the founder of Dulwich College stipulated in his will that the school should always be under the control of someone bearing the name Alleyn.

Discussing in *Surnames* the mysterious word *hollin-priest*, this, says Professor Weekley, 'suggests a pious hermit among the hollies: it is found in Cheshire where *Hollin-* names such as Hollingshead are numerous; but it is perhaps for *holy priest.*'

In Arthurian Romance Elain or Elen is described as sitting along or alone in a sea girt castle on a throne of ruddy gold: it is said that so transcendent was her beauty that it would be no more easy to look into her face than to gaze at the sun when his rays were most irresistible. The feast of All Hallows was at times mentioned as Alholen, seemingly an alternative plural: but the hallows were the immaterial souls of the dead, the ellies, the fays, the fairies: it is in fact impossible to distinguish between Helen the historic and Helen the Fay.

The existence of St Helen's Chapels on the Scilly Islands and at Land's End, a district known to the Hellenes as the Cassiterides, provokes a wonder as to the truth of the time-honoured tradition that Britain was colonized by Hellenes and that London was once entitled 'Troynovant'. That the Greeks traded with the Cassiterides for tin is, I believe, not a matter of controversy: according to the Greek historian Diodorus, 'Those Britons who dwell near the promontory of Bolerium live in a very hospitable polite manner which is owing to their great intercourse with foreign merchants.' Tyndal, the earliest translator of the Greek Testament into English, asserts that 'the Greek agreeth more with the English than the Latin': there is also, of course, the familiar testimony of Caesar that in their public and private accounts the Druids 'make use of Greek letters'. There is further some seeming connection between *ichneia*, the Greek for tracking, and the prehistoric British *Ichnield* Street, a name for long associated with the Iceni, but now set aside as insoluble.

Among the phenomena of Celtic mythology are numerous identities with tales related by Homer, a fact which perplexed Sir Walter Scott: discussing one such instance he suggests, 'Perhaps some Churchman more learned than his brethren may have transferred the legend from Sicily to Duncrune, from the shores of the Mediterranean to those of Loch Lomond.' It is not my province to discuss the problem whether Hellenic influences reached these islands by culture-deep overland, or by direct sea contact: that the goddess Nehalennia was associated with the sea is sufficiently evidenced by the well-merited votive tablet inscribed to her by Secundus Silvanius of Britain. Whether this chalk merchant sailed from Newlyn or from London is unknown, but, as Newlyn does not provide chalk and London merchanted large quantities, the probabilities are in favour of London.

That Nehalennia was the Little St Helen of London is somewhat implied by the various forms under which a Maiden Lane in east

London is recorded. That this Lane (now destroyed) took its title – not from a midden heap – but rather from an inn-sign, or possibly a shrine, is implied by significant variants of the name. In 1282 it figured as Englenelane, which implies either Angel Nelane or else Angel Nel Lane: in 1332 Nel seems to have dropped out and the name appears simply as Engleslane, i.e. Angels Lane. But in 1339 Nel comes back again in the form Ingenelane, the preliminary Inge being evidently the Norman-French form of *angel*, i.e. *ange*. In 1310 this maiden – obviously an ange or angel – appeared as Ingelane and its ultimate form was Ingestrate, i.e. Ange Street. It is possible that traces of the angelic Nelane or Nellie may survive at Nelldale Road in Bermondsey and it might prove worthwhile to inquire into the origin of the East Anglian name Nelson, for which Professor Weekley proffers no explanation.

In all the four shrines or tablets now illustrated, Nehalennia is associated with an animal which is certainly a dog, seemingly a greyhound. In North Wales there is, still standing I believe, a table stone known locally as *Llety-y-filiast* or 'the stone of the greyhound bitch': 'This name,' says Dr Griffith, 'was given in allusion to the British Ceres or Keridwen, who was symbolized by the greyhound bitch.' An animal which is unmistakably a greyhound bitch appears on some of the coins of pre-Roman Britain and the greyhound would thus seem to have been a national emblem.

It is officially supposed and taught that all our early British coinage, some tracing backward to 200 BC, was merely a degraded imitation of a certain Greek stater issued by Philip of Macedon. If this were so, it would imply a potent Greek influence in England where alone in

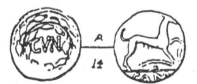

[Figure 31: Coins of Nehalennia. From John Evans, *The Coins of the Ancient Britons,* 1864, and John Akerman, *Ancient Coins – Hispania, Gallia, Britannia,* 1846.]

305

Britain such coins have been found: it is however manifestly absurd to suppose that the clear-cut charioteer of the Greek stater could by carelessness and incompetence have become 'degraded' into so excellent a greyhound bitch as is here portrayed.

The lettering CUN which occurs in both examples may be connoted with the word *kennet* meaning a greyhound. According to Professor Weekley, the name Kennet is a Norman diminutive of *chien* a dog. Herodotus speaks of a race called Kynetes or Kynesii, both of which terms, as Sir John Rhys says, 'have a look of Greek words meaning dogmen'. According to Herodotus, 'The Celts are outside the Pillars of Hercules and they border on the Kynetae who dwell the farthest away towards the West of the inhabitants of Europe.' Ancient writers locate the Kynetes in the West of Spain, which, says Sir John Rhys, 'suggests a still more important inference – namely that there existed in Herodotus' time a continental people of the same origin and habits as the non-Celtic aborigines of these islands.' There are in England two rivers Kennet and one river Kent, both assigned to a Celtic root of unknown meaning: of the county Kent or Cantium there is no accepted etymology.

It might thus seem possible that Nehalennia of the Greyhound was a pre-Celtic goddess and that the greyhound was not only a tribal emblem but likewise a royal appendage: not only in England but likewise in Ireland place-names having reference to the dog are so persistent that Sir John Rhys surmised the dog was originally a totem of the country. There used to be a tradition that the Isle of Dogs, now a peninsula, once an islet, in the Thames, derived its name from the greyhounds and spaniels of Edward III: later the mythical 'king' was said to be Henry VIII and later still Charles II. Nowadays this is considered aprocyphal and one theory is that the Isle of Dogs derived its name from the possibility that 'so many dogs were drowned in the Thames here'. Norden's map of 1593 shows the place as 'Isle of Dogs Ferme' and it seems scarcely probable that this was a spot conspicuously dangerous to the health of dogs.

Proud Kenilworth of Warwickshire figures in Domesday as Chinewrde: *wrde* is here evidently *worth* or *farm* and the *chine* is either the Norman *chien* or perhaps *chuyn*, the Celtic for dog; we thus get the equation Kenil farm or Dog farm. It is just possible that the Ullen

Street in the Isle of Dogs neighbourhood perpetuates a trace of Helen or Nehelennia of the Dog. The triple evidence of the stone of the greyhound bitch; the appearance of this animal in our prehistoric coinage and its reappearance on the altars of Nehelennia argues in any case a high and unsuspected antiquity.

The fact that roads were indubitably named after Elen may perhaps justify the speculation that to this same source of fecundity (symbolized by Nehelennia's fruit and flowers) are attributable the river names Hollinbourne, Alan, Allan, Alaune, Alone, Aln, Elan, Ilen, Len, Lyn, Leen, Lone, and Lune. It is an accepted etymology that all these names are in all probability from the Keltic *alain, alwyn* or *alwen* meaning exceeding fair, lovely, bright, and to account for this adjective one may safely postulate a divinity.

Irish mythology tells of a certain golden-haired hero named Bress, which means *beautiful*; whence we are further told that every beautiful thing in Ireland, whether *plain*, fortress, or ale, or *torch*, or woman, or man, was compared with him so that men said of them 'That is a Bress.' If this process were elsewhere prevalent (it probably was) we have here an explanation of Helen meaning torch and of *ailean* meaning a green plain: the Irish form of Helen is Aileen and to the same source may perhaps be assigned the Welh *llan*, Cornish *lan*, meaning a sacred enclosure.

In the words of Isaac Taylor:

> One class of local names is of special value in investigation relating to primeval history. The river-names, more particularly the names of important rivers, are everywhere the memorials of the very earliest races. These river-names survive where all other names have changed, they seem to possess an almost indestructible vitality. Towns may be destroyed, the sites of human habitation may be removed, but the ancient river-names are handed down from race to race; even the names of the eternal hills are less permanent than those of rivers.

It is an old-standing joke against etymology that consonants mean very little; vowels nothing at all: this as regards consonants is untrue, but as Professor Weekley rightly says, 'Dialects do as they like with the vowels.' He cites as examples the surnames Long, Lang, Lung, Leng, 'and possibly sometimes' Ling.

It is well known that our 'blind' ancestors paid divine honours not only to rivers but likewise to trees. Place-names such as Allington in Wilts are assigned to *ellen*, an old word for elder tree, and the name is thus interpreted to have meant elder tree hill: similarly Lindon in Dorset is interpreted as flax town. But linum or flax does not grow upon a site till it has been long previously inhabited, and it may be that the linden or lime tree, as also the elm or ullum, and the holm or holen oak, were named after Helen.

In Scandinavia the linden or lime tree was supposed to be the favourite haunt of elves and cognate beings and it was considered not safe to be near it after sunset. According to Skeat, the holm oak acquired this name from a resemblance to holly; *holin*, the medieval name for holly, was, he adds, 'sometimes corrupted to holm or holy'. It would thus seem that holin, holme and holy are all radically akin: the hollyhock was so named because it came from the Holy Land.

There is a tradition that the site of the world-wonder Temple of Diana at Ephesus was originally a small and primitive tree shrine standing on the marshy ground of the river delta, and that in the seventh century BC a stone building was erected over and around it. In view of Rice Holmes's belief that probably every primitive British town owed its nomenclature to a presiding fairy guardian, it may be that London itself may be traced to a prehistoric tree-shrine and that the London Stone now preserved in Cannon Street may mark the approximate spot.

Although the name London is Celtic, it is believed by some authorities that prior to the Roman invasion nothing in the nature of a settlement existed. It is however quite likely that a dun amid the swamps at the delta of the Thames was dedicated to Nehalennia, for this divinity was certainly worshipped in the delta of the Rhine, where she was regarded as 'the tutelary deity of fishermen and the bestower of fruitfulness'. There is an old English word *line* which means to fecundate, and that Nehalennia or St Niwelinae of the dog was the same as Line may be further inferred from the archaic word lynehound or limehound: which animal, according to J.O. Halliwell, was a common hound or sporting dog.

The loss of an initial vowel such as in the case of *lone* or *alone* is extremely frequent: Lena is a customary contraction of Helena; Ellenburgh (Maryport) a town on the River Ellen or Alne figured in Domesday as *Line*halle, in 1200 it reappeared as Ellinhale. In view of the patent connection between Nehalennia, Helen and London, it is not an irrational suggestion that the primitive dun of the fisherfolk took its name from Elen the Fair sitting lone and alone on her throne of ruddy gold. For the 'Lon' of London there is at present no known or accepted etymology: the *don* means by general acceptance the *dun* or fortified hill upon which the ancient settlement stood.

17

Britannia and St Paul's

Alan V. Insole

I T IS A strange thing that we in Britain neither know the origin of the name of our country, nor apparently make much effort to find out. An old encyclopaedia once described Britannia as a 'Roman goddess', and this arrant nonsense has been vaguely accepted by all educational authorities, so that generations of the children of this great Commonwealth are allowed to grow up in total ignorance of what is, after all, the most important aspect of a country's history – its origin; and also one of the things hostile propaganda is always most anxious to make obscure.

The root of the great words 'Britain' and 'Britannia' is in their consonants Br – t, and therefore in dialects varying not only locally but over long periods of time, the root word might have been written or spoken as Brat, Bret, Brit, Brot, Brut, or Bryt. It is obvious that the word Britain, Brytan, or 'Great Britannie' (*c.* AD 1600) derives from the same source as Brittany, just as do Briton and Breton. Both have similar Arthurian legends; both have an Insula-av-Alan where Arthur was buried; both have great stone circles found nowhere else; both Welshmen and Bretons understand each other to this day. All this points to a common origin for the name Br–t (and the Arthurian legends) at least as old as 2000 BC.

Brut, the name of the traditional first Trojan king, may have been a title meaning king-paramount, similar to the Anglo-Saxon royal title Britwalda. Humphrey Lhyud (AD 1570) was of the opinion that the ancient name of our island was the Cymric Welsh *Prydain*. This suggests that the impact of Latin and Saxon, to say nothing of change of pronunciation over a thousand years, caused confusion between the consonants t and d; and that Brut or Brit equates with Brid; all are titles of the Great Mother. We therefore find the common origin in

Crete where the Mother Goddess was called Britomart. Britomart was, like Britannia, associated with Diana. She had a divine son, who was first known as Dionysus and later as Pluto; and just as the Greek Bacchus turned into Pluto, so did the British horned god in the midsummer pageantry.

In the early agricultural epoch the wise-woman was not merely the mother of the clan, but in every respect its chief. There were no prophets or priests when she was the voice of the Oracle. People went to her when in trouble; she announced auspicious days for hunting, sowing, ploughing and festivals. She would have been the first individual dependent on others for her food. When there was a successful hunt, or a herdsman killed a domestic beast, they did not give her a portion, but brought the whole animal or carcass to be sacrificed upon her altar.

The first sacred object that has been found associated with an image of the Great Mother was a tribal phallus. Now in the ancient world a phallus was believed to have magical powers, especially of warding off the evil eye, bad spirits and even savage animals. Hence they were often erected, like a barber's pole, over the doors of houses and the entrances to villages. There were huge ones outside the gates of Rome and on the chariots of Roman generals. The phallus which protected the gate of Belin in London survived until the seventeenth century and became known as the Billingsgate Bosse. The local porters would insist on passers-by kissing the Bosse or else they picked them up and bumped them on the seat against the stone.

But, as from the earliest times, the cross of three sticks had similar powers, they too were erected at entrances to the town and on the approaches to the shrine of the Great Mother. This is the origin of the great London crosses and those around Glastonbury. Only a few like Charing Cross were Christian and were called 'Eleanor' crosses after the queen (but strangely even that name is of the ancient root L + N).

Another London Stone that survived nearly to the seventeenth century was known as 'Paul's Stump'. It was set close to the site of Wren's cathedral, but it seems to have lost all sense of its ancient sanctity and even its legends. Nevertheless it must have once been of much importance to have survived so many stormy centuries in the city's centre. It was probably one of the last relics of the sacred enclosure on Lud's Hill. St Paul's Cathedral would originally have been a solitary oak tree, or a Holy Oak in a grove near which the Great Mother had her altar and tended her sacred fire. Very early in the evolution of the shrine two stones were set up on either side of the altar or beside the tree, which were the 'heap and pillar of the witness', upon which men swore oaths, and which by extension became boundary stones.

These were the customs of that remote period known as the 'tree and pillar cult' and arose from the fact that it was:

> the custom for the person who took an oath to place his hand under the 'thigh' of the adjurer. This practice arose from the fact that the genital member, which is meant by the euphemistic expression 'thigh', was regarded as especially sacred ... No more impressive ceremony could therefore have been performed in early days than for a man to touch the symbol of creation ... even at the present day this form of oath is to be found amongst certain Arabian tribes, who actually swear by the 'Phallus of Allah'.[1]

This form of oath-taking must have lasted far longer in north-west Europe than we have been led to believe, because we get from it such important words as 'testament', 'to testify', and the French 'temoin', etc. In fact, the Old Testament originally consisted of the 'two stones of the testimony' (Exodus 32:15), yet when the Christians added a third it still remained two.

We may therefore picture the Great Mother sitting under her tree, above her any bird with red feathers, such as a robin or woodpecker, and later the domestic fowls when roosting were regarded as thunderbirds and of sacred omen. She would have had in her keeping the sacred stone – possibly in the form of a stone-headed mace. There would have been a bundle of torch-crosses leaning against the tree ready for the runners in case of danger. Her dog would have been lying at her feet ready to warn of the approach of strangers, and her geese would have been wandering in the field nearby.

At first sight it is hard to realize that in this simple rustic scene will be found nearly all the elaborate symbolism of a great gothic cathedral. The earliest known temple was in Crete and from the *Hagia Trida* sarcophagus we know it was a kind of small roofless erection with an altar and a pillar standing in front of a small roofless building, in the middle of which was a sacred tree, and that amongst the furniture found there was a double-headed axe. We also know that the male played only such small parts in the rites as porters or spectators.

The next stage in the evolution will be found in the temple of Het-Ben-Ben at On (Cairo) in Egypt. There at one time was the sacred Persea tree under which the goose laid the egg which hatched into a phoenix. 'A vignette in the papyrus of Ani shows a pylon-shaped building between double pillars:[2] Here the tree had fallen into decay and been replaced by a building.

The temple of On was the model for Solomon's temple. An old Jewish legend tells us how David, when keeping sheep, was carried up to Heaven on the back of a colossal rhinoceros and delivered from this position through the help of a lion, whereupon he vowed to build a temple of the dimensions of that animal's horn.

Here is another version of the story of the lion fighting the one-horned unicorn. The unicorn took David to Heaven and the lion brought him back to earth. Solomon's temple when built consisted of two pillars 'Jachim and Boaz' on either side of a huge 'porch' or tower which dominated the whole building. The building was sixty cubits long by twenty in height and breadth; the porch was one hundred and twenty cubits high by twenty wide. The whole story seems to be another instance of Judah stealing the birthright and the blessing from Israel, for the building was constructed with the friendly aid of the kings of Tyre, who were worshippers of Baal and would never have helped to build a temple to a God vowed to destroy Baal worship. Moreover we know from the correspondence of the Pharaoh Akenaton that there was a sun temple at Jerusalem already famous some three centuries before the time of David.

The next stage in evolution was when the two pillars became the Twin West End Towers, and the 'porch' that replaced the sacred tree became the central spire, still with its thunderbird on top. Inside we still find the Tree of Life as oracle in its form of the lectern, i.e., a thunderbird upon a thunder pillar – in Durham Cathedral it is a phoenix – holding on its wings the two testaments, and over all still flies the Red Cross of the Heavenly Twins. The cross within the circle that symbolized the Great Mother will still be found on the regimental flags which have replaced the ancient stones of the standard.

In the course of evolution the Great Mother gradually fades away into the realms of shades and symbology. This began when men usurped the functions of the prophetesses. At first a man could only be accepted and recognized as a seer provided he married the seeress and even then he had to adopt feminine dress. It was for this reason that Hercules and his priests wore female garments, and on occasions Alexander the Great appeared dressed as the Goddess Diana. Little by little as the male replaced the female in all religious ritual not only did the seeresses disappear, but the prophets also, until only the priests remained: and to this day they still keep up the ancient fiction that they are female by wearing long robes originally intended to disguise the male.

But before the final disappearance of the Great Mother from her temples and shrines she herself underwent several evolutionary changes. With the coming of the solar cult and its divine kings she lost much of her importance both in the religious and social spheres. In the cult of the Heavenly Twins she appears associated with the sun but by Roman times she changes from a solar emblem to a lunar goddess. In place of the maiden of the sun she appears as Diana the chaste huntress. Traces of this change will be found in Britain as in the post-Roman shrine to Diana at Maiden Castle, and also in the legends of St Paul's.

All too often the orthodox historian considers mythology and legend to be outside the sphere of historical research. But however vague and legendary may be the change of the sun maiden into Diana, there is no doubt that this change was an unmistakable historical fact when related to the character of the women of Britain. In the solar epoch religious nudity was 'common usage' and no British woman in those days would have given a thought about being seen unclad, but a thousand years later any male who peeped at an English hunting woman while in her bath would have been likely to learn that her language and her wrath transcended even that of the chaste Goddess herself.

In London when the sacred tree decayed and became a stump it was likely to have been replaced by a stone, which acquired the name of Pol or Pul which was an ancient title of the sun god, and so became Old Pol's Stump. E.O. Gordon in her *Prehistoric London* (Covenant, 1925) gives reasons to believe that on the site of St Paul's there was an oracle of the hunting days as far back as 3200 BC; and that it became a stone circle about 1900 BC; and that the pointer to the south-east was the famous London Stone still preserved in the walls of St Swithin's Church. The London Stone has often most exasperatingly been called a 'Roman milestone', one can only hope our children will not be taught to believe it to be of Russian origin! At Stonehenge the pointer stone was a phallus, and phallic rites were rainmaking magic. It is therefore interesting to note that the London Stone used to be at St Swithin's, who, as we still believe, gives us a wet or dry harvest.

The above dates are astronomical calculations made by the Rev. John Griffith, from the mounds of ancient London. There were the White Mount (now the Tower), Parliament Hill, Penton Hill, Tothill (now Westminster) and Primrose Hill.[3] The calculations indicate that the solar cult was imposed upon the May–November months about a century earlier in London than at Stonehenge, as calculated there by Sir Norman Lockyer.

That St Paul's area of London had been a sacred enclosure of that particular open-air type is certain. Henry VIII abolished the right of sanctuary at Westminster, but even he was not powerful enough to abolish it within the City. There it lasted until the close of the reign of James I, in spite of the fact that latterly it became a public nuisance and a haunt of malefactors and that the monastic buildings had long since disappeared. The right of sanctuary, however, was not in the cathedral itself, but in the nearby St Martin's-le-Grand. St Martin was said to have been cut up and eaten in the form of an ox, his festival being 11 November, the Feast of the Dead. 'This is clear evidence that St Martin merely took the place of the God Hu who was symbolical of that animal.'[4] It also points to the extreme antiquity of London's sanctuary.

Between St Martin's and St Paul's was an open space in which stood two crosses, St Paul's and the Broken Cross. This was the place of the meeting of the folkmoot – London's open-air parliament. As late as the fourteenth century, this bit of land was of greater national importance than any building erected up to that time. There, according to Stone Age custom, the citizens of London met to elect the kings of England before they could be crowned at Westminster. We have records of the election of Edward IV, Stephen, Edward the Confessor, Edmund Ironside and others; even William the Conqueror submitted to the formula of election before being crowned at Westminster.

Another example of continuity of custom in London, and one even older than the above, took place on the festivals of St Paul. In January a doe and in June a stag were taken to the cathedral where they were met at the West Doors by the Dean and chapter wearing garlands of leaves or roses on their heads. The deer was then slain on the steps of the cathedral to a fanfare of trumpets and the proclamation of a public holiday. The head and horns of the beast was set on a spear and taken in solemn procession to the high altar. This ceremony lasted until the time of Queen Elizabeth I.

This is a typical example of an official 'explaining away' when we are diverted from the actual truth by the overwhelming desire for moral welfare. In the fourteenth century the Roman Church was at the apex of her power, and for centuries had been gradually suppressing all rites savouring of heathenism, and would certainly not have permitted a new and obviously pagan custom to have been started, nor would the very conservative Londoners have accepted it.

That it was an ancient custom is clear from the instructions sent by Pope Gregory the Great to Bishop Miletus in AD 601 when he (Miletus) was engaged in building the first Roman church on the site of St Paul's. The Pope expressly instructed Miletus as follows:

> Let the shrines of idols by no means be destroyed. Let water be consecrated and sprinkled in these temples; let altars be erected and relics laid upon them because if these same temples be well-built, it is necessary that they should be converted from the worship of evil spirits to the service of the true God, so that people not seeing their own

temples destroyed may displace error from their own hearts and recognize the true God meeting in the familiar way at the accustomed places: and because they are wont to sacrifice many oxen to devils, some celebration should be given in exchange for this.[5]

The sacrifice of the deer at St Paul's *precisely* fulfilled the Pope's instructions, and gives added weight to the words of E. Hull on this subject:

> The solemnity and sacrifice of the buck, the garlands of flowers worn by the clergy and the blowing of horns in the city, and the importance of the days in the Cathedral life as those of its patron saint, all point to some function of a more universal nature than the private payment of a debt for a piece of land. It was evidently a ceremony in which the city as a whole had a part. Camden's suggestion that the custom went back to the worship of Diana the huntress gives a more reasonable explanation.[6]

It is true that Sir Christopher Wren was disappointed at being unable to find any remnants of a Temple of Diana when he was clearing the foundations of the ruined Old St Paul's. He may not have realized that a still earlier cathedral was destroyed by the Great Fire of AD 1136 and that the still older church of Miletus was destroyed when the Danes sacked the city in AD 839. Moreover as the 'sanctuary' was in St Martin's he may not have been looking in the right place. Tradition has it that a still older third-century church preceded that of Miletus, but that St Martin's was pre-Roman.

Again, Sir Christopher Wren was looking for a temple of the Roman period and type, forgetting perhaps that before the Great Fire of Rome, in Nero's reign, the ancient Roman temples were built of wood. But the ancient sacredness of St Paul's district lay not in any building but in the open space. It may quite possibly have been that in Roman London what was called the Temple of Diana was actually a grove of trees within the open space, which certainly seems to have been the case of the famous shrine of Diana at Nemi outside Rome.

Yet another example of the extraordinary continuity of custom in London will be found in the symbolic structure of its civic

government. Until the rise of Puritanism, Midsummer Day was celebrated all over Britain. In country places Michael in rustic pageantry
still came down from his mount to slay the dragon. In London was
held the great procession of the Midsummer Watch. Even when this
was abolished in Elizabeth I's reign, London's Day with the Lord
Mayor's Show was transferred to Michaelmas when the sheriffs were
elected.

In the old religion of the Heavenly Twins, the Storm God with
his thunderbolt or stone mace, his phallus that became the sword,
were accompanied by the twelve Gods of the Mount, and by the
Naked Horsemen. When in AD 1189 the port reeve of London
became the first Mayor, we find the civic government evolved out of
the ancient pattern; the Lord Mayor with his mace and sword, his
aldermen and his twin sheriffs. To this day, on state occasions at the
Guildhall, the mace and swords are laid out in the form of an Andra's
Cross.

This symbolic connection with pre-Roman Britain in more
complicated detail is clearly to be traced in the actual pageantry of the
Midsummer Watch, as held in the fourteenth, fifteenth and sixteenth
centuries. The procession of the Midsummer Watch consisted of
several thousand men, but no clergy; it marched from St Paul's Cross
– Old Paulie – round the city and back to the same point.

In the procession, first came a company of Morris dancers, then
twelve 'hobbye-horses' and after men in armour followed by drum-
mers with a very tall canvas giant. After this came three hundred
archers and others. Then a band of musicians with fifty naked boys,
dyed black like devils, with darts to goad the followers of Pluto.
Pluto was a large figure in a decorated cart seated under a canopy.
'He himself being naked, with drawn sword in his hand.' Clearly in
an earlier age this London 'Pluto' would have been the Horned
God, and gives us an exact parallel to the change of Bacchus into
Pluto.

Another band of steel-clad halberdiers marched next, preceding the
Prophets, with the Tree of Life sprouting from the belly of a recum-
bent male figure, and by certain mechanisms the Prophets turned
about from side to side.[7]

In an earlier time the prophets would have been Arch-Druids. This is a very strange survival of the prophets who had been so long ousted by the priests.

Then came other marching men and carnival figures preceding choristers on foot in white surplices, in front of a stage on which a very beautiful little girl under a canopy represented the Virgin Mary with four boys chanting Lauds – clearly the Maiden of the Older Cult. Next came a band of halberdiers with a stage on which was St George in armour, choking a big dragon and delivering St Margaret.

Then after more soldiers and musicians came twenty-four grave personages – mostly aldermen – all dressed in black velvet with chains of gold and mounted on 'small naggies' – a faint memory of the days when only the ass was available for important persons to ride upon. Then in contrast to the solemnity of such equipment and demeanour came the Lord Mayor's two henchmen. They rode upon 'great stirring horses' clothed in red, white and gold with huge head-dresses of plumes, some of which stood upright and some which flowed down their backs. Then the sword-bearer carrying the sword of the city preceded the Lord Mayor in crimson damask, and behind the two sheriffs, also on horseback, with crimson surcoats.

The above account from R. Liddesdale Palmer is a mixture of periods but it shows how clearly the whole ceremonial was marked with the traditional pattern and colour of the cult of the Heavenly Twins. The Watch moreover was held on the great day of Michael and was purely pagan throughout, with the flower festival of the Stone Age mingled with the bonfires of the Solar Cult and the thousands of lamps from the cult of Diana.

In 1598 John Stow published an account of how London celebrated Midsummer Day in his time:

> In the evenings after the sun setting there were usually made bonfires in the streets, every man bestowing wood or labour towards them; the wealthier sort also, before their doors near to the said bonfires, would set out tables on the said vigils, furnished with sweet bread and good drink, and on the festival days with meals and drinks plentifully, whereunto they would invite their neighbours and passengers also to

sit and be merry with them in great familiarity, praising God for His benefits bestowed on them. They were called bonfires as well of good amnity amongst neighbours that being before at controversy, were there, by the labour of others, reconciled, and made of bitter enemies, loving friends . . . Every man's door being shadowed with green birch, long fennel, St John's wort, orpin, white lilies, and such like, garnished upon with garlands of beautiful flowers had also lamps of glass, with oil burning in them all the night; some hung out with branches of iron curiously wrought, containing hundreds of lamps alight all at once which made a goodly show.[8]

It is curious that for nearly a thousand years under the Roman Church Britain held tenaciously to her ancient customs, but with the advent of Protestantism she let the old customs fall into abeyance. Thus in throwing off the political yoke she accepted the spiritual. Little but her national symbols and Orders of Knighthood survived. Of these nothing shows more clearly the continuity of custom than Britannia and her attributes, all of which can be traced back not only to Cappadocia, like St George, but to that lost civilization in Asia from which the Indo-Europeans first came. Amongst the Phoenicians she was called 'the Daughter of the Phoenix', and the Lycaonians of Asia Minor called her Barate. Here the Phoenix, like the Swan, seems to have replaced the goose.

On the Lycaonian coins Barate is depicted as a robed woman seated on a rock or ship amidst waves, and says T.A. Waddell:

She holds the cornucopia or horn of plenty . . . and beside her chair on board ship is a shield-like Sun Cross, or St George's Cross within the sun's disc designating her to be of the Solar Cult . . . On the other coins of Cilicia, Lycaonia, Phoenicia, and other Phoenician colonies she sometimes holds a sceptre or standard cross . . . and she sometimes carried a torch . . . which explains the lighthouse figured beside Britannia on the old pennies . . . In the Vedic hymns all the attributes of Britannia are accounted for, her titularship of the waters, her Neptune's trident, her helmet and her shield; her cross on her shield as well as the cornucopia which . . . takes the place of the corn-stalk on the British coins.[9]

On some of the coins are stamped the words 'The Commonwealth of the Lycaon Barats', showing that even then Britannia was a special symbol for a Commonwealth of free people. T.Λ. Waddell also tells us that the Trojan Barate bore the title 'Parthenos'. She is sometimes represented on early Hittite seals with the weapons of the chase. Thus she became confused with or identified with Diana. One legend says she sailed west and when she reached Crete she was pursued by the unwelcome attentions of the Minos and escaped by retiring to the sea, sailing to the Island of Aegina, and disappeared there at the spot where now stands the Temple of Diana.

The legend of Barate or Parthenos also throws some light on the underlying symbolism of the Acts of the Apostles. St Paul came from Tarsus, whose original name was 'Parthenia'. He was connected with Diana of Ephesus and he was mistaken for Mercury (the ruler of the Twins in astrology). Paul like Parthenos 'passed through Phoenicia'; and Syria and Cilicia and came down to Troy, on the way to Macedonia: and so to Athens where he is said to have converted both Dionysus, and Apollos. Like Parthenos he sailed to Crete and was driven away. Moreover he sailed in the good ship, named after the Heavenly Twins, Castor and Pollux; and so to Rome where there was, beyond the walls, another famous Temple to Diana. Thence, as some authorities declare and others deny, he came to Britain. Whatever be the truth of that, the fact remains that St Paul not only became the patron saint of London's great shrine to Diana, but the church of St Paul-without-the-walls at Rome to this day remains, for reasons unexplained, under the unique patronage of the kings of England.

In turn the legend of Diana, Roman in origin, replaced the older Brit or Bride. Britannia is indeed none other than The Great Mother herself, the oldest figure known to mankind. She presided over the seas at the dawn of the agricultural age. She is almost the sole great figure of the past to survive without being Christianized. Surely it would put new heart into efforts in these grim days to realize – once again – that the great symbol of our Mother Country is immortal, for she alone has survived millennia of storm and was already here – in Britain – and hoary with age, before the first legendary dynasties of Sumeria or China.

18

Parliament Hill and the Druids

Ross Nichols
Chosen Chief of the Order of Bards, Ovates and Druids

Foreword

In 1965 the Order of Bards, Ovates and Druids, reformed in 1964, began its series of observances of the Spring and Autumnal Equinoxes and of the Summer Solstice upon Parliament Hill, Highgate, as the most ancient and important Gorsedd site near London. Since 1717 indeed the Autumnal Equinox has been celebrated in one way or another, for a long time upon Primrose Hill, Regent's Park; and observances of some kind at Stonehenge for the Summer Solstice seem never to have altogether ceased. Nevertheless since the Ministry of Works has begun to keep out the general public from the solstice dawn for which the temple was designed and to which they have in fact a prescriptive right as owners, Stonehenge has recently seemed unfit to be used as the main temple for this rite. Moreover London is the main centre of this country now, as the Stonehenge region was for the late Wessex culture of the fifteenth-century BC; and ceremonies should be held with their public in mind.

The following, slightly adapted from talks given at the various festivals by the Chief, are based upon considerable research together with traditional lore handed down through his office as Chief. Few people in Highgate seem to be aware of their own traditions in these matters, so this work is offered to fill an apparent gap.

1. A Talk upon the Llandin or Parliament Hill in 1965

Your Worship, Companions and Friends.

You stand on the most distinguished eminence of London, that which named the city. There are two high places, twin heights of the older London, this and the Penton. Highgate Hill, perhaps because of its springs and ponds, was not it seems a centre in the same way; it might well however have been the abode of a mother goddess. Llandin in old Welsh is *Lyndin*, the Lake City, the old name of London; Penton is the Hill of the Head or the Holy Hill. The Llandin is the higher, the dominating hill ringed with mound and ditch; the Penton had a well and was almost certainly crowned with a stone circle orientated to the May sunrise, where preparations were likely to have been made with ceremonies for the main Gorsedd upon the Llandin.

By legend this mounded and ditched hill is Britain's Areopagus. Around it was the old city of *Caer Troia* or *Troia Nova*, the migrated form of Troy, whose inhabitants had been led here by Brutus, grandson of Aeneas who fled from Troy. He is said to have landed at Totnes in the far West near the Brutus stone. Here St Paul is said to have preached and he is certainly one of London's two apostles, the other being Peter who appeared in vision on Thorney Island and then dedicated the church-abbey of Westminster himself. St Paul's sword of decapitation is part of the arms of the City of London.

This Port of Llandin, or *Londinium* in its Latin form, was famous for the numbers of its merchant ships, mentioned by Tacitus about AD 60. Strabo mentions them as trading corn, cattle, iron, hides, slaves and dogs to the Seine and Rhine. By the end period of the Roman occupation, by AD 359, there were some 800 vessels solely engaged in exporting corn. The town was the seat of the chief administrative official, the Vicarius of the Province.

Over all this the Llandin and Penton presided, with the lesser and more artificial hills of the *Bryn Gwyn* ('White Hill' or Tower of London) and the Tot Hill. They formed a triangle, the long side of which pointed directly from here towards the south-east. The line passes through Boadicea's Tumulus, Parliament Hill, Gospel Oak and the Penton to the *Bryn Gwyn*. Up here might well be held therefore the ceremony of midwinter's dawn solstice. Below you lies Gospel

Oak, that is, the Druid Oak under which Edward the Confessor sat and renewed the City of London's charter, oathing upon the Gospels.

At the grove at Highgate nearby we have the probable site of a Druid college. In the Penton is an ancient telescope-well said to have been used by Merddin (Merlin) for his calculations. Perhaps the holy well, Deans Yard Westminster, was of similar use. Telescope-wells of the same kind are used still; one is at Mount Wilson Observatory.

This area held one of the earliest memories of a fight for freedom. It was only after sacking *Londinium* with great thoroughness that Boadicea, the mother-queen of the Iceni, was eventually defeated, probably at Battle Bridge, Agar Town, now part of Camden Town. Her army was encamped here, it is said, and thence swept down to the fight. They may well have brought her body up again; her grave is said to be in that tumulus, on the north-west slope of the hill. She fought for the old right of a matrilinear succession against the usurping and tyrannous Romans, and if she did not finally succeed, she at least made them pay a terrible price. Her spirit was triumphant; on a stone just below us, to the south-east, was recorded that this was, and is, one of the places of free speech, and on the hill or the fields around us have been held numberless public assemblies, some most vital to English history.

The Witan of the area met on this hill for centuries; it must then have been rather like the terraced Tynwald in the Isle of Man. Following on this, here the electors met to choose their MPs; they did so until 1822. So you see that, although largely ironed out now, these circular terracings, mound and ditch, meant something linking past with present. We still need the Stone of Free Speech to remind us of the ancient right.

Other great meetings here have usually struck a similar kind of national note. Here a great concourse of citizens representing the City of London came and welcomed Elizabeth I as the new queen rode to her capital. General Monk's army made this a main organization point on his way down from Scotland to reorganize government, so as to put into effect the general wish for a restoration of the monarchy.

In the eighteenth century London's train bands deployed here for exercise in periods of national danger.

324

Names famous in our history cluster here. Upon the hill of Highgate Dick Whittington is said to have sat and heard his chime-message predicting his success. He has quite definite historical links up here in the fifteenth century, although his cat-totem may be a take-over from earlier medieval symbols. The great Francis Bacon died here as Lord St Albans, as the result of an experiment it is said. Cromwell and Ireton and Nell Gwynn all lived hereabouts. There are other names famous in art and literature: Andrew Marvell, the poet, George Morland, the prolific painter of farm and domestic scenes, William Blake, ancestor of the poet who was one of the Order's Chosen Chiefs, above all the Sage of Highgate, Samuel Taylor Coleridge, at number three, the Grove.

Upon this historic spot, then, which presided as it were over London's beginnings and still presides, we appear on the old assembly place of Ancient Druids for the first open-air public London ceremony of the reshaped Order of Bards, Ovates and Druids, as the earlier reformed shape of the Order appeared for the first time in 1717 on Primrose Hill. Then John Toland had united at least ten areas of Druidry into one Order, and ever since Druids have met there. On this more dominating height we proclaim again the truth of Universal Majesty, Verity and Love Infinite, with the weight of the still older triple-formed traditions behind us. Our Bards may be seen in blue, our Vates in green; the Druid has the inner robe of white. In these forms we wish to unite with our Breton, French and Welsh companions in an augury we hope of greater unity.

The regulations for our meetings were laid down by Aed Mawr, the founder of the Order in its western form, many centuries ago. 'A Gorsedd of the Bards of Britain must be held on a green spot, in a conspicuous place, in full view and hearing of country and aristocracy, in the face of the sun, the Eye of Light, under the expansive freedom of the sky, that all may see and hear.'[1]

There are a decreasing number of green spots. Stonehenge is polluted with gravel; the *Bryn Gwyn* or Tower of London is paved; the Penton's top is a reservoir – not inappropriate for a feminine-type hill, yet not a natural thing. Here, although the old rivulet has been diverted for the reasonable purpose of forming ponds, we have still the Parliament Fields, where we may meet and parley in the ancient circle carrying out the timeless ceremony that marries the order and its teachings to a locality, wherein she who represents Earth makes her gifts and the civic area receives and welcomes us.

Here we hope later we may meet and make friends with some of you. Unity and harmony are what the world needs today as much as it has ever needed them. For these we stand, and for the promotion of them in ourselves, in this land; for we cannot lead others in this path if we have not travelled it ourselves.

2. The Winter Orientation from the Hill

'The Ancients wrote it in the earth' is an old Druid saying: that is, they made symbolic constructions to signify meanings, which only those of a later age understand who are trained in symbolism or have an instinctive imaginative grasp. This has been realized concerning Stonehenge; what is more surprising is to find such a concept written in natural features.

Looking on a map at the sites of the summit of Parliament Hill, the traditional site Gospel Oak where Edward I is said to have confirmed the laws of England, the top of the old Pen Ton earlier said to have been crowned by a Druidic construction and now holding a reservoir, and the old White Mound, the *Bryn Gwyn* or site of the Tower of London, we find, as said before, that they fall into a straight line. When one realizes that this line points within a degree or so to the place of the midwinter sunrise, light is thrown upon the crucial importance of the Llandin in the concepts of our ancestors.

Manifestly, man did not create these hills. But having the preoccupation with orientations that does characterize the Stone Circle civilization and its successors, a race that found such an extraordinary natural phenomenon would naturally conclude that all three hills, and especially the Llandin, as that from which the rest were sighted, were infinitely holy, and chose the most distinguished as a natural preordained centre for government or cult. As at Stonehenge, no signs of a prehistoric settlement having been found, it seems fair to conclude that it was a sanctified assembly place, probably for government or meeting-place of kings over a wide area, like the Hill of Tara in Eire.

326

Perhaps indeed the higher, nearby Highgate Hill was devoted to a deity and so unfit for man to assemble upon; repeatedly in the earlier Mediterranean island sites we find that temples are not so much upon holy hills as on lower heights near them, high hills being for gods or goddesses.

The midwinter sunrise or sunset at the south-east or south-west was a direction as much valued for the cult as the sunrise place at the north-east. In the case of Stonehenge it seems clear that it is orientated to the winter sunset as much as, or perhaps more than, to the midsummer sunrise. If we can distinguish it would seem that the winter observances were the earlier and linked rather with moon and other emblems of the mother goddess.

It seems therefore that on Parliament Hill we have not merely traces of a very large *gorsedd*-place, a place of circle gatherings (*cor* or *gor* means 'circle'), aboriginal for the London area, but also an obvious site for an early cult, perhaps of the sun as mother rather than father – the birth of the 'small sun' of midwinter, after all, suggests motherhood, and the sun in Eire is a goddess . . .

This is where we should hold a Winter Solstice observance; but the weather having changed from the near-Mediterranean type of 2000 BC, we hold it less heroically in a London hall. However, we make up for it by celebrating up here as well as we can the Summer Solstice ceremonial in its three solemnities of Vigil, Dawn and Moon.

3. Talk upon Parliament Hill at Alban Eiler, 20 March 1966, at noon

Your Worship, my Lady Mayoress, Companions and Friends.

For the second time we of the Order of Bards, Ovates and Druids greet you of the northern heights and the legendary city at the festival of the Spring equinox or *Alban Eiler*.

What is this festa with the strange title that we are celebrating for you today, when the civil authorities are beginning the yearly manipulation of the calendar that makes our noon one p.m.? It is the equality of day and night in the season when the day – the sun – is winning. This event is one of the sixteen sightings that our ancestors worked out on the mystic dial of Stonehenge. Ever since the eighteenth century Druids have been declaring that Stonehenge was a calculating scheme aimed many ways; this was repeatedly scoffed at as arbitrary fancy, just the kind of thing that people led by the 'imaginative' Dr Stukeley, a leading archaeologist as archaeology then went, and Chief of the Order, would say.

Then, some three years back, an American researcher put Stonehenge sightings together with a working-back of the positions in the heavens to 1500 BC – the estimated date of Stonehenge – into Harvard's computer and behold, the sighting lines of the sunset and sunrise, moonset and moonrise, for both solstices and equinoxes, were correct (to within a tiny fraction of error, probably due to the shifting of the stones over three and a half thousand years).

This had quite an amount of publicity, e.g. in *Nature*. No one, however, made any amends to the Druids, who had always indicated these truths, I noticed. In one age, a mystic statement is truth and experiment is lies, as with Galileo; is it an improvement when computer truth must be right and any occult or mystical pronouncement is automatically discounted?

At this season, then, recorded in these islands at least as long ago as 1500 BC, we show you again some signs of the meaning in the *Alban Eiler*. Rays at these seasons were magical and propitious; some scientific inquiry has recently been made indeed into the effects of angles such as trines (120°) and squares (60°) and it seems to find significance in these, just as in the *Bryn Celli Ddu* in Anglesey, where the angulations from the hidden cup in the line of light of the longest day are obviously marked by twelve stones. Just now the ray-angle is one said to favour growth; it is a season propitious to planting and quick firm formations.

Alban means 'light'; it is used to denote the four festivals of the astronomical year, when the sun is furthest north or south, or his swing is equal between darkness and light in some form. *Eiler* means 'of the earth'; it is the sphere of earth we are conscious of at this time, its force and its transforming face.

The ancients conceived earth as afloat in water, and the next *Alban* is concerned with the *shores* – *Alban Heruin*, the ever-trembling and moving shore of the earth, the place of eternal change and balance between the rising and the falling, the Summer Solstice. But beyond the shore is the mysterious depth of ocean, into which all waters seem to flow, which grows darker with the shorter evenings – and *water* is the sphere of the Autumn equinox, *Alban Elued*, the year descending into ocean.

Three elements have been signified – Eiler the Earth, Elued the Water, and the eternal swinging and changing between them, Heruin, signifies the transformation of fire. But at the fourth the figure changes; we raise our eyes to the sky at night and see the fixed centre of all things, the star of the north that signifies perpetual dark, the sky's quarter where the sun never shines, where the axis is fixed round which move the circumpolar stars and those 'wandering stars' the planets; and this is the high place of air, *Alban Arthuan*, the light-time that is of darkness or night and belongs to the Great Bear. We have a saying in the Order 'Arthur is dark to us' – and here is some of its meaning.

This is a scrap from the vast mound of the hereditary lore that can now be given out as circumstances become fitting. This Order is ready to give further to all who will seek sincerely. Much is given by symbolic ceremonies, not words. You have seen the fire of spring burning in the censer – primed now with English herbs and resins, by the way, as has not for long been done: you have seen the trefoil that is the form of the footprints of the Spring Goddess in many forms, presented by the Young One, the Mabin of the Order; then the Lady of Spring's seeds and buds have been given and scattered for growth. The Lady and the Presider represent season and patronage respectively. The Presider used to be a local lord and the Lady's actions were magical.

Early in February, we showed the first ploughing and the washing of the Earth-Mother's face; now in March comes the liberation of buds and leaves, yet still seeds are being sown. In May, at Beltane, come the full spring flowers. This festival we may hold at Glastonbury. So we pass, in alternate Albans and Fire Festivals, through the year's arches in a rhythm marked out, giving you something of the old and the permanent that is living and therefore also new.

There is here behind me the new version of the old Banner of the Order with its visible presentation of the truth; the Three Rays, the gateway trilithon, the mound of the ancestors, the three fields of knowledge – the springing seed, the ripening grain, the calm blue hills, and over all the eightfold sun of many colours. It is this banner's first out-of-door appearance, and this therefore again is something of an occasion.

We shall now hold a brief eisteddfod of poetry, before the closing ceremony; this will give you the hailing of the four quarters in the names of the correct archangels and the saints of the four lands that are Brittanic. When we unite in thought for others, we should be glad if you would contact in a ring by clasping hands, since this always ensures more beneficent power.

4. Talk at the Vigil 21–22 June 1967, given by the Chosen Chief beside Boadicea's Tumulus

We are here to celebrate a great Queen on the nineteen-hundred-and-sixth anniversary of her death, beside her reputed tomb. I would like to give you a rehearsal of the main facts of her remarkable struggle for freedom and justice.

The Claudian conquest took place AD 43–4. In AD 61 Britain had therefore experienced the yoke of Roman military rule for some eighteen years and found it increasingly burdensome and unjust.

It was in Nero's time that the able and aggressive Suetonius Paulinus became military governor. The demands of Rome for money became clamorous and moral scruples under such an Emperor were weak. Many well-to-do Britons had fled to Anglesey, and the Druids were agitators in the resistance there to Roman rule. Suetonius decided to quell the Anglesey area of refugees early in AD 61 – perhaps March; he crossed England and in the face of desperate resistance slaughtered the rebels, especially a great crowd of unarmed Druids, who for some time terrified the Roman soldiers by their aspect and hostile magic.

Meanwhile the civil administrators had grasped the whole fortune of the late Prasutagus, Boadicea's husband, for Rome, and violated Boadicea's daughters. Now the peculiar feature of Boadicea's kingdom of the Iceni was that it was matriarchal, that is, the elder of these girls was the heiress to the throne: Prasutagus had merely been consort. Rome with its patriarchal tradition, refused to recognize the daughter's rights. This, and the outrageous taxation demands, caused Boadicea to rise in rebellion with a confederacy of East Anglian tribes. She sacked St Albans, then London, in early July, acting in obvious collaboration with the Anglesey Druids.

As Suetonius had marched back with the memory of the Druid curses still ringing in his ears he had been met by the news, as though in their fulfilment, for he had killed those whose Order forbade them to take any part in war. Suetonius decided to abandon these cities, having forces inferior to the vast army of charioted tribesmen that Boadicea led. With great skill he chose his ground near Islington, King's Cross area, where Battle Bridge keeps the memory. It was an enclosed site wherein the wheeling British chariots would have no space to manoeuvre. He awaited her attack.

Tacitus has the maddening habit of describing battles in some detail without giving a hint of where they occurred. Now Hampstead and Highgate forest areas were then continuous with Epping Forest, and in Essex was Boadicea's stronghold. A recent book on Boadicea places the great battle between Boadicea and Suetonius far away in the Midlands; but there really seems little ground for upsetting the earlier location. According to this earlier version, she simply led her forces across, and their resting and rallying place was on Parliament Hill, in all probability. They descended thence upon this enclosed Roman terrain by chariot and waggon, a journey of some five miles, early in August in the year 61.

The Celts were over-confident in their chariots and numbers. They even brought their families to witness the victory.

The Roman war machine, ably handled, won: the 'tortoise' of locked shields, the spears and daggers, progressed pitilessly upon the Celts, now hampered by their discarded chariots and waggons, unable to escape. There was great slaughter. The defeat was final.

After the event it was normal for Celtic forces to withdraw to their camping place; and Boadicea's suicide, to avoid the gross indignities put upon the defeated by Rome, whether it occurred on the battle-field or on Parliament Hill, would have meant a funeral pyre, for this people burnt their dead, thus releasing the spirit from the earthly shell as soon as possible. Reincarnation, or rather metempsychosis, was a distinctively Celtic faith; those who died bravely or in brave protest were received with honour in the land of the *Sidhe* and returned soon to earth with noble parentage. Whether this Neolithic chamber ever contained these royal ashes is very doubtful – there were no burial signs when it was opened up. Nevertheless the fact that Boadicea's name is attached to it may perpetuate a memory of her dying or being burnt hereabouts.

The Iceni were a Brythonic race of the first Iron Age mixed with the Parisii people, from the Seine, of the second Iron Age. They were a cultured folk in dress, ornaments and weapons. Boadicea is described as very tall, with a commanding aspect, a strong voice and yellow hair, which fell past her waist.

Boadicea's goddess was Andate: the name is also given as Adraste and Andarte; this, and her own name as Boudicca, both mean 'victory' or 'victorious'. There is a votive altar at Bordeaux linking Andate with the name Boudicca. A very ancient and widespread belief is reflected in the account of her divining from the running of a hare.

The Celtic god of war was 'Camulus', it is interesting to note; compare the names Camulodunum (Colchester) and Camelot. The old form seems to have been Camhael – which is a form of the name of our Druidic President (Dr Charles Cammell).

The name of Boadicea's Chief Druid has come down to us as Sywedydd, meaning 'the one learned in the mysteries'. He it was who prepared the poisons for Boadicea and her daughters to take, so that they should not be seized as prisoners for exhibition in one of the triumphal processions of Nero's Rome.

If there is one figure rather than another in our history which can fulfil the idea of Britannia as shown on our coinage, Boadicea's surely does so. Her evidently statuesque form with its majestic decorative Celtic helmet of the period is a much truer model of what we would like to think of as an embodiment of national courage, than was ever in fact the model used, Emma, Lady Hamilton, Nelson's friend, beautiful as her face was.

It seems appropriate that the fullest book until very recently upon Boadicea was written by a Druid, Lewis Spence, the great antiquary and a recent President of the Order.

We shall now place this wreath of oak-sprays and red roses to Boadicea, Boudicca or Boudega, defender of liberty against oppression, and then we will speak of and read a list of those great Druids who have passed on . . .

To the Memory of
A GREAT NATIONAL LEADER
QUEEN
BOUDEGA
who died hereabouts AD 61
after the joint revolt of Iceni and Druids
against Roman outrage and oppression.

Laid by the
ORDER OF BARDS, OVATES AND DRUIDS
MCMLXVII

Notes on Contributors

Geraldine Beskin is happy researching almost any aspect of the Western Esoteric worlds of the last 150 years. Film and television companies, as well as authors, witches and magicians frequently consult her encyclopoedic knowledge of the occult world. She has a significant collection of esoteric first editions and has been collecting the artist Austin Spare since the 1970s. Aleister Crowley was a friend of the founder of the Atlantis Bookshop, of which Geraldine's family first took ownership in the 1960s. With her daughter, Bali Beskin, she maintains a home from home for researchers from their delightful shop in London's Bloomsbury. Her interest in Crowley in particular, as well as the lives of other famous magicians, has enabled her biographical talks to be given internationally to discerning audiences.

Carol Clancy is a cockney from the East End of London. Her family has lived here and worked on the river for more than 200 years. She has had a life-long love affair with her native city, full of beauty in unexpected places.

Gareth Knight is one of the world's foremost authorities on ritual magic, the Western Mystery Tradition and Qabalistic symbolism. He trained in Dion Fortune's Society of the Inner Light, and has spent a lifetime rediscovering and teaching the principles of magic as a spiritual discipline and method of self-realization. He has written about fifty books, including translations from the French, on topics as diverse as Christian Qabalism, history of magic, Arthurian legend, Rosicrucianism, tarot, the Inklings (J.R.R. Tolkien, C.S. Lewis et al.), faery traditions and the feminine mysteries. His blog and a full list of his books can be found on his website: www.garethknight.net.

Caitlín Matthews is the author of over seventy books including the forthcoming *Lost Book of the Grail*, and a two-volume study of *The Mabinogion, Mabon and the Heroes of Celtic Britain* and *King Arthur and the Goddess of the Land*. She is co-founder of the Foundation for Inspirational and Oracular Studies dedicated to the sacred arts. She teaches internationally on a range of subjects including shamanism, myth, ritual and aspects of the Western Spiritual Tradition. Her website is: www.hallowquest.org.uk.

John Matthews has been a full-time writer since 1980 and has produced over 100 books on myth, faery, the Arthurian legends and Grail studies, as well as short stories, a volume of poetry and several successful children's books. He has devoted much of the past forty years to the study of Arthurian traditions and myth in general. His best-known and most widely read works are *Pirates* (Carlton/Athenaeum), No. 1 book on the *New York Times* best-seller list for twenty-two weeks in 2006, *The Grail, Quest for Eternal Life* (Thames & Hudson, 1981), *The Winter Solstice* (Quest Books, 1999), which won the Benjamin Franklin Award for that year, and *The Wildwood Tarot* (with Mark Ryan). His book *Celtic Warrior Chiefs* was a New York Public Library recommended title for young people, and the more recent *Arthur of Albion* won a Gold Medal from NAPPA, a gold Moonbeams Award and a BIB Golden Apple Award.

John has been involved in a number of media projects, as an adviser and contributor, and was the historical adviser to the Jerry Bruckheimer movie *King Arthur* (2004). He shared a BAFTA award for his work on the educational DVD made to accompany the movie.

Bernard Nesfield-Cookson was educated at a Rudolf Steiner school in London and at the universities of Jena, London, and Bristol. He was the principal of Hawkwood College, an independent centre for adult education in Gloucestershire until his retirement. He is the author of *Rudolf Steiner's Vision of Love* (Aquarian Press, 1983) and *William Blake: Prophet of Universal Brotherhood* (Aquarian Press, 1987).

Nigel Pennick is a writer and lecturer on ancient and modern mysteries, an authority on northern European geomancy, runemaster, practising geomant and traditional symbolic craftsman. A founder and coordinator of the Institute of Geomantic Research, he organized five Cambridge geomantic symposia, and has coordinated an international conference on labyrinths. He has written many books including *Games of the Gods* (Rider, 1988) and *Practical Magic in the Northern Tradition* (Aquarian Press, 1989).

Chesca Potter was born in Lancaster in 1958. She worked as a freelance artist from 1985, after graduating from Edinburgh College of Art. She has illustrated numerous books, including *The Grail Seeker's Companion* (Aquarian Press, 1987), *The Western Way* (Arkana, 1985/6), *Mabon and the Mysteries of Britain* (Arkana, 1988), *Arthur and the Sovereignty of Britain* (Arkana, 1990). She collaborated with Mark Ryan on *The Greenwood Tarot* (Aquarian, 1996) and with John Matthews on *The Celtic Shaman's Pack* (Element, 1995). She has also published several articles on earth mysteries, and a booklet on *Mysterious King's Cross* (1988).

Robert Stephenson is a Londoner who has taught and written about his native city for over twenty years. As a qualified City of London Guide and a tour leader and trustee at Kensal Green and Brompton cemeteries, he lectures widely about funereal history and on London.

Robert John Stewart is a Scottish author, musician and composer, living in Glastonbury, Britain, and in Seattle, USA. Author of forty-five books on music, mythology, and magical subjects, both fiction and non-fiction. He has also recorded and produced numerous musical albums and CDs, appeared many times on television in Britain and the USA, and has created music for feature film, television, and theatre productions. His website is: www.rjstewart.org.

Caroline Wise has a passion for London, especially the old gods and goddesses and the legendary foundations of the City. She has been an esoteric bookseller, once owning the Atlantis Bookshop, and has

337

produced many conferences on folklore, such as the Wildwood series in the 1990s, and major goddess events. She now works as a publisher. Caroline compiled the book *Finding Elen, the Quest for Elen of the Ways* and has contributed to others. She gives talks on the women occult pioneers of the nineteenth and twentieth centuries, and of the great goddesses of the ancient world. She lectures and leads walks and workshops on mythic London.

Notes and Sources

Chapter 2: New Troy: London Before History

1. Quoted in Lewis Spence, *Legendary London*, Robert Hale, 1937, hereafter simply referred to as Spence.
2. Geoffrey of Monmouth, *History of the Kings of Britain*, various editions, including that of Lewis Thorpe, Penguin Books, 1976.
3. Acton Griscom (Ed.), *Historia Regum Britanniae of Geoffrey of Monmouth*, Longmans, 1929.
4. J.R.R. Tolkien and E.V. Gordon (Eds.), *Sir Gawain and the Green Knight*, Clarendon Press, 1925.
5. Rev. Peter Roberts, *The Cambrian Popular Antiquities*, E. Williams, 1815.
6. Virgil, *The Aeneid*, Robert Fitzgerald (Trans.), Harvill Press, 1984.
7. Spence.
8. ibid.
9. Raphael Holinshed, *The Survey of Modern London*, 1788.
10. Sir John Rhys, *Celtic Heathendom*, London, 1888.
11. See the Gazetteer below.
12. *Brut Tysilio*, Peter Roberts (Ed.), *The Chronicle of the Kings of Britain*, London, 1811.
13. Anthony Roberts, *Sowers of Thunder*, Rider & Co, 1978.
14. William Blake, *Poetry and Prose*, G. Keynes (Ed.), The Nonesuch Press, 1975.
15. ibid (see: *A Descriptive Catalogue.*)
16. Plutarch, *Moralia*, Vol. V, F.C. Babbitt (Trans.), William Heinemann, 1957.
17. *The Mabinogion*, J. Gantz (Trans.), Penguin Books, 1979.
18. Spence.
19. ibid.
20. Lewis Spence, *The Mysteries of Britain*, Aquarian Press, 1970.
21. Edward Hatton, *New View of London*, 1708.
22. Quoted by Spence.

Chapter 3: Goddesses of London

1. Geoffrey of Monmouth, *History of the Kings of Britain.*
2. Discussed by John Clark in *The Temple of Diana*: www.academia.edu/5937963/The_Temple_of_Diana. Also see *Interpreting Roman London: Papers in Memory of Hugh Chapman*, Oxbow Monographs in Archaeology, Oxbow Books, 1996, pp. 1–9.
3. William Camden, *Britannia*, 1610.
4. Walter Thornbury, *Old and New London*, originally published Cassell, Petter & Galpin, London, 1878.
5. John Stow, *Survey of London.*
6. See: archive.museumoflondon.org.uk/Londinium/analysis/religiouslife/structures/.
7. R.E. Witt, *Isis in the Graeco-Roman World.*
8. See: archive.museumoflondon.org.uk/Londinium.
9. See: cathedral.southwark.anglican.org/.
10. http://www.stbrides.com/history/43---1000.htm.
11. *Our Lady of Willesden*, Catholic Truth Society, 1980.
12. *ASSAP News*, May 1987.
13. Metropolitan Museum of Art, New York: *Statues of the Goddess Sekhmet.*
14. Stow, *Survey of London.*

Chapter 4: The Guardian Head

1. R.P. Weston and Bert Lee, 'With Her Head Tucked Underneath Her Arm', Francis, Day & Hunter, 1934.
2. *The Mabinogion* (MAB), Lady Charlotte Guest (Trans.), David Nutt, 1910.
3. *The Welsh Triads* (TYP), Rachel Bromwich, (Ed. and Trans.), University of Wales Press, 1961.
4. MAB.
5. C. Kerenyi, *The Gods of the Greeks*, Thames & Hudson, 1951.
6. ibid.
7. Kerenyi, *The Heroes of the Greeks*, Thames & Hudson, 1959.
8. Pausanius, *Guide to Greece*, Vol, 1, p. 152, Peter Levi (Ed. and Trans.), Penguin, 1971.
9. Julius Caesar, *The Conquest of Gaul*, V, 18, S.A. Handford (Trans.), Penguin, 1951.
10. MAB.
11. TYP, p. 352.
12. Caitlín Matthews, *King Arthur and the Goddess of the Land*, Inner Traditions, 2002.
13. Matthews, *Mabon and the Guardians of Celtic Britain*, Inner Traditions, 2002.
14. Matthews, *King Arthur.*
15. Geoffrey of Monmouth, *History of the Kings of Britain*, VII, 4, Lewis Thorpe (Trans.), Penguin, 1966.
16. TYP, p. 88.

17. ibid., p. 89.
18. ibid., p. 387.
19. MAB.
20. Geoffrey, p. 166.
21. MAB.
22. Matthews, *Mabon*, p. 164.
23. ibid., p. 107.
24. TYP, p. 241.
25. Bartrum, *13 Treasures*, Elliol Cetl, 1063.
26. TYP, p. 5.
27. John Matthews, with additional material by Caitlín Matthews, *Taliesin: the Last Celtic Shaman*.
28. Emyr Humphrey, *The Taliesin Tradition*, p. 16, Black Raven, 1983.
29. Geoffrey, pp. 176–7.
30. TYP, p. 229.
31. A similar thing is said of the Irish god, Lugh, in the Second Battle of Mag Tuiread. 'They made a *cro* of Lug', meaning an enclosure or protected space: Nikolai Tolstoy, 'Merlinus Redivivus', *Studia Celtica*, XVIII/XIX.

Chapter 5: Templar London

1. Archbishop William of Tyre, *History*, I.
2. Rev. Professor T.G. Bonney, 'Temple Church, London, etc.', *Abbeys and Churches*, Vol. II, London, 1891.

Chapter 7: Merlin in London

1. R.J. Stewart (Ed.), *The Book of Merlin*, Blandford Press, 1987. Contains articles on Merlin and British legends by various authors. See also the second anthology *Merlin and Woman*, Blandford Press, 1988. Both volumes are drawn from Merlin Conferences, held in London in the 1980s.
2. Rachel Bromwich (Trans.), *The Welsh Triads*, University of Wales, Cardiff, 1961.
3. See also R.J. Stewart, 'Merlin, King Bladud, and the Wheel of Life' in *The Book of Merlin*. The relationship between Merlin and Mabon is discussed in depth in Chapter 15 of *The Mystic Life of Merlin* (see Note 5 below). The mythic and legendary significance of the Welsh *Mabinogion* is examined by Caitlín Matthews in *Mabon and the Mysteries of Britain: An Exploration of The Mabinogion*, Arkana, 1987, and *Arthur and the Sovereignty of Britain: King and Goddess in The Mabinogion*, Arkana, 1989.

4. Geoffrey of Monmouth, *The History of the Kings of Britain*, various translations. The modern standard is set by Lewis Thorpe, Penguin, 1966. A detailed commentary on the *History* is found in J.S.P. Tatlock's *The Legendary History of Britain*, University of Berkeley, California, 1950.

5. R.J. Stewart, *The Mystic Life of Merlin*. A detailed commentary upon the esoteric, magical, cosmological and legendary content of the *Vita Merlini* of Geoffrey of Monmouth, with an edited version of the translation by J.J. Parry, Arkana, 1986. Particular emphasis is given to the shamanistic, initiatory, and potentially practical aspects of the Merlin traditions for the present day in meditation, visualization and inner disciplines. Many of these concepts are developed in *The Merlin Tarot* (book and full colour deck of cards) by R.J. Stewart, illustrated by Miranda Gray, Aquarian Press, 1988. In this deck and book, the visual imagery of the Merlin tradition is restored and analysed in the context of tarot, mythology, cosmology, and story telling.

6. Various translations of *The Mabinogion* are available, including that by J. Gantz, Penguin, 1976. It is worth comparing the various translations; Gantz is the more precise academic translation, but that of Lady Charlotte Guest (first published in the nineteenth century) is often more true to the poetic spirit of the original tales.

7. Harold Bayley, *Archaic England*, Covenant, 1919. See also the same author's *Lost Language of London*, Jonathan Cape, 1935. Bayley's books are of a vast organic or holistically rambling nature, full of valuable source material, but tending to be diffuse and occasionally highly speculative. Perhaps the worst example of this school of writing is Elzsabeth Gordon, *Prehistoric London*, Covenant, 1925, in which no linguistic or comparative excess or spurious connection has been omitted. A more accurate writer, though still tending to draw vague analogies, is Lewis Spence, *Legendary London*, Robert Hale, 1937.

8. George Daniel, *Merrie England in the Olden Time*, London, 1841.

9. Harriet Crawford (Ed.), *Subterranean Britain*, John Baker, 1979.

10. *The Birth of Merlin, or The Childe Hath Found his Father*. A Jacobean comedy attributed to William Rowley and William Shakespeare, new edition, R.J. Stewart (Ed.), with a commentary on the Merlin legends within the play, and additional chapters by Denise Coffey and Roy Hudd. Foreword by Professor Harold Brooks, Element Books, 1989.

11. R.J. Stewart, *The Prophetic Vision of Merlin*. A detailed commentary upon the medieval 'Prophecies of Merlin', with a new edited version of the translation by J. Giles. The origins, initiatory techniques and possible meanings of the bardic prophecies are discussed, with particular emphasis upon their relationship to the present day.

Chapter 8: William Blake's Spiritual Four-Fold City

Abbreviations:
FZ = *The Four Zoas*; J = *Jerusalem*; M = Milton; MHH = *The Marriage of Heaven and Hell*.

All textual references are to *Blake: Complete Writings with Variant Readings*, edited by Sir Geoffrey Keynes, Oxford University Press, 1966 and subsequent editions. Quotations are given by the page number in Keynes (K), followed by the abbreviation of the work, then plate, and finally line number(s). Thus the lines in *Jerusalem*:

Why stand we here trembling around

Calling on God for help, and not ourselves, in whom God dwells,

Stretching a hand to save the falling Man?

will be located as K672 J43: 12–14. However, in the case of *The Four Zoas*, which has no plate numbers, references are given by section and line, thus the lines in *The Four Zoas*:

That Man subsists by Brotherhood & Universal Love.

Not for ourselves but for the Eternal family we live.

Man liveth not by Self alone . . .

are located as K374 FZix: 638–641.

1. William Blake was born on 28 November 1757, in London, and died, in London, on 12 August 1827.

2. K218.

3. K216.

4. K709 J71: 7.

5. K708 J69: 40.

6. Blake insists that the most vital activity of the human mind is the imagination. For him it is the very source of spiritual energy. He is convinced that it is divine and that those who exercise it partake in some way in the activity of God. Indeed, for Blake the imagination is nothing less than God, Christ, as He operates in the human soul. In the imagination Man's spiritual nature is fully realized. Coleridge, though not expressing himself with such apocalyptic certainty, is of a very similar view:

    The primary imagination I hold to be the living Power and prime Agent of all human Perception, and as a repetition in the finite mind of the eternal act of creation in the I am. S.T. Coleridge, *Biographia Literaria*, J. Shawcross (Ed.), Oxford, 1973, Vol. I, p. 202.

7. K657 J31: 19–20. Moral virtue in the Old Testament sense.

8. The allusion to the new 'Bedlam', on Lambeth Road, gives us the dates 1812–15.

9. Urizenic (adj.) derived from Urizen, one of Blake's great mythological figures. He is a complex figure with many shades of meaning. For purposes of the present essay we may understand Urizen ('horizon', 'your reason') to represent abstract reasoning, analytical reductionist thought.

10. K656–7 J31: 6–11.

11. See Margoliouth, 1951, p. 157.

12. K657 J31.39.

13. i.e. drains.

14. K657 J31: 17–18.

15. ibid., 20–1.

16. ibid., 28.

17. See Bronowski, 1972, p. 138.
18. See Ault, 1974.
19. John Locke, 1632–1704.
20. See Damon, 1979, p. 273d.
21. cf. K636 J15: 14–17, and Nesfield-Cookson, 1937, pp. 130, 165–6.
22. K595.
23. cf. K483 M4: 6–8.
24. Elizabeth Burton, 1967, p. 214.
25. William Pitt (1759–1806), known as the 'Younger Pitt'. Son of the Elder Pitt. Chancellor of the Exchequer (1782–3); Prime Minister (1783–1801 and 1804–6).
26. Kathleen Raine, 1979, p. 148.
27. K212, 'The Chimney Sweeper'.
28. K211–12.
29. K216.
30. K384.
31. K383.
32. James Boswell, *Life of Johnson*, 1791.
33. Keynes suggests that 'temper' is probably an abbreviation of 'temperance'.
34. K323 FZvii: 118$_2$8.
35. George, 1925, p. 244.
36. K117.
37. K212.
38. George, 1953, p. 53.
39. K709 J71: 7.
40. K818. Those who mistake matter for reality have no more than 'single Vision'. Letter to Thomas Butts, 22 November 1802.
41. From the sonnet 'The World'.
42. K217.
43. K170.
44. K830. Letter to William Hayley, 7 October 1803.
45. For purposes of this essay we may understand Blake's mythological figure Los as being the poet/artist; the faculty of soul we may equate with Creative Imagination. See also Notes 6, 9 and 51.
46. K672 J43: 12–14.
47. K154 MHH, Plate 14.
48. cf. K521 M32: 6.
49. K331 FZviia: 453.
50. K485 M6: 1.
51. J. Middleton Murry gives us a very good idea as to what Blake meant by Art in his maturer years:

> *Art, for Blake, is the Imaginative Life in its totality, nothing less. A compact confession of what he meant by art will be found on the Laocoön engraving . . . The fundamental proposition is this:*

The Eternal Body of Man is The Imagination, that is, God Himself, The Divine . . . Jesus; we are his Members.

It manifests itself in his *Works of Art. (In Eternity All is Vision)* . . . K776. Engraved about 1820.

Art, in fact, is a new order of life: the order of life which (Blake believed) Jesus meant by Eternal Life. It is to live in accord with the Divine Vision, as a member of the One Man, through continual Self-annihilation . . . When every activity of life attains to the condition of the pure and selfless artistic activity, then we are totally regenerated, true members of the Eternal Body of Man which is the Imagination.

Golgonooza is a symbol of the redemption of the Universe of which the individual man is a member, into unity by the Imagination . . . Golgonooza is the Art which expresses the Divine Vision (as Blake sees it) in the reality of the regenerated Universe; or of the Universe striving towards regeneration through Man.

The Art of Golgonooza is, then:

. . . not art in any sense ordinarily attached to the word; it is nothing less than a new kind of Life. When Blake said, on the Laocoön engraving, that 'Jesus & his Apostles & Disciples were all Artists. Their works were destroy'd by the Seven Angels of the Seven Churches in Asia, Antichrist, Science', he did not mean that there had been so many 'works of art' consigned to destruction by some evil power; he meant that the new way of life, the way of Eternal Life, life permeated and eternally renewed by the all-comprehending, all-renewing Imagination; a way of life which Blake believed had been lived by Jesus and his true disciples had been overlaid and lost through the deadly operation of that Rational Principle, which, seeing the Ratio in all things, sees itself only. The life Imagination, once supremely manifest in Jesus, had been denied and cast out. And so, in the deepest sense of all, wonderful 'works of art' had been lost. They had been destroyed.

J. Middleton Murry, 1933, pp. 199–202.

52. K462 'On Reynolds'.
53. Edwin Muir, *An Autobiography*, 1954, p. 33.
54. K649–50 J27: 1–16.
55. Most of the places enumerated by Blake in the four stanzas quoted may be found in Rocque's London survey of 1745. The outer 'pillars' – Islington, Primrose Hill, St John's Wood and Kentish Town – were all within a two-and-a-half mile radius of Golden Square.
56. K650 J27: 33–6.
57. K665 J38: 54.
58. Bronowski, 1972, p. 50.
59. See Note 51.
60. K647 J24: 25, 31–5. Blake sees the 'Moral Law', as laid down by the reason-bound ego, as being a direct consequence of blindness to the spiritual, eternal core in man. The morality preached by 'natural religion' can only be relevant to 'natural' man and can have no relevance to spiritual man. It is to such blind morality that Blake is vehemently opposed. What he fights to establish is a morality born from with man's spiritual insight, his intuitive imagination. cf. Nesfield-Cookson, 1987, p. 40.

61. K481. Preface to *Milton*.
62. K374 FZix: 638–41.
63. K651 J27: 77–80.
64. K673 J43: 70.
65. K647 J24: 42–3, cf. K720 J79: 22.
66. K652 J27: 85–8.
67. K485 M6: 1.
68. See Damon, 1979, p. 363 b–d. Also Howard, 1976.
69. K632 J12: 42.
70. See Notes 6, 45 and 51.
71. K632 J12: 43.
72. K684 J53: 19.
73. K485 M6: 2.
74. K211 'The Clod & the Pebble', line 1.
75. K631 J12: 24.
76. K283 FZii: 126–9. On several occasions Blake speaks of the material sun (as distinct from the spiritual sun) as being the 'sulphur sun' – the powerful mephite odour which sulphur, when burning, emits is traditionally associated with hell-fire.
77. K287 FZii: 273–5, 282–6.
78. K286 FZii: 240.
79. K333 FZviib: 12–24.
80. K632 J12: 25–37.
81. cf. K494 M13: 35.
82. K665 J38: 29, 31–4. Blake sees London imaginatively as a living being, her streets blood-vessels, the people on the streets thoughts.
83. cf. K665 J38 – the whole passage, lines 29–59.
84. Doskow, 1982, p. 83.
85. K665 J38: 48.
86. ibid., 49.
87. Doskow, 1982, p. 83.
88. K480 M1: 13–16.

Bibliography:

Ault, D., *Visionary Physics. Blake's Response to Newton*, Chicago and London, 1974.
Beer, J., *Blake's Humanism*, Manchester and New York, 1968.
Blake's Visionary Universe, Manchester and New York, 1969.
Bloom, H., *Blake's Apocalypse*, London, 1963.
Bowra, Sir Maurice, *The Romantic Imagination*, London, 1963.
Bronowski, J., *William Blake and the Age of Revolution*, London, 1972.
Burton, E., *The Georgians at Home*, London, 1967.
Damon, S. Foster, *A Blake Dictionary*, London, 1979.
Damrosch, L., *Symbol and Truth in Blake's Myth*, New Jersey, 1980.

Deen, L.W., *Conversing in Paradise*, Columbia and London, 1983.

Doskow, M., *William Blake's Jerusalem*, London and Toronto, 1982.

Erdman, D.V., *Blake. Prophet against Empire*, Princeton, 1977.

Frosch, Th.R., *The Awakening of Albion*, Ithaca and London, 1974.

Frye, Northrop, *Fearful Symmetry. A Study of William Blake*, Princeton, 1969.

Fuller, D., *Blake's Heroic Argument*, London, New York and Sydney, 1988.

George, M.D., *England in Transition*, 1953.

London Life, 1925.

Howard, J., *Blake's Milton. A Study in the Selfhood*, New Jersey and London, 1976.

Johnston, K.R., 'Blake's Cities' in *Blake's Visionary Forms Dramatic*, Erdman, D.V. and Grant J.E. (Eds.), New Jersey, 1970.

Lindsay, J., *William Blake*, London, 1978.

Margoliouth, H.M., *William Blake*, Oxford, 1951.

Mellor, A.K., *Blake's Human Form Divine*, Berkeley, Los Angeles and London, 1974.

Murry, J.M., *William Blake*, London, 1933.

Nesfield-Cookson, B., *William Blake. Prophet of Universal Brotherhood*, Wellingborough, 1987.

Paley, M.D., 'William Blake, the Prince of the Hebrews, and the Woman clothed with the Sun' in *William Blake. Essays in honour of Sir Geoffrey Keynes*, Paley, M.D. and Phillips, M. (Eds.), Oxford, 1973.

Raine, K., *Blake and the New Age*, London, 1979.

Sabri-Tabrizi, G.R., *The 'Heaven' and 'Hell' of William Blake*, London, 1973.

Schorer, M., *William Blake, The Politics of Vision*, New York, 1946.

Witke, J., *William Blake's Epic: Imagination Unbound*, London and Sydney, 1986.

Chapter 9: Towers of Sound and Light

1. R.J. Stewart, *The Underworld Initiation*, The Aquarian Press, 1985.

2. Stewart, *Living Magical Arts*, Blandford Press, 1987.

3. Stewart, *Advanced Magical Arts*, Element Books, 1988.

4. Gareth Knight, *The Rose Cross and the Goddess*, The Aquarian Press, 1985.

5. Peter Ackroyd, *Hawksmoor*, Hamish Hamilton, 1985.

Chapter 13: The Mythology of London
Gazetteer of Sacred Sites in London

1. Walter Thornbury, *London Recollected, its History, Lore and Legend*, Vol. 1, Alderman Press, 1985.

2. See S. Grian, *Brighde, Goddess of Fire*, Brighde's Fire, 1985.

3. Parts of this entry are adapted with permission from *London Walkabout*, by Andrew Collins, Earthquest Books, 1984.
4. Samuel Palmer, *St Pancras*, London, 1870.
5. A.D. Webster, *Regent's Park and Primrose Hill*, Longman, 1911.
6. D. Goode, *Wild in London*, Michael Joseph, 1986, p. 12.
7. A. Farmer, *Hampstead Heath*, Historical Publications, 1984.
8. P. Mills, *The Archaeology of Camden*, ILAU, 1982.
9. E.O. Gordon, *Prehistoric London*, Covenant, 1925, pp. 131–2.
10. ibid.
11. Nigel Pennick, *Earth Harmony*, Century, 1987.

Chapter 15: London in the Time of Arthur

1. See John Evans, *The Coins of the Ancient Britons*, 1864, pp. 205, 242, 243, and elsewhere.
2. Ibid., p. 416.
3. Beale Poste, p. 43.
4. Ibid., pp. 283–5.

Chapter 17: Britannia and St Paul's

1. M.F. Farbridge, *Biblical and Semitic Symbolism*, p. 7.
2. Sir E.A. Wallis Budge, *Gods of the Egyptians*, Vol. 1, p. 148.
3. E.O. Gordon, *Prehistoric London*, Covenant, 1925, p. 150.
4. Lewis Spence, *The Mysteries of Britain*, p. 171.
5. Bede, *Ecclesiastical History*, Bk. 1, Ch. 30.
6. E. Hull, *Folklore of the British Isles*, p. 164.
7. Quoted by R. Briffault, *The Mothers*, Vol. III, p. 162.
8. John Stow, *Survey of London*, W.J. Thoms (Ed.), 1876.
9. T.A. Waddell, *Phoenician Origins of the Scots and Britons*.

Chapter 18: Parliament Hill and the Druids

1. Iolo Morganwg (1747–1826).

Further Reading

These are just a selection of the many hundreds of books about London. Many are concerned with history and architecture, but those included here are about the secret, hidden side of the city – the subject of this book:

Ackroyd, Peter, *Hawksmoor*, Abacus, 1986.
    London, the Biography, Chatto & Windus, 2000.
    London Under, Chatto & Windus, 2011.
    Thames: Sacred River, Chatto & Windus, 2008.
Ashe, G., *The Ancient Wisdom*, Macmillan, 1977.
Ashton, J., *The Fleet*, London, 1888.
Barton, Nicholas, *The Lost Rivers of London*, Historical Publications, 1962.
Bayley, Harold, *The Lost Language of London*, Covenant, 1925.
Belloc, Hilaire, *The Historic Thames*, I.B Tauris, 2008.
Blatch, M., *A Guide to London's Churches*, Constable, 1978.
Boswell-Stone, W.G., *Shakespeare's Holinshed*, Chatto & Windus, 1807.
Brentnall, M., *Old Customs and Ceremonies of London*, B.T. Batsford, 1975.
Brooks, J.A., *Ghosts of London (The East End, City and North)*, Jarrold, 1982.
    Ghosts of London (The West End, South and West), Jarrold, 1982.
Caine, Mary, *The Kingston Zodiac*, 1978.
Chambers, M., *London, the Secret City*, Ocean Books, 1985.
Clayton, Antony, *The Folklore of London*, Historical Publications, 2008.
Cohen-Portheim, P., *The Spirit of London*, Batsford, 1935.
Collins, A., *London Walkabout*, Earthquest Publications, 1984.
Coverley, Merlin, *Occult London*, Pocket Essentials, 2008.
Duncan, A., *Secret London*, New Holland, 2009.
Dunn, Aidan Andrew, *Vale Royal*, Goldmark, 1995.
Fairfolt, F.W., *Gog and Magog: The Giants in Guildhall*, John Camden Hotten, 1859.
Farmer, A., *Hampstead Heath*, Historical Publications, 1984.
Foster, R., *Patterns of Thought: The Hidden Meaning of the Great Pavement of Westminster Abbey*, Jonathan Cape, 1990.

Gibson, Adrian, *The New Jerusalem*, Bantam Press, 2002.

Goode, D., *Wild In London* Michael Joseph, London, 1986.

Gordon, E.O., *Prehistoric London: Its Mounds & Circles*, Covenant, 1914. *Prehistoric London*, Covenant, 1925.

Hayward, R., *Cleopatra's Needles*, Covenant, 1925.

Kent, W., *London Mystery & Mythology*, Staples Press, 1952.

Lethbridge, T.C., *Gogmagog: The Buried Gods*, Routledge, 1957.

Lewer, D., *The Temple Church*, Pitkin Pictorials, 1971.

Matthews, J., *Spring-Heeled Jack*, Inner Traditions, 2016 (forthcoming).

Michell, J., *The Traveller's Key to Sacred England*, Alfred A. Knopf, 1988.

Mills, P., *The Archaeology of Camden*, ILAU, 1982.

Pearman, H., 'Caves and Tunnels in Kent' in *Records of the Chelsea Speleological Society*, Vol. 6, 1984.

Pennick, Nigel, *Tunnels Under London*, Cambridge, 1981.

Platts, B., *A History of Greenwich*, David & Charles, 1973.

Popham, H.E., *Quaint Survivals of Old London Customs*, C. Palmer, 1928.

Richardson, J., *Highgate*, Historical Publications, 1983.

Roud, Steve, *London Lore*, Random House, 2008.

Sinclair, A., The Albion Triptych: *Gog. Magog. King Ludd*, Hodder & Stoughton, 1967–88.

Sinclair, I., *Lud Heat,* English Language Society, 1986. (Ed.) *London: City of Disappearances*, Penguin, 2006. *Blake's London: The Topographic Sublime*, Swedenborg Archive, 2013. *Swimming to Heaven: The Lost Rivers of London*, Swedenborg Archive, 2013.

Stow, John, *The Survey of London,* J.M. Dent, 1967.

Street, C., *London's Ley Lines*, Earthstars Publishing, 2009. *London's Camelot and the Secrets of the Grail*, Earthstars Publishing, 2009.

Tatlock, J.S.P., *The Legendary History of Britain,* Gordian, 1974.

Thorley, Anthony, *Legendary London and the Spirit of Place*, Archive Publishing, n.d.

Thornbury, Walter, *London Recollected, its History, Lore & Legend*, Vols. I–V, Alderman Press, reprinted 1985.

Webb, S., *Unearthing London*, History Press, 2011.

Williamson, Dr G.C., *Curious Survivals*, Herbert Jenkins, 1922.

Wilson, S., *Lotus in the Mud – A Pagan View of the Horniman Museum*, privately printed, London, 1987.

Do you wish this wasn't the end?

Join us at www.hodder.co.uk, or follow us on
Twitter @hodderbooks to be a part of our community
of people who love the very best in books and reading.

Whether you want to discover more about a book
or an author, watch trailers and interviews, have the
chance to win early limited editions, or simply browse
our expert readers' selection of the very best books,
we think you'll find what you're looking for.

And if you don't,
that's the place to tell us what's missing.

We love what we do, and we'd love you to be part of it.

www.hodder.co.uk

@hodderbooks

HodderBooks

HodderBooks